ON THE INDIAN HILLS

ON THE INDIAN HILLS

OR,

COFFEE-PLANTING IN SOUTHERN INDIA

BY

EDWIN LESTER ARNOLD

GYAN

Published by

Gyan Publishing House
5, Ansari Road
Daryaganj, New Delhi-110002
Phone: 011-47034999, 9811692060
E-mail: books@gyanbooks.com

Distribution Network
gyanbooks.com
India, USA, Canada, UK, Australia, France

ISBN: 978-81-212-7987-1 (PB)
First Published, 1893

2nd Impression 2023

Printed at: Gyan Press, Delhi.

ON THE INDIAN HILLS
Author: EDWIN LESTER ARNOLD

ON THE INDIAN HILLS.

A COFFEE ESTATE.

ON THE INDIAN HILLS

OR,

COFFEE-PLANTING IN SOUTHERN INDIA

BY

EDWIN LESTER ARNOLD

AUTHOR OF
"THE WONDERFUL ADVENTURES OF PHRA THE PHŒNICIAN,"
"A SUMMER HOLIDAY IN SCANDINAVIA," ETC., ETC.

A NEW EDITION, WITH ILLUSTRATIONS.

LONDON:
SAMPSON LOW, MARSTON & COMPANY
LIMITED,
St. Dunstan's House,
FETTER LANE, FLEET STREET, E.C.
1893.

PREFACE.

I COMMEND these sketches of adventurous life in a little-known corner of India with more confidence because they bring out in a simple but picturesque fashion the natural variety and woodland features of a great region, whose immense resources for forestry, plantations, and hunting are even now hardly comprehended by Indian authorities. My son, who has put these pages together from long-ago-collected material of notes made in all the novelty and rough experiences of pioneering in the southern jungles of Hindostan, has, happily I think for his book, nothing to say of the beaten tracks of Indian travel; and it is for this reason, because he breaks fresh ground, and because he describes with the pleasant simplicity of letters written for home reading strange and curious phases of jungle-life in these vast and half-explored woodlands of the Madras peninsula, that I am emboldened to express my own pleasure in reperusing his book, and glad to commend it to all who love the East and enjoy plain tales of the Asiatic hills excellently told.

EDWIN ARNOLD.

CONTENTS.

CHAPTER		PAGE
I.	Outward Bound	1
II.	The Threshold of the East	7
III.	On Sinbad's Sea	26
IV.	Ceylon and its People	55
V.	A Mountain City	71
VI.	Up the Coast	86
VII.	On the Road to the Jungle	103
VIII.	At Work	141
IX.	Jungle Days	160
X.	"Under the Sun"	179
XI.	A Feeble Folk	190
XII.	Building Tabernacles	202
XIII.	The Trackless Woods	216
XIV.	Jungle Society	231
XV.	Hard at Work	244
XVI.	Birds, Beasts, and Savages	252
XVII.	The Fever-fiend	266
XVIII.	Jungle Festivities	278
XIX.	Death and Bright Life	291
XX.	Road-making	301
XXI.	Through Water and Fire	321
XXII.	Vanquished by Fever	327
XXIII.	Homeward Bound	337

LIST OF ILLUSTRATIONS.

PAGE

A Coffee Estate ... ... *Frontispiece*

"He wears the Livery of Sin without a Blush" ... 59

A Moonlight Ford 115

The Samee Tree 195

The Sunday Rendezvous 274

An Anxious Moment 319

ON THE INDIAN HILLS.

CHAPTER I.

OUTWARD BOUND.

THERE is so much strange and curious in these chapters which I have put together, albeit' they deal with districts under ægis of the British flag, and within less than two weeks' direct steaming of the English shores, that I shall no doubt be excused for passing lightly over the familiar preliminaries. Every one knows of an outward bound passage down the Thames, of the last sight of one's native shores—that moment dedicated in silence to an infinitely delicate sorrow,—of the rugged coast of Portugal,—and then the Straits.

It is only when well into the Mediterranean that you get the first breath of the East in the sea-wind, and a sight of things which tell you you have at last stepped out of the old new world into a sphere more full of novelty and wonder than any conceived by the wildest dreams of ancient geographers.

The morning of the 25th of August found us off the coast of Africa, steaming along against a fresh head wind. When we first came up after breakfast the land was a misty purple line on the horizon, but as time went on our course took us nearer and nearer, and the mountains and hollows unfolded before us a rich and varied panorama, which we watched as it rolled slowly along. We looked hard for a glimpse of Algeria, that "diamond set in an emerald frame," as the poetic Arabs call their steep town of white houses and green woods, but when the ship's bearings were taken about mid-day we were sorry to find that we lay a long way to the eastward, and must have passed the town soon after daybreak. However, the coast was beautiful—a long, serrated range of dark mountains sloping right down into the sea, and broken up and crossed in all directions by deep forest-covered ravines and gullies. Here and there we passed open clearings, where the bright green of waving corn crops could be seen amongst the olive trees and quiet little homesteads, more Dutch than Algerian in appearance, peeping out from the terraces on the steep mountain sides.

A few land birds fluttered to the ship during the day, mostly grey wagtails and shore larks; but they seemed to come from the northward, and were all tired when they first reached us, perching on the rigging or shrouds, whence they could hardly be frightened off. After a time they rapidly recovered their strength, and ran about the deck, searching for insects amongst the ropes and lumber, with very few signs of fear. Fresh water seemed to be what they needed most, some of them even venturing into the hen-coops in order to obtain a drop of the precious liquid. Curiously enough, they would not leave the ship, although the land was plainly in sight about a league away to the southward. Several times I frightened them up, in the hope of starting them for the shore while it was still near; but they preferred to cling to the vessel as a harbour of refuge, and only flew round and round, with their musical call-notes, settling again in some other part of the rigging. Besides the land birds, there were here a good many large brown sea-gulls flying over the steamer—dull, heavy-winged birds of sombre hue, always sailing mournfully about, rising above the crests of the waves and skimming down the hollows, every now and then plunging after a fish, and once more following in our wake to pick up the refuse thrown overboard by the cook.

After Cape Bougiarone we lost sight of land for a time, but enjoyed a beautiful starlight night in passing across the mouth of the deep Gulf of Stora, on which the harbour of Constantine is situated. I believe the only streams in Algeria where trout are to be found flow into the bay close to the town of Collo. Here, too, the most lovely and valuable kinds of red coral are dredged, the rights of fishing for which have caused much bloodshed.

Beyond Tunis the coast loses a great deal of its rugged grandeur, and the hills become more undulating, with larger surfaces of cultivated ground; the cork and olive woods that clothe the uplands about Algeria growing scarcer. I noticed some palm-trees on the sky line at one time, which interested me considerably as the first sign of approaching the veritable East.

Then for the next three days we had to amuse ourselves as best we could in the usual indolent fashion of steamboat travelling, as we were out of sight of land the whole time, with nothing to be seen but the blue arch of the sky overhead and the darker blue of the sea below. It is a strange feeling to be in the centre of a great waste of waters for a long time. It seems as though the ship were the whole world, and the merest trifles in the way of novelty are eagerly welcomed. The ladies appeared to get on better than the men: they are more accustomed to laborious idleness, and their nimble fingers were always suitably employed in working crewels of extraordinary flowers for their Indian homes, or on that mysterious open-work embroidery which they manufacture by the yard, but which always vanishes directly it is ready to be worn. As for our less ready hands, we employed them for a greater part of the time in writing voluminous diaries and letters for posting on the first opportunity from Port Saïd or Suez to friends and relations in England, or by taking part in an occasional game of tennis or quoits.

Amongst the incidents which our solitude magnified into excitements were the passing birds that came to the ship. One of these was a hoopoe. It was discovered circling round and round with a short jerky flight, every now and then giving a plaintive whistle bearing some resemblance to its English name, but pronounced in a very low, musical tone. Being considered an authority on birds and their names, I was called up to identify it, in which I had no trouble, as it would not be easy to mistake the lovely orange crest of gracefully curved feathers, the delicate banded plumage of soft black and white, and the long slender bill of glossy black. We tried to persuade the strange visitor to settle, so that we might observe him more closely, but though tired he was wonderfully shy, flying round the vessel with nervous wings; at one minute hovering with drooping feet over the bulwarks, and almost making up his mind to perch, but never quite screwing his courage to the sticking point—our least movement causing the bird to utter his plaintive whistle and sail away for a couple of hundred yards, whence, however, he soon came back to hover over us. He followed us for twenty or thirty miles without once venturing to rest, and then disappeared as suddenly as he had arrived.

About 6 p.m. on August 30 we were delighted to notice the deep blue-black of the sea giving way to water of the most beautifully delicate pale green tint, with the crests of the small waves, raised by a gentle south-west wind, looking golden in the low sunlight. The greenness of the water is a sure sign of being in soundings, and so shallow is it all along this Egyptian coast that large ships often cannot approach within twelve miles. The bottom is gradually but surely rising, probably by deposits of mud and sand brought down by the mighty Nile from the interior of the continent of Africa, and some day it may be possible to annex it from the kingdom of Neptune and turn it into fresh fields for the Fellaheen of Egypt.

We had seen, for a long time before getting into shallow water, a far-extending low bank of white clouds stretching along the southern horizon, flat and straight beneath, and broken and rough on the upper surface. These were the invariable signals of land, never to be noticed anywhere but over a coast; so we "unbuttoned" our eyes to the utmost, and shortly before the sun went down clearly made out some tall palm trees, and then the long low line of the sandy Egyptian coast. In one place we perceived against the brilliant evening sky what seemed to be a large clump of bamboos, but on passing nearer we made them out to be a fleet of feluccas, with their black hulls hidden under the dark bank. Just as we were going down to dinner, somebody who had been looking in the right direction exclaimed that he made out Port Saïd lighthouse. All eyes were soon turned to the point indicated, and there we could just discern a fine slender needle rising from the sea about fifteen miles ahead. An officer assured us we should be at anchor very shortly after dinner, and we went below with the delightful prospect of getting a run on shore and stretching our cramped legs. Lycurgus told the Spartans there was nothing like hunger and fatigue for seasoning their black broth, and, to adapt the stern lawmaker's words, there is nothing that makes land so pleasant as a couple of weeks on the sea; for, though charming enough for a time, one comes to know every plank and nail of the ship much too well, and a promenade of a couple of hundred times up and down the deck becomes monotonous beyond a limited number of days.

About eight o'clock we were off the twinkling lamps of Port Saïd, with the magnificent electric beam in the lighthouse shining in the darkness like a huge firefly; and after our patience had been sorely tried while waiting for a pilot to take us into the harbour, we entered, to drop anchor into the mud of Egypt.

A long avenue of red and green lanterns, fixed to floating buoys on the right and left, marked out the deep channel leading up to the anchorage, but it was so narrow that we could almost touch each lantern in turn, and we had to proceed with the utmost care. Above us the light threw out its brilliant rays, and quite entered into rivalry with the moon, which was shining in the opposite quarter of the heavens. Ahead of us lay the flat sandy Egyptian shore, with a few scattered palms and then a crowded town of miscellaneous buildings, with innumerable lights burning, dimly visible minarets, and the masts of fifty great merchant ships all crowded together. The night was very quiet, and as we stole softly on, almost the most sound was the water lapping against the pilot's boat, which we were dragging along; but occasionally a scrap of a sailor-song in some foreign language, or the barking of wandering dogs, reached us, and the voices grew louder as we neared the town. We passed a silent Turkish ironclad, looking very grim in the moonlight, moored so as to sweep the approaches to the canal with its heavy guns, and then about eleven o'clock we reached our anchorage, and came to rest within twenty yards of the long landing-place in front of the esplanade.

Soon thirteen of us, all embryo coffee planters, were stowed somehow in a single fragile native boat, which had besides two remarkably dirty Italian rowers. Luckily, the basin was as calm as a mill-pond; for our gunwale dipped within a couple of inches of the water, and a slight tip to either side would have swamped us and made some vacancies in the various companies we had the honour to represent. As it was, we arrived safely at the landing-place, and after some fourteen days afloat were once more on dry land.

CHAPTER II.

THE THRESHOLD OF THE EAST.

THE first thing I noticed was the sand. We plunged in ankle-deep before we had made half a dozen steps. Toiling through it anyhow, we gained a long well-lit boulevard with innumerable cafés and taverns all about. We visited one where some French women on a stage were singing and playing—both very badly—and tried some lager beer, which tasted much like the rinsing of old ale barrels, and for which we paid something like a shilling a glass. After listening to two or three songs, we went out and up the principal street in the town to make some purchases, for which purpose we accepted the services of a very diminutive Arab boy with a very large reed basket, who offered to carry our things.

Port Saïd is strong in shops where tobacco, cigars, jewellery, and photographs of the neighbourhood are sold. These are generally kept by Frenchmen, who did not appear to be overflowing with super-abundant respectability. The tobacco sold is usually

Turkish and fairly good, though much better can be got in London; it is, however, cheaper, as there is no duty or very little. The photographs of the Canal with which every shop is stored being very novel and interesting, nearly every one buys some to send back to England. But much cannot be said for the sham Turkish jewellery; it is, first of all, remarkably ugly in design, never made of the material it lays claim to be, and more expensive than that which can be bought any day in Regent Street.

Two of us, myself and a huge Scotchman from the very far north, started off into the native quarters in search of Arab curiosities.

Luckily the moon was shining brightly and bathing the upper parts of the whitewashed houses in silvery light, though it made the narrow streets below even more dark by comparison. As we went along through the deserted roads ankle-deep in sand, we disturbed innumerable dogs—disgusting animals, employing themselves in eating all the day's refuse and garbage of the town. They seemed to have a particular hatred of "pale faces," and snarled or howled as we went by in an unpleasant manner. One gaunt mangy animal came slouching after us for a long way, slinking along in the shadows behind, and barking when we stopped. The houses in the poorer parts seemed very nondescript, partly French, partly Italian, with Turkish arabesques in places; their open raised courts and circling balconies reminding one a little of Moorish villas. They were nearly all two storied, painted grey or drab to the top of the door, and the rest whitewashed.

We found a few native shops, but, as we might have guessed, they were chiefly food stores for the poorer classes, who seemed to have little superfluous cash, or inclination to spend it on ornaments or fine raiment.

These shops were nothing more than recesses under the houses, with counters across them; and upon innumerable shelves, nails, etc., on the walls, were dried fish, tomatoes, melons, and artichokes, stored or hung, in great profusion. In one of these we spied some particularly fine water-melons hanging on a peg—beautiful great fruits with cool pale-green rinds, striped with darker green. Unfortunately, although the shop was quite open, there was no one to be seen in it; but when we thought of the flaring sands of the Canal to-morrow, and then of a week of roasting in the Red Sea, we determined to have some at any cost; so we went boldly in, and we were just arranging that W—— should climb up and get them down, after which we would leave some change on the counter, when we caught sight of something wrapped up in a blue bournous with a faint resemblance to the human form, lying under a table in the corner. I gave it a poke with my stick, and it promptly started up, showing the black face of a curly-headed Nubian. The fellow had perhaps been dreaming of the bastinado, and thought we were the Khedive's officers come for him; at all events, he rubbed his eyes and took a long time to wake up and understand what we were there for. When we left the shop with half a dozen melons on a stick, he came out and stood to watch us down the moonlit street, as though he still doubted our purposes.

We obtained a good idea of the town, and from the number of doubtful houses and low drinking shops, came to the conclusion that it was just the sort of spot which might be expected from a place grown up in half a dozen years, and populated by a great concourse of French and Italians, backed by the Egyptian and Turkish labourers employed on the construction of the Canal.

Arriving at the outskirts of the town, where the

open maidan country commenced, and nothing was to be discerned but sandy wastes in front, dotted with scrubby bushes, we saw a group of dogs gnawing the white bones of a dead buffalo, and I was just telling W—— how a young Englishman had been stabbed in the back a couple of weeks before, somewhere in this neighbourhood, when three slouching ruffians, armed with sticks, stepped out of the shadow of a tumble-down Moorish house, and came towards us. We walked on, and, luckily perhaps for us, matters did not come to blows; but we were rather near it, for one of the men had already ranged up alongside of the hot-tempered Scotchman, and said something which was quite unintelligible, but evidently aggressive. Somebody would have had a broken head in another minute; but just at the right time a diversion appeared in the persons of two of the ship's officers, who came towards us, and the rascals, seeing the odds against them, disappeared in the shadows. The officers told us it was rash to go about the town at night, except in considerable parties, and the outskirts were especially to be avoided, as they were infested with ruffians of every nationality who had very small scruples about cutting any one's throat if there was a chance of "swag," and then tucking him away in a hole in the sandy desert. A considerable number of people had mysteriously vanished lately, and nothing was ever heard of them again. When we eventually reached the more civilized localities under the pilotage of the officers, W—— said that if we had only been going to stay here another night, we might have made up a party to rout out some of the thieves, and have a fight on the maidan. Eventually we fell in with the rest of our friends, who had been shopping busily, their little Egyptian boy with the big basket having nearly as much as he could carry. This poor little lad nearly fell into the talons of "justice;" for, while we were all in a shop purchasing various articles, two zaptiehs came along, and seeing him sitting on a doorstep close by, with a basket full of valuables by him, jumped at the conclusion that he had stolen them, and proceeded to "run him in." In vain the frightened lad explained that he was carrying them for "the Franks;" the policemen, probably with an eye to sharing the spoil between them, wanted to march him off, and if one of us had not happened to come out of the shop and to see the trio vanishing down a by-street, we should have been minus all our purchases. As it was, we quickly rescued Mustapha, and recompensed him liberally for his fright and services.

These Egyptian gendarmes are decidedly imposing to look at. Their uniform is pale sky-blue; their trousers are white on the first day of the week, but drab for the rest. They wear French military caps with peaks in front, and sword bayonets at their sides. In the daytime they stand expectorating and smoking at the street corners, and at night they collect in the open police stations, where a dozen of them may be seen with their feet on the backs of neighbouring chairs, smoking bad cigarettes and, if they can afford it, drinking absinthe. Occasionally a couple of them sally out and make a tour of the quietest and best-lit streets, but on the whole their conduct is considerably like that of Dogberry and his watch. If they meet a thief they bid him stand, and if he won't stand, they let him go.

It was past 2 a.m. when we came to the conclusion that there was nothing more to be seen or bought on shore, and went down to the landing-place, where our boat was waiting for us with the men asleep in the stern sheets. We were soon on board the *Almora*, and found that the unwonted exertion of three hours on land after a fortnight of idleness had told on us heavily. We were as sleepy as possible, and our mattresses were quickly on deck, each occupied by its owner in the usual light flannel sleeping-suits of hot countries.

Before turning in, I went forward to see the coal for the engines brought on board. It was a most curious and fantastic scene. Close alongside were moored half a dozen large open lighters, each piled with a mountain of fuel. On these boats scores of dusky forms were hard at work filling baskets, which a continuous string of Arabs and Egyptians carried up one sloping board, emptied down into the coal bunkers, and immediately returned by another sloping board for a fresh load. The moon shone brightly on the men at work in the barges, and made them look like gnomes toiling in a mine. As they came on deck the yellower light of the lanterns glittered on their naked bodies; none of them wore more than a waist-cloth, and the perspiration streaming down them cut channels in the glittering coal dust, with which their skins were thickly covered. Everything was densely sprinkled with this dust; ropes, coops, deck, were all alike jetty black, but the afterpart of the ship was protected by canvas screens, which kept the passengers from the general griminess. The coolies seemed to be working hard, though no task-masters were visible; so probably they were doing piece-work, *i.e.* getting paid by the job—always the best arrangement with Asiatics when possible, as they exert themselves to get through their allotted share, which tells both in favour of themselves and of their masters. I stood at a respectful distance, watching these streaming black figures toiling up and down the ship's sides with their heavy burdens, until at last, like Lot's wife, I was turning into a solid pillar, not of salt, but of Welsh coal, becoming in fact rapidly jet black from the crown of my fez to the soles of my boots; so I beat a retreat, and soon afterwards was stretched on my mattress on the saloon skylight, sleepily listening to the howling of the jackals and dogs, who kept up rival choruses until the moon went down, and the sky began to grow grey in the east with the first touch of dawn.

It seemed I had hardly fallen asleep, when my arm was lightly touched by a white-turbaned "boy" with a cup of coffee and some biscuits. "Chota hazri, sahib," he said, and added he had woke me by order of some of the other sahibs, who were going ashore again before the ship started. It was a lovely, cool, fresh morning, with the sun just coming up over the far-stretching sand wastes on the Arabian shore. To the northward lay the limitless blue-grey sea we had so lately crossed, with a few white sails dotted about. Nearer to us was the picturesque but untidy Port Saïd on the one side, and a miniature forest of tall masts in its harbour; while beyond spread the tawny, monotonous desert, where nothing grows but stunted thorn bushes, and nothing breaks the level expanse but the white bones of camels or buffaloes that have been turned out and left to die. From amongst these shelters now and then village dogs crawled. They seemed to have been sleeping after their disgusting meals, and the increasing light disturbed them, for they came slowly forth, and, sniffing the air once or twice, slunk away with a sidelong trot, keeping by instinct in the hollows and shadows.

In the town animation returned rapidly. First, a tall Arab, in a long flowing blue bournous, came down to a strip of sand close to our moorings, and proceeded to make careful ablutions, regardless of foreign eyes. Then, having washed and dressed, he spread a small bit of gaily coloured carpet, and kneeling down on it, proceeded to say his morning prayer. He was careful to turn his face towards the spot where he supposed

Mecca and the shrine of his prophet to be, but if he faced two or three points too much to the northward, let us hope it did not mar the effectiveness of his worship. Squatting on his heels, with his hands clasped in front of him, he seemed for a moment buried in thought; then, placing his hands on the sand in front of him, he bent down and touched the ground three times with his forehead. Then came a few more minutes of what appeared to be profound meditation, though doubtless the votary was repeating prayers to himself, after which he slowly turned his head to the right and to the left; a little more meditation, another deep bow to the sand, and he had finished, and jumping up, shook the dust from his carpet, and strode away over the maidan to his hut and breakfast of maize or water-melon.

Soon afterwards came a long string of camels, starting for some distant journey. Emerging from the outskirts of the town with their turtle-like heads high in the air, and their elastic step, they crossed the plain and disappeared among the sandhills. Then, as the sun rose higher in the sky, the brown children came out of the houses to play and squabble, waking up with their noise the mongrel dogs curled up in out-of-the-way corners, and the Egyptian soldiers who had been on duty all night; while women in blue gowns and men of all nationalities poured down to the harbour, or filled the narrow streets with a strangely mixed Eastern crowd; for the day's work had fairly begun.

Finishing my coffee and biscuits, I joined a small party of passengers bound for fresh adventure, with whom I soon reached the landing-place, and we became the cynosure of a score of natives, who wanted to do anything or everything for me—and backshish. Selecting a little Egyptian girl in a blue chemise but nothing else, with a pretty face and bright eyes, I made her show me the way to the post-office.

Of all things at Port Saïd, these little Egyptian girls are the nicest and prettiest. They wear simple blue gowns like the older women, but no face-covering. They have gentle, quiet manners, to strangers at least, and never make rude remarks about "foreign devils," as their brothers do, but are, nevertheless, fully alive to the value of money, and always ask for four or five times as much as they expect to get. You beckon to a small damsel and request her to carry you a melon to the ship. She jumps at the prospect of the back-shish, but with an eye to getting as much as possible, says, "Yes, sar, s'pose you give me five shillings." Then if you look stern and offer her twopence, she says, "Very well, sar," and up goes the melon on to her head (they carry everything there, no matter how heavy or fragile), and giving her robe a hitch up under her scarlet girdle, she steps out over the soft hot sand in a way that puts the heavier "Britisher" on his mettle to keep pace with his little guide. It is a pleasure to see her walk; she holds herself as straight as an arrow, and treads as lightly as a gazelle. The small Egyptian boys are also often bright and pretty, but regular little rogues, and both girls and boys lose their good looks only too quickly.

About nine o'clock the sun was powerful, and I was beginning to feel so much interest in breakfast, that my little Egyptian girl was dismissed with a gift which put an extra sparkle into her eyes, and I rowed off to the *Almora*.

Many tourists and travellers—to say nothing of all the outward and homeward-bound Anglo-Indians—have long ago seen and traversed the great ditch whereby M. de Lesseps has made Africa an island. That short cut has become more important to the commerce and influence of Great Britain than any piece of water in the world, and at least seven-tenths of the shipping going from Port Saïd to the Red Sea flies the white or red ensign of England. It was high noon when we again felt the gentle tremor sent by the revolving screw through our ship as we slowly passed inward from Port Saïd. Getting clear of the wharf, a little plot of ground, with two or three mud shanties on it, was pointed out as boasting the proud title of British soil. This bit of land, when the Canal was in course of construction, stood valued at £800, but so little was thought of the undertaking that the patch was not bought until the Canal became a success, and then the land had so much risen in value that it was finally taken by our Government for £26,000. We crept past this and some large new buildings, where the French tricolor was gaily fluttering in the sea-breeze, and entered the mouth of the Canal. The harbour gradually narrows as the steamer passes down between the town and a long line of ships in dock on the port side, until almost imperceptibly the vessel is in a narrow lane of water, with open country on both hands. On the left stretches a well-nigh boundless plain of drab level mud—not a stone or a blade of grass breaking the vast expanse; all is of one dull unbroken colour, excepting some scattered patches of grey salt, left when the sea last subsided. On the right opens a great expanse of shallow water, connected with the Mediterranean. Along the margins and sandbanks in the centre stood long lines of flamingoes and pelicans. At first it was difficult to believe those could be birds which remained so still and were in such vast numbers. They looked more like the scattered white fragments of some broken sea-wall, but through a telescope we could make out each tall bird, standing on one leg, with his head turned aside, watching, no doubt, the shoals of little fish swimming about in the neighbourhood. At a rough guess there must have been about six or seven thousand of these huge white waders in sight at once, and our sportsmen burned to make closer acquaintance with them. On the surface of the lake there were also many other kinds of water-fowl; among them the ubiquitous curlew—as wide awake and shy as his kindred are everywhere—and the lesser stint, flying along the margins in little packs of seven or eight, but vanishing the moment they settled, their brown and grey plumage harmonizing so exactly with the mud and sand.

The first five miles of the Great Ditch are as straight as an arrow—the narrow ribbon of steel-blue water stretching away over the hot brown plain like a band of iron upon a cotton bale. The banks on both sides lie very low, while the Canal itself is so narrow that to catch sight of any water at all from a ship's deck it is necessary to lean over the bulwarks, and then one perceives a few yards of liquid on either side. What impresses the mind most is the terrible ease with which the channel could be blocked by any nation that might desire it. Imagine a mutiny in India or an effective *jehad* stirring up the Mohammedans of Afghanistan and the Northern Provinces! It would then be of the utmost importance for us to command free and rapid means of transit through the Canal; but if Russia wished to put a spoke in our wheels, what would be easier than for her to send a merchant steamer with a cargo of anything conveniently heavy, and have her sunk—by accident, of course—in a narrow part? It would stop the whole traffic for a week or more, for even an English steamer lightly aground at the bows has several times blocked the way for a couple of days.

The width of the Canal ought to be doubled, and will be some day; it must also be lined with stone or concrete right through for the whole eighty miles.

Its present section is curiously shaped. The bottom is seventy feet wide, or should be, though I suspect the sand drifts in considerably. On either side the banks slope up sharply for twenty feet, and then shelve off at an angle. The central channel is thus about twenty-six feet deep in the centre, with ten or twelve feet of very shallow water on either side. The effect of each steamer passing through is certainly damaging. As the vessel glides along, nearly filling up the deeper parts, her bows seem to force a body of water ahead, and the element rushes down from the shallow shelves on either side, uncovering a narrow muddy beach, where the pebbles roll over and over as they are left behind, and numerous astonished little fishes kick and splash in a vain endeavour to regain their native sphere. Then, when the ship has passed, turgid waves come tumbling after her, scouring along under the banks, and sweeping fishes, sticks, and stones pell-mell into deep water. The fretting of the banks is thus constant, most of the loose material getting into the channel, whence it has to be laboriously removed by steam-dredgers. Although there is a nominal depth of twenty-six feet everywhere, it is found in practice that a ship drawing more than twenty-four feet is liable to come to grief. Some little time ago a large steamer with telegraph cable on board ran the gauntlet with a draught aft of twenty-four feet seven inches, but she had to steam at full speed and scraped her keel nearly the whole way through. There would have been great delay if she had stuck, as she would have had to discharge half her cargo before she could go ahead or astern. When the Canal is widened and paved with stone the exact depth will be always known, and the authorities will be able to refuse a passage to all craft exceeding the limits.

About five miles after leaving Port Saïd we come

to the first station. On one bank there is a huge board with "Gare, limite nord" printed in long black letters, and a quarter of a mile away stands another board, on which is inscribed "Gare, limite sûd." Between them the Canal runs of double width, and there appear numerous mooring-posts and buoys. The traffic is worked on the block system, as upon a well-conducted English railway. At each of these *gares* a small cottage stands for the Canal guard, connected by telegraph with the other stations up and down the line. When a ship is reported to be coming up from the next station, the caution signals —two black balls one above the other—are hoisted on the neighbouring flagstaff, and any ship that arrives downwards is obliged to stop and haul into the siding until the one approaching from the opposite direction has passed. This is, of course, a tedious affair, especially to the captains of steamers who have an eye to economizing the coal, half the value saved under a certain amount allowed by their company being their perquisite, the other half going to the chief engineer. But it is the only plan by which the Canal could be worked at all, as two ships cannot pass in any part excepting at the Bitter Lakes. Passengers seldom object, as it gives them an opportunity for some fishing over the sides, and longer time for recovery among the victims of the *mal de mer*. We, however, were not detained at all, but went straight through several *gares*, where large Indian mail and troop ships lay waiting to see us pass. As we glided slowly by, our bulwarks only a few feet from those of the other ships, of course we all crowded to the side, and the homeward-bounds doing the same we had a curious transient glance at each other, giving and taking flying messages, etc., amid cheery badinage and bits of home or foreign news.

As we still steamed along, the banks grew higher on both sides until the surrounding country was hidden from view, and then it became really hot. The sun was high overhead, and flared down till the pitch between the planks of the deck turned soft and bubbly. The water of the Canal shone like brass, for the vessel moved between steep bare brown banks of baked mud, which reflected the heat in a way that was decidedly trying. Every now and then we passed a gap in the banks, and felt for a moment a breath of wind. But such a wind! It came panting and red-hot across the burning desert like a blast from the gates of the lower regions, bringing with it, too, a blinding storm of hot sand, that beat against our faces, drying them into the semblance of parchment. Nearly all our passengers effected a retreat to their cabins, where they spent the time till the sun went down, lying in their berths, as lightly clad as possible, fanning themselves and drinking iced claret. But the sun is not deadly to the temperate, and, seen in its natural blaze of Egyptian light, the Canal was still a thing of immense interest; for though certainly not beautiful, it represents a splendid enterprise, and now that it is achieved it is difficult to think how the world can have got on so well without it. Fancy ever again jolting over the desert from Alexandria to Suez in an omnibus under such a sun as this! Yet that is how we used to get to the Red Sea.

At tiffin nobody could eat much. Nothing was heard but sighs and languidly toned requests for "iced pawnee," while the punkah creaked and flapped overhead, keeping the parboiled sufferers just in existence. A slice of water-melon seemed truly a prodigious meal, and we got back on deck to find the steamer passing the station at Kantara. At this spot there is a really pretty little building on the right-hand side amongst tall palms, half-hidden in creeping vegetation and vines. It is an oasis in the desert, and at the same point an old Syrian road —once the great highway between Egypt and Palestine —is crossed by the Canal. The road is still used to some extent by the natives, picturesque groups of whom may be seen standing on the bank, waiting to be ferried over on a railed-in platform drawn from bank to bank by ropes.

Here ancient and modern modes of travelling are seen working side by side. A cluster of motionless grey camels, with burdens of outlandish goods, tower up amongst burnoused and turbaned Arabs, who lean on their long staves and watch from under their bushy eyebrows the big black ship of the "Franks," with her tall masts and mazy cordage, pass silently along, moved by some invisible and magic power, coming from lands outside the orthodox world, the haunts of fog and mist, and going to the equally unknown land whence Solomon the dread king obtained his ivory and peacocks.

We were not detained at Kantara, but steaming still forwards soon passed one of the larger Arab villages on the left bank. At a little distance it was impossible to say with certainty whether the dull brown heap in a hollow of the plain near the Canal was the work of scavengers or housebuilders, but coming nearer we made it out to be a collection of a hundred tumbledown, flat-roofed mud hovels, scattered about without the smallest attempt at regularity, and varied by numerous piles of refuse, the accumulation of ages, the odour of which we could catch even a couple of hundred yards away. The architecture of these dust-heaps is of the most simple kind, as the builders, not having yet reached the art of making windows, content themselves with a door, effected by cutting a hole in the most convenient side of the square mud pile. The only inhabitants visible in the glare were a couple of camels and some ragged brown children in dirty blue garments, who ran out to gaze on us, scampering along the bank and yelling for backshish. I threw a huge "captain's" biscuit to the biggest, which was at once pounced upon by a crowd of small Egyptians, and when last seen they were still fighting over this unheard-of luxury. All the afternoon we steamed along between the sultry banks on either hand, catching accidental glimpses, through the gaps, of a sandy desert beyond, with its scattered thorn bushes and skeletons of camels, but perceiving no signs of life save an Arab or two stalking along the Canal—his dusky black figure showing up well against the pale blue sky—or the drowsy signalmen in the station-houses. In many places the sand at the edge of the water was marked with the trails of strange water-creatures and footmarks of animals, which might be those of jackals and even gazelles, for they sometimes come down to the brink. We passed several dredging machines at work—huge cumbrous affairs, worked by steam, the mud being got up in an endless circle of buckets which empty themselves into a long iron shoot, whence the stuff finds its way to the adjacent plains. Greater efforts should be made to grow plants and trees upon this soil. There is already a scanty show of reeds in places along the Canal, and they materially assist in keeping the channel open by binding the sand together and preventing its slipping; but if melons or any kinds of grasses could be persuaded to establish themselves on the neighbouring soil, the dredging machines would probably find their work much lightened.

We still went smoothly and slowly along between the banks, with the saffron hue of the Eastern afterglow lighting up the sky. We glided round numerous turns, past the ugly Château Eugénie, built for the

Empress when she opened the Canal, and rarely used since—nor is it wonderful, for the sand lies banked up to the top-story windows on one side, and there can be little pleasure in inhabiting a house where your garden blows from one part to another according as the wind drifts it. At nightfall we took a final sharp turn and entered the first of the really beautiful Bitter Lakes. The steamer was now in a land-locked water—not the smallest sign of entrance or exit to be seen anywhere—dry desert all around us, excepting in one quarter, where there was quite a dense wood of palm and nebbuk trees, with white houses peeping between them. This was Ismailia, where the chief Canal officials live in preference to Port Saïd. We anchored for the night about two miles from the town, and there were soon some half-dozen feluccas alongside, their long lateen sprits flapping against the ship's side and rigging, as the evening breeze rocked them to and fro, while their crews shouted and yelled, causing considerable confusion in the darkness. A party who went ashore gave rapturous accounts on returning of the donkey rides they had enjoyed, and of numerous adventures with dogs, jackals, Egyptian policemen, and boatmen, which made us wish, too late, we had accompanied them.

The next morning, just as the sun rose, our anchor was lifted, and after running aground once in attempting to turn, we steamed away to the southward. The water of the lake displayed the most beautiful blue-green colour, contrasting strongly with the spotless yellow and white of the sandy shores. Ismailia looked quite rural and pretty under the warm sunlight, amongst its green trees, with the great palace of the Viceroy towering above them. Let us hope that the groves of Ismailia will spread themselves, for these lakes, which before the Canal was opened were dry beds of salt, may now favourably influence the climate and generate the much-needed moisture. Nothing but moisture is needed, for it is found by actual experiment that the sand of the desert, unlike the hard sand of the sea-shore, is perfectly fertile—nothing, in fact, but the "top soil" of a tract of country in a very fine state of pulverization, which will grow anything with irrigation. We now carefully picked our way down an avenue of buoys, and then regained the Canal.

Here we were in fairyland. The high banks of the preceding day had vanished, and in their place spread a level tract of land on either side, broken up into thousands of little azure lakelets and bays. In the background the sand formed great smooth yellow hills, without a spot or mark of any kind upon them. In the foreground the waters had encroached upon the desert, and all around us were little lagoons and pools, of the bluest turquoise tint, though scarcely a foot deep. Little peninsulas of sand jutted into them, and little sand cliffs fringed their sides. In their centres rose liliputian sand islands, on which, encouraged by the brackish water, grasses and thorn bushes made tiny forests. In these miniature lagoons fishes great and small disported themselves, and as the rolling waves made by our passage broke on the sandy beaches, the shining fry were thrown up on dry land, where they were quickly pounced upon by hungry sea-swallows—graceful little lavender-and-white birds—which flew on either side of the ship as she passed along. After breakfast we entered again into the region of high banks, but now they were no longer the brown clay of yesterday, but soft, bright, wind-smoothed sand sloping into the water, where grew on either side tall hedges of reeds, so near the ship I almost succeeded in picking some. Gliding past these we entered another broad lake, much larger and deeper than the last, where the land trended so far away that it became nothing but a yellow streak on the horizon; and here a pleasant breeze, with less hot sand in it than usual, fanned our faces and raised little curling waves under our bows. Until the water from the Red Sea was first let into these lagoons they were in much the same state as the Dead Sea is now. The water was so densely impregnated with salt that it is said the workmen used to stick their spades upright in it (this, however, requires to be taken with even still more "salt"), while the bottom was composed of nearly as much saline sediment as sand or mud. The French engineer took advantage of this, and saved himself more than eight feet of digging; for immediately the fresher water was admitted it diluted the solution and reabsorbed so much salt that the bottom of the lake sank many feet downwards, and thus spared half the labour of cutting a passage.

Altogether, an intelligent observer cannot but enjoy the Canal passage, and be very much impressed with the hugeness of the undertaking and the enormous amount of energy required to have kept going that army of labourers—men of all nations and tongues—and to have fed them in such a wilderness. Perhaps the only mistake connected with the great highway was the erection, at a prodigious expense, of extensive shipping docks and harbour works at Suez. These docks were built under the impression that the Canal would render that town a great emporium and coaling station, but they are now a proof of how risky it is to prophesy "until one knows;" for, instead of increasing the importance of Suez, the Canal has well-nigh ruined it. Once everybody came to Suez, when it was the real harbour of the Red Sea and the station whence passengers and mails started across the desert for Cairo and Alexandria. But now, shorn of its glory, it sees the commerce of the world go by within arm's-length, and yet stagnates and decays for lack of trade, since few ships make use of the big harbour, Port Saïd being the real northern port, as Aden is the southern one of the Red Sea. There are several reasons why Port Saïd has thus sucked up the prosperity of Suez—the chief being that where steamers stop their passengers will land and trade become brisk, and steamers only stop where they can get coal cheapest and find the best provisions. The promoters of the Suez Docks overlooked the fact that coal-laden ships coming from England would naturally prefer to unload their cargoes at Port Saïd—thus sparing themselves four days' journey at least through the Canal and back, and saving the Canal dues, which, being very heavy, would of course add largely to the price of the coal unloaded at the southern end. It is for this reason the steamers discard the Red Sea town for the northern one, with its cheap coal and European provisions. If M. de Lesseps only had Aladdin's lamp, he might do a useful thing by rubbing it, and, on the appearance of the Djin, getting him to remove all the harbour works from the Suez entrance to the Mediterranean port.

CHAPTER III.

ON SINBAD'S SEA.

AT the sandy town of Suez our good ship did not stop for even a moment, but slackened speed just enough to permit a little snorting and puffing steam launch, with the agent and our letters, to overtake us, and then, steaming out of the Canal, picked our way amongst the dredgers, the broken-down coasting ships, etc., which were the only occupants of the docks, and finally emerged into the Red Sea. The only visible reason why it should be called Red is that, on the Egyptian side, there rises a long range of fine sandstone hills of a warm pink hue, running all along the coast. As for the sea itself, it is, of course, as blue as the heaven above it, and no more of a ruddy tint anywhere than the Black Sea is inky or the White Sea milky. The opposite shore to Suez lies as flat as a billiard-table for about twenty miles all round. The guide-books say that somewhere on it may be seen a well overshadowed by trees, this being the spot where Moses rested after crossing the sea with the children of Israel. But in fact, twenty or more places in the Gulf of Suez are pointed out as the true spots at which the Hebrew Lawgiver crossed; the most favoured one being about thirty miles south of Suez, where there is a good landing-place on both sides—a great cleft in the cliffs, with a sand "shoot" leading down into the water.

So few ships now pass round the West Coast of Africa and cross the equator that the time-honoured custom of receiving a visit from Neptune is occasionally moved by common consent round to the head of the Red Sea, where his majesty now ofttimes holds his court, and comes on board outward-bound ships to pay his respects and shave those passengers who have never been through the Canal before. In the evening, after leaving Suez, we were invaded by a crowd of finny monsters, with a fishy old gentleman at their head, whose disguise could not hide the countenance of the jovial ship's doctor; while his majesty's barber, with a bucket of soapsuds and a chopper for a razor, was well played by the under steward. Besides a crowd of courtiers, there were sepoys with handcuffs for the unruly; but the "griffins" came up as their names were called, and took their shaving very quietly, while the barber cracked innumerable jokes at their expense. The young ladies were also called up to be shaved, but, as the barber said, "Beards are like ideas—men only have them when they grow up, and women never have any;" so as there was nothing to shave, they were allowed to shake hands with Neptune and hasten away; after which we had some dancing, in which the courtiers were continually tripping over each other's tails, and then fireworks were let off from the stern, during which performance the king and his retinue retired, a final blue light, sent adrift in a tube which went bobbing astern, being pointed out to the youngest of the passengers as "Davy Jones's" private gig taking him away. With this imposing ceremony ended our passage through the Great Ditch.

The next day was Sunday, and we had church on deck under the saloon awning, the grey-headed captain reading the service from a desk covered with the dear flag of our country, and Mount Sinai away to the left soaring rosy and bright in the hot sunlight, while the fresh waves were running bubbling by the port-holes.

Afterwards there was fire drill, which alarmed those of the ladies who did not know it was only a make-believe. We were just dispersing after the final hymn had ended, when the fire-bell was heard ringing loudly —that sound so dreaded by sailors. Of course, there was a rush forward to see what was the matter, and we found the native crew cutting wildly about, chattering and gesticulating like monkeys. In about a minute, or less, the brass caps were screwed off the two steam-pumps, and twenty yards of tubing fixed to each, down which the water quickly made its way, throwing up little jets from every defective seam as the pressure increased, until it came to the far end by the saloon, where a lascar was holding the nozzle overboard, or we should have been swamped. At the same time two hand-pumps were fixed on either side of the ship forward, with plenty of tubing running to the main hatch and second-class cabin, and heavy leathern pipes with perforated leaden muzzles were trailed overboard for obtaining a plentiful supply of water. Every one seemed to know his duty. The whole ship's company—including the twenty "boys" or waiters who stood in a long line at the gangway, and the carpenter, who appeared with an axe ready to break open any number of doors or hatches—had their posts, and occupied them, so that if the fire had been genuine we should have been pouring heavy volumes of water on it in less than three minutes.

When this was over the captain held an inspection of the crew, which proved an interesting spectacle. The ship's company of a large Indian steamer such as the *Almora* is a very mixed collection of human beings. To begin at the top, there are the captain and his four officers, all Englishmen. Besides these, there is the chief engineer, who ranks with the first navigating officer, and three or four assistant engineers—all Europeans—their duty being entirely confined to the engine-room. There is also an English doctor, generally a very pleasant man, who has a remarkably easy life on the outward voyage, rarely finding anything to do but lie on his back reading a novel, or perhaps once and again being called upon to feel the pulse of some young lady; though coming home he often has his hands full, attending to a cargo of fever-stricken Anglo-Indians. An upper and under steward, with an English stewardess and a ship's clerk, make up the list of Europeans.

The number of Asiatics was much larger, and their nationality more varied. First in rank was the head boatman or serang, a corruption of the Persian word for a general. His dress consisted of snowy-white trousers of the usual native cut, baggy towards the waist, but very tight round the ankles, where they formed many wrinkles, and contrasted strikingly with his bare brown feet. His white jacket was tied in round the waist with a gay red scarf, and round his neck hung a silver chain with a whistle attached, on which he was able to produce a set of signals completely understood by the crew. This distinguished individual came from Bombay, whence all the best native sailors are drawn. The two boatswain's mates —tindals in Hindustani—were clad in much the same way, and exerted themselves strenuously at the Sunday review in ranging their long line of clean-clad lascars down one side of the deck. There were some sixty of these men, whose sole duty lay in attending to the sails and gear of the ship. Not half so many English sailors would have been required; but the British physique is, of course, superior to that of the Indians, whose sole diet consists of rice and cakes, though some are glad enough to eat flesh when they can get it—even the flesh of unclean animals. The reason why the pig is considered unclean is well known. Mohammed once called a great council of the beasts and birds of the earth to hear him preach. They all attended, and so great was the eloquence of the Prophet that they with one accord were converted to the faith, with the exception of the cow and the pig, who, for reasons of their own, declined to be influenced, and entered a protest against the proceedings. At this Mohammed was very naturally enraged, and forthwith cursed them, and proscribed their flesh to all true believers. In order to avoid the results of roughly breaking this command, the lascars have resort to a simple process. When a pig is bought by subscription or received as a present from the officers, he is conducted to the bows and slaughtered in accordance with the most orthodox rules of Islam, the butcher drawing his knife across his throat and muttering a solemn, "In the name of Allah the Compassionate." The pig is at once tied by the legs to a strong rope, pitched overboard, and trailed through the water for an hour or more, after which time a lascar goes up to the line and proceeds to haul it in, saying as he does so, "Jáo súar, idhar áo machchi," that is, "Go away, pig; come hither, fish." After this formula the "fish" is supposed to be clean enough for all practical purposes, and is soon cut up and converted into stew.

From an officer I learnt that the crew's usual food on the voyage was rice, dried fish, and a sort of pulse called dal. When in harbour or exposed to cold weather they sometimes received a sheep or pig as a present; but he told me that some time before he had been instructed by the managers of the company to go through the ship's books, and find the average cost of feeding the lascars each day, the result of his investigations being that the average per head per diem was only three half-pence! For this reason, amongst others, natives are employed in preference to English sailors; for, as he said, though the Englishmen are more reliable in danger and better able to work in rough weather, their feeding was almost as costly as that of passengers.

Besides the ship's lascars there are Sidi boys—regular negroes from the neighbourhood of Zanzibar—whose chief duty consists in shovelling coal into the furnaces far away down at the bottom of the ship. Probably none but they could stand the heat; but they seem to like it, and though never clean, except for parade on Sunday, they are a cheerful set, living all day in a roasting temperature, and sleeping at night on the iron grating of the engine-room or in a coal-bunker, as happily as though it were a bed of feathers. The Agwallas consider themselves rather superior to the Sidis, their chief duties being to do the rough work of cleaning the machinery and acting as the hands of the English engineers. They are all Mussulmans, and mostly from the neighbourhood of Bombay, as are also the "boys" who wait in the saloon and second cabin; in fact, most Indian ships are manned by Mussulmans, as the Hindoo is generally too effeminate for rough work, and has, besides, religious scruples about crossing the kala pani, or black water, as he calls the ocean.

Though I have mentioned the "boys" last, they are the finest men, the best fed, and the smartest dressed of any natives on board the ship. As to their honesty and general behaviour I have not much to say. They are attention itself at meals, standing behind one's chair with folded arms, and watching with eagle eyes for an empty plate or glass. Being always barefooted—no Indian ever comes into the presence of a superior with his feet covered—they move about quite noiselessly, and, in fact, nothing could be better than their waiting. At off-times they are also very obliging and willing, though perhaps some of it may be due to the prospect of the tip of ten or twenty rupees which each passenger gives his own particular "boy" at the end of the voyage.

Their chief amusements are having their hair cut, or rather shaved, and playing draughts, over which they become quite absorbed. Saturday afternoon is the favourite time for the hair-cutting operations. I frequently went forward to watch the *modus operandi* at the main hatch, where the "boys" congregated. The barber, a good-looking fellow with long black cat-like whiskers, shaved the "believers" with great dexterity, but at a pace that made me thankful not to be under his hands myself. Sitting down on his heels in front of his customer, who also squatted, he gave him a little round hand-glass to watch all that was done, and then, razor in one hand

and the other resting on the head of the victim, he rolled it about from side to side, and soon removed the bristles of a week's growth, taking care, however, to leave that single lock of hair above the forehead by which the Angel of Death draws true believers up to heaven. The shaving over, and the Mussulman's skull being as smooth as a cannon-ball, the barber proceeds to put the finishing touches by extracting all superfluous hairs from the ears, nose, etc., and then cracking every finger-joint in turn; nay, for a couple of cash more, he will thump his customer all over, that being considered the most refreshing part of the whole operation. In spite of the terrible pace at which he is obliged to work to shave the whole crew in turn, he rarely makes a false stroke or inflicts a single cut.

On the whole the company of the ship was a very interesting collection of human beings, their officers seeming well contented with their work, everything being done at the proper time, and very little talking being necessary. In cold weather the natives are apt to get benumbed and stupefied, like bees in winter; but in the tropics, where the ships sail during the greater part of the time, they are perhaps as good as Europeans.

For the next two days we were out of sight of land. We now began to feel genuine equatorial heat and the resulting lassitude—white linen jackets and trousers for the men, and various pretty light dresses for the ladies, coming into fashion in our little society. The ship's officers had donned their hot-weather uniform on the first Sunday after passing through the Canal, and now looked both cool and neat in snowy white, with gold buttons and bands on their sleeves. They also laid aside their blue-peaked caps, and took to broad-brimmed white pith hats of a regulation pattern, very necessary for them, as they were constantly exposed to the rays of a roasting sun. For my own part, I found nothing so comfortable as thin white flannel. It was pleasant during the day, and when the sun went down and the usual heavy dew began to fall, it saved me from the chilly feeling which many other "griffins" on board experienced. I am sure of this, that whatever the outside clothes are made of, it is the height of rashness to wear anything but flannel or wool next the skin in the tropics.

For a head covering anything will do, as the passengers remain under the awning all day long; but it is best to wear something light, with good ventilation, since even a temporary exposure may result in a bad headache. Those who have never lived in the East can form no idea of how hot the sun can be, and what a power the orb has when it shines straight down. They have a vague sort of notion that it is "very warm," but perhaps they will appreciate it more if they were to remember that once or twice a steamer going through the Red Sea in hot weather has been obliged to turn and steam against the wind, simply to save the lives of those on board. Such, of course, is an exceptional case, and as a general rule the heat will be found bearable, though no one can afford to trifle with it.

While the sun was high up in the sky, the glare on the sea was so great that no land could be seen on either side; but when the sun went down in the west, he dropped behind the craggy Libyian hills, which loomed out inky black against the pale yellow "Libyian glow," about which artists and tourists rave, and which is certainly beautiful, though scarcely equal to the crimsons and greens of a sunset in the fjelds of Norway. When the sun sank down, the hills would come out in black profile against a pink and yellow sky, and twilight would deepen rapidly; but after fifteen or twenty minutes the sky began to get brighter and brighter, till it almost seemed the sun was coming back, and then the "after-glow" faded and darkness settled down on everything—the stars glittering out one after the other till the sky was as brilliant as the phosphorescent sea, and the dew began to fall heavily on the ship, soon soaking anything that was exposed to it.

By the 5th of September we were in the neighbourhood of "The Islands," and the water being shallow, we saw a great abundance of fishy life and many new birds. About six o'clock, when roused from my mattress on the saloon skylight by my "boy" with coffee and biscuits, the sea was alive with fishes of all sorts and sizes, and the perfect stillness of the surface enabled me to watch their various movements. The biggest fish were sharks. There were six or seven of them half a mile away on our starboard bow—but half a mile seems no distance on the open sea—rolling and plunging about in circles; every now and then one would rush up from deep under-water and throw his huge length several feet into the air, falling back with a resounding splash amid showers of spray. Fishes are usually supposed to lead a dull, pleasureless life, and few people would suspect any members of the tribe of actually romping, yet these "salt-sea robbers" were as clearly as possible having a game, and enjoying themselves in the early sunlight before the serious business of the day began. For my part, I believe there is a great deal more in the fishy mind than most people think. Nearer us there were sundry shoals of fish about the size of the Cornish rock bass, also leaping about; but as two or three porpoises were rolling in the neighbourhood, I expect they were more bent on escaping their enemies than playing. Everything that was not amusing itself was intent upon devouring some weaker victim.

In the air there were hundreds of little black-and-white sea-gulls, all pouncing upon the shoals of shining silver fry that the larger fish chased and compelled to leap into the air to avoid them, many being snapped up by the gulls before they could fall back. They seemed to be having a lively time between the fish and the birds, but perhaps it gave those that escaped a good appetite to prey in turn on yet feebler denizens of the deep. While every fish in the sea appeared to be thus dividing his energies between escaping from his pursuers in air and water, and eating as many as possible of his relations who happened to be smaller than himself, the gulls were being chased about and compelled to drop their booty by piratical-looking birds that seized it before it sank in the water. The eyesight of these birds and the gulls is most acute. There were many of them sailing round the *Almora* as high, at least, as her topmasts, and on the watch for any food that might be thrown overboard. How they knew they might expect any is a difficult question, but there they were; and having nothing better to do, I fetched a long, deep sea-line, and, baiting the last hook with bacon, soon had it trailing astern. To me the tiny speck of flesh was quite lost in the bubbling caldron of foam and spray turned up by the screw and meandering far away in our wake. I had not even a notion of whereabouts it was; but the gulls high up, who could scarcely even have seen me throw it overboard, caught sight of it at once, and came plunging down like hawks, picking it up without a moment's hesitation, though they "declined the hook with thanks."

Amusing ourselves with the numerous birds and fishes around the ship, we spent another roasting hot day, steaming quietly along till about 1 p.m., when we were off the "Twelve Apostles"—a group of islands standing boldly out from the sea in a long line, very evenly placed, and about a mile apart, like a gigantic row of nine-pins. The first one seen in coming from the northward is a mere steeple of grey rock, with the waves dashing nearly over it; but the others are much larger—the largest of all, and the central one, seeming about a couple of miles in circumference. They appeared to be clothed with short scrub and grass in places, but generally were very craggy and steep, in parts the cliffs rising straight out of the sea to a height of two hundred feet, while in others the sides sloped down, seamed with what looked like veins of black lava. I doubt if they are inhabited at present, but perhaps something might be made out of them—a fish-tinning manufactory could be started, for which there would be plenty of material in the surrounding sea, as we had been witnessing all the morning. If the sardine is found as low down as this, from what I have seen of the sardine fishery and preserving manufactories along the south coast of France and in Corsica, I should think these islands would be a very promising spot in which to commence operations. We cleared the lowest of the group just at sunset, and the long line of ragged pinnacles, lit up with the last red light, formed a striking picture till darkness hid them from us.

Early next morning we ran into a regular tropical downpour, though the sea was as calm as a mill-pond, and the sun just rising above the Arabian table-land. The *Almora* was for a time the centre of a miniature deluge; the rain, every drop as big as a bean, beat upon the awning and ran off the edges in an unbroken sheet that quite hid the sea from view. K——, whose mattress was next mine, hearing the noise, sleepily muttered that he thought it was going to rain, but when roused, we agreed that it was a great opportunity for adding a shower bath to our usual morning tubbing; so we went forward to the main hatch, where many of the gentlemen were congregated in light costume, getting the lascars who were scrubbing the decks to pump upon them with the fire hose.

At 7 a.m. the weather mended, and as the mist rose, we got a clear view around, and found we were steaming down a wild bare coast about ten miles on our port side. Long sandy beaches, strewn with rocks, alternated with rugged hills and precipices all the way until the two shores—Africa on the right and Arabia on the left—closed in rapidly upon us, and we seemed to be running down to the small end of a wedge. In appearance there was little to choose between either coast, both being equally rugged and barren—the result of the uncertain way in which the rain falls. For nine months or more, the land will be consumed with fiery heat, which reduces the soil to the condition of dust or sand. Then, perhaps, a small black cloud comes out of the sea, spreading as it goes, till it covers the whole sky; and then "the floodgates of heaven are opened," and nine months' rain descends in three or four days, furrowing the earth with water-courses, and washing all the soil away to the hollows or the sea; in fact, just such a rain-storm as we had witnessed that morning.

Perim was reached after breakfast—the island which divides the exit of the sea into two channels. Either passage is practicable for large ships, but the left one, being the widest, is most frequently used, and we steamed through it safely, yet had to keep the sounding-lead going, as very strong currents sweep these narrow inlets at certain seasons, and move sand-banks from place to place in an unpleasant manner. The day may even come when they will close up the mouths and turn the Red Sea into an inland lake, as has, beyond doubt, been done at the northern end by the Mediterranean. There is so little to be said about Perim itself that every one who feels bound to mention it takes refuge in the one stock story on the topic. The story is simply this. A French commander, on his way to annex the valuable little island to "la belle France," dropped in at Aden, and spent a jovial night with the English commander. He seems to have let out some hints of his purpose, for two hours before the too-talkative Frenchman got his frigate under sail the next morning, an English gunboat had stolen out of harbour, having on board as cargo a flagstaff and a Union Jack. When the Frenchman at length arrived at the goal of his ambition, one can well imagine the *sapristis* he uttered, when his eyes caught sight of the British flag fluttering from the summit of the highest peak in the early morning breeze. Here history merges into romance, some versions of the tale being that the French and English shook hands, and sat down to as good a breakfast as their means afforded, and others maintaining that the little episode nearly plunged the two great countries into war. Anyhow, as we passed in the *Almora* the British flag was still flying, and doubtless will fly there for ever. The only use of the island is as a foothold for a fort to dominate the straits, which, however, we have put off building. Nothing of agricultural value grows on it. It is a flat, barren, muffin-shaped place, with a dingy white lighthouse, backed by a dingier barrack in the centre. There is no soil, I believe, but a few dwarf cocoanut palms are grown in the barrack yard, and a small scrubby plant, with tiny yellow flowers, finds a scanty living amongst the cracks of the rocks. There is not even a supply of fresh water, but all wanted for drinking purposes has to be condensed from the sea-water. On the whole, I am glad I don't live at Perim.

As we left the island behind us, we emerged into

the Sea of Sinbad, changing our course from nearly due southward to a few points north of due east as we bore up for Aden, and meeting a strong breeze, which we had not felt inside, but which threw up a considerable swell in a very short time and sent some of the ladies below, though most of the gentlemen stayed on deck and watched the rugged Arabian coast to the northward of us passed slowly by. If the inside of the country were as uninviting as the outside, no one would desire to see more of it.

At five o'clock the same afternoon we reached Aden, and "easied" into the great land-locked bay that lies inside "Steamboat Point." Immediately we were seen approaching, long before we had finally dropped our anchor, flights of crows and kites started from the shore to inspect us, and, reaching our rigging, the former birds perched and set up an uproarious cawing to their friends on shore. This was my first introduction to the Indian crow, that famous bird which is to India what the sparrow is to England, but, indeed, even more noticeable and conspicuous than the latter. Only a little slower than the stream of kites and crows came a number of tiny canoes, impelled by Abyssinian boys, who, with a single paddle, working first on one side and then on the other, drove their primitive log "dug-outs" over the waves to the ship, where there was soon a flock of them, all shouting at the top of their voices, "I dive, sar! I dive, sar!" till some one threw overboard two or three small silver coins. As they touched the water a dozen little blacks sprang eagerly after them, going down like stones, and totally disregarding the sharks which abound in the bay. Canoes and paddles, left to their fate, bobbed about on the water, until one by one the black heads came to the surface, and black hands held up the coins, all of which had been safely recovered from the bottom of the sea. Then, as soon as every little savage had recovered his paddle and tumbled back into the canoe, the shouting began again, "Have a dive, sar, have a dive!" till we were deafened. Some had lumps of coral or shells with them, which they brought on deck to sell, scrambling up the ship's side by a slack rope as easily as monkeys; but they asked ridiculous prices for everything in the expectation of being beaten down. Their heads were covered, in many instances, with a hard white substance a couple of inches thick, looking like china clay. For some time I could not make out what this was, and was more puzzled to notice that some had the usual short, curly black hair, while on other heads, though equally curly, it was tawny gold. Afterwards I found it was owing to the lime with which they plaster their hair, for an obvious purpose, once every two or three months. This must be an uncomfortable process, and bleaches the hair to a dirty yellow when removed after a week or two. They were not at all bad looking, many of the little fellows having graceful forms, light-brown skins, and regular features. They are all from Somali-land, or the interior of Abyssinia, and come over in Red Sea trading vessels.

When one has mentioned that Aden is a burnt-out cinder, with, however, a good deal of warmth still left in it, and that nothing lives in the neighbourhood which can possibly avoid it, except crows and mosquitoes, all is said about it that there is to say. It is a sort of small edition of Gibraltar; only the "key of the Mediterranean" is of a pleasant neutral tint at a distance, with traces of vegetation, while this is of a torrid brown, painful to look at, without a single redeeming feature. How it came to be called Aden, which in Arabic is "Paradise"—the Eden of the Bible—I do not know, unless the joke was committed by some unfortunate resident in a fit of sarcastic spleen. We went ashore, of course, in a large party, but we took the precaution to make a good dinner first, and gave the "cinder" time to cool down after sunset before we started.

When the moon at length arose, we hailed "No. 1 boat," and, filling our purses, tumbled in and were rowed ashore. What a wonderful power moonshine has in softening ugliness and rounding off deformity! It is sometimes useful not to know too much. Too much light spoils a great many things, Aden amongst the number; but in the uncertain, charitable rays of the moon the great pile of lava, with its contorted strata and tall pinnacles, looks actually imposing.

Once on shore, our first thought was the post-office, which we reached only to see closed, it being then rather late in the evening; but, at the suggestion of the ship's doctor, who happened to be with us, we made for the agent's office, and soon found ourselves on an open sandy plain, with a semicircle of white houses round one side, well lighted up, and the harbour on the other. These houses were nearly all hotels, or shops for supplying goods to the ships anchoring off Steamboat Point, and mostly kept by the Parsees, who devote their lives and the large amount of wit Providence has given them to making money—"honestly if possible." At the agent's office—a large shop where everything, from postage stamps to ship's tackle, could be purchased—we stamped our letters, and then adjourned to a neighbouring hotel. We spent the remainder of the evening discussing "Beaconsfield and Salisburys," as somebody translated B. and S., while relays of Abyssinians pulled the huge punkah overhead, or stood behind our chairs fanning us with peacock-feather fans, in expectation of the sahib's magnanimous bounty.

The punkah is worth a word. It is an invention made to keep Englishmen in India as much below the boiling point as may be. In the ceiling of every room in a better-class Indian house there are strong hooks, to which short ropes are fastened, supporting a long thin teak board, which swings freely backwards and forwards. To the lower edge of the board is fastened a fringe or curtain, varying according to the tastes of the owner. Generally it is a foot or eighteen inches of brown holland with red braided borders, but sometimes the stuff is much more magnificent—pale cloth of gold, for instance, fringed with a deep border of white and scarlet flamingo feathers. From the teak board a bridle of two ropes is connected with another long cord, which passes through a hole in the wall, turns over a grooved wheel, and descends to the verandah or some other convenient place, from which it can be worked by the punkah-wallah, who sits on his heels pulling the line back and forth. At first, to those not accustomed to the ceaseless "flap, flap" of the heavy fringe, it is apt to give them a strong inclination to go to sleep, but after a time it becomes an absolute necessity, the slow creak of the wheel mixing with the hum of the night insects outside, and the currents of cool air being so essential to one's comfort that without them, should the punkah-wallah strike, or some accident happen, the Anglo-Indian is liable to a fit of temper. I pity the poor coolie who has the rope-pulling to do. He gets about fourpence a day; his occupation quite prevents him from going to sleep, and yet must be dreadfully somnolent work; but if he should succumb, and indulge in a peaceful "forty winks," he is generally rudely awakened by an empty soda-water bottle being thrown at him, or the butler being sent out with a stick to "oil the machinery."

Considerably after midnight, those who had taken most brandy and soda-water proposed to seize some donkeys that were standing on the sand below our verandah, and ride in a body to the great tanks built somewhere at the back of the island, or to scramble up to the highest peak in the neighbourhood and wait for sunrise, of which we should have a splendid view. But those who were not so full of Dutch courage, and who had chiefly confined themselves to cheroots and story-telling, were sleepy, and supported a counter proposition for getting on board and going to bed; so, after some discussion, we paid the "lawing" and walked down to the harbour, where we found our boat, and the crew asleep in her, swathed in their white bournouses.

The *Almora* was anchored just astern of a fine French frigate, the *Marseille;* so, before going on board, we ordered our boatmen to row slowly round the latter, and getting under her gleaming port-holes, we struck up the "Marseillaise," our voices rolling over the still water and awakening a wonderful echo from the rocks on shore.

"Allons, enfants de la patrie,
Le jour de gloire est arrivé,
Contre nous de la tyrannie,
L'étendard sanglant est levé:"

so we sang, till the Frenchmen came upon the stern of their vessel, and launched into a well-sustained "God save the Queen," which they sang capitally, quite "taking the starch out" of our performance; after which *rapprochement cordiale* we cheered them, nearly swamping our boat by all standing up at once, and finally got on board our ship, where we were soon buried in much-needed slumber.

On the second day from Aden we were running along the northern shore of the large island of Socotra, which appeared to be one of a group of six or seven; all the others, however, mere rocks, while the big island itself is nearly a hundred miles long by forty across in the broadest part. It seemed a most fertile spot, with white cliffs along the seaboard and green tracts of open country further inland.

The chief trade, I believe, is in aloes, which are largely used for paper-making, and it grows the dragon's-blood tree, from which a medicinal gum is obtained. The population is about four thousand, mostly Arabs, though there are some rich Banian traders located on the hills. Although the island at present belongs to the Sultan of Keshin—of whom probably very few people have heard—we have lately made a treaty with him by which he promises never to cede Socotra to any foreign Power, and never to allow any settlement to be made upon it without the consent of the British Government, which, needless to say, would not be given, as the island lies right in the road to India. Practically, that treaty and the small annual subsidy we pay to the Sultan places the island in our hands.

Then we lost the protection of Socotra cliffs and the far-away Cape Guardafui, and got out into the open sea, where we soon found ourselves in for a "capful of wind," as sailors pleasantly call a good gale. It blew hard and harder every hour, till it scarcely seemed weather could be any worse. The ship heeled over and raced through the water, with huge curling waves chasing her on either side, every now and then sending a blinding shower of spray sweeping across the bows, or landing a few tons of water on the deck, where it careered about in an unruly flood, washing armchairs, cushions, novels, and everything movable, down into the lee-scuppers. Above all rose the creaking of the yards, the whistling of the wind amongst the cordage, varied by the occasional breaking of china, the quacking of the ducks, and mournful remonstrances of the inmates of the various pens and cages forward as they lurched about from side to side.

Very few remained on deck for the first day or two, but I thoroughly enjoyed the blow. It certainly was very rough—rougher than I have ever seen the sea, even in the German Ocean or the Mediterranean under a tearing *mistral*. The big green waves came on board of us every five minutes, setting everything floating about the deck, and driving all hands from cover to cover like rabbits across the open. About mid-day, when the wind was end on, and we were plunging heavily through the sea, our fore square-sail gave way to an extra strong puff of wind. One moment the great sheet of white canvas was bellied out without a wrinkle in it, straining the ropes and making the spars creak, and the next we heard a sound like blasting in a stone quarry, and, looking up, saw the best part of the sail flying away down the wind like a lady's handkerchief, while all that remained was a collection of streaming ribbons that fluttered and lashed about in the gale.

This sort of thing went on for a couple of days, and then ended in soft breezes, which blew till we got into shallower water near the Maldive Islands. The milder weather brought the ladies out of their cabins one after the other—looking, alas! as if care or something else had been feeding on their "damask cheeks," but they picked up rapidly when they had breathed the fresh air for a little while and tasted several good meals. A little later we were able to point out to them some faint threadlike things on the horizon as palm-trees growing on the low coral reefs of the "hundred thousand islands," and about noon we were steaming very slowly and carefully through the most southerly of the great upper group of atolls called by the general name of Lacadives.

Fortunately we got the best of passing glances at this interesting group, and were duly grateful, as steamers often keep far out in the broad "ten degrees channel" where nothing can be seen of them. Every spot of these strangely created lands was covered with a dense forest of palm-trees, from which the few thousand fishermen who inhabit them derive a considerable revenue in cocoa-nuts, oil, toddy, and fibre, all of which they convey in open boats to Colombo and the ports of the Indian coast. The effect of salt water at the roots of these trees is curious. In one place we approached a small atoll, with the usual forest of palms growing down to the water's edge, but one patch, about a hundred yards square, was of a dark brown colour, giving us the impression the trees had been badly burnt or singed just there, until we came quite close to the island, when it turned out that there was a small sandspit running along one part of the face, and separated from the atoll by about twenty yards of water. The palms on the older, and possibly deeper, soil of the latter were of the ordinary glossy green; while those on the sand-bank, whose roots were probably deep under water, were of a dull, sombre brown, though to all appearance growing.

The flying-fish had been very numerous since we left Aden, but we saw them to most advantage when the sea was calm, as it was here. At other times they seemed to go deep down, only coming up to the surface occasionally in twos or threes. When, however, the sea was a sheet of glass, and our vessel passed through the water like some great marine monster, the sight was most interesting and novel. The fish rose in scores all round us. Leaning over the ship's side, I could see far in the green depth great herds of them swimming backwards and forwards, each shoal under the guidance of an old and cautious leader, who had doubtless had many narrow escapes from the jaws of large members of his species or the ravenous dolphin. They would swim this way and that—now diving down, till I could hardly distinguish their shadowy forms, and now coming up nearer the surface in their efforts to elude or outpace the steep black sides of the monster who had invaded their dominions. After a time the leader would give some sort of signal —a peculiar twist of his expressive fins perhaps—and all the shoal would turn their heads from the ship. Then I could just make out a great wriggling of tails as the fish shot upwards through the water with arrow-like rapidity. Another second and they had reached the surface, and, spreading their great side fins, their impetus carried them away over the surface of the waves with an easy, rapid flight. The distance which some of the largest and strongest fish accomplished was really astonishing; one, a fine fellow of about a pound weight, sprang out of the water just as I happened to be looking at my watch, and I took the opportunity of timing his flight, which was close upon four minutes from rise to fall. During that time it must have covered a distance of at least half a mile, which seemed a very remarkable performance, seeing the fish made no pretence to actual flying, keeping its fins out nearly at right angles from its body the whole time, and trusting to the impulse received in the starting rush through the water. Frequently they avoided breaking crests by rapid side turns which could not have been better done by swallows on the wing. As a rule, however, their flight was quite straight—nothing more than a long glide about a foot above the surface, but offering a very curious sight when there were several hundreds on the wing at once, crossing and recrossing each other like house martins over the shallows of an English brook in summer time.

Since leaving Suez no one had thought of reposing between decks, everybody sleeping in the open, the ladies having all the "after skylight" to themselves, separated from the rest of the ship by a screen of canvas and Union Jacks. We used to see them flitting from their cabins below to their mattresses behind the awning like shrouded ghosts, and then things would settle down quietly in their dominions;—the lanterns were put out, and silence held an "ancient solitary reign," broken only by occasional sounds such as the strange, melodious cry of the look-out men in the bows and on the bridge, passing the word to "keep a bright watch ahead" after every bell that rang the half-hours of nautical time. Occasionally, it is true, there would be a disturbance among the sheep and poultry in the forward part of the ship, or a cock would wake up suddenly and send a solitary crow echoing over the still sea, which would rouse the ducks, who quacked out a vigorous remonstrance against being disturbed, and were in their turn upbraided by the whole flock of geese, who seemed to use very strong language. Then, perhaps, the fair sleepers on the other side of the curtain would raise an alarm of "black beetles," and we heard smothered shrieks and screams, and a dozen cries of "Throw it overboard!" "Kill it!" "Stamp on it!" "Don't hurt it!" "Call the stewardess!" etc. Of course we all jumped up, and though no one dared to go to the rescue, some of us pushed brooms, mops, etc., under the bottom of the curtain, while others ran to fetch the stewardess or doctor, or anything else they could think of in the ardent chivalry of the moment. The cockroaches certainly were not nice — huge, great fleshy creatures, three or four times the size of their English brethren, with an ample allowance of spiky legs and waving antennæ. They swarmed all over the ship, and anything animal or vegetable left within their reach became speedily tainted with their unsavoury presence; so we showed them very little mercy, condemning all those we caught to a watery grave.

The last day of the voyage was a charming one.

We were steaming along over the strangest "ground-swell" I ever encountered. The sea was beautifully smooth, but as far as eye could see furrowed by long, unbroken undulations. Our course being directly at right angles to these curious vibrations of some distant storm, we at one time were apparently gliding down the gentle slope of a watery ridge for a couple of hundred yards, and then as gently steaming up the corresponding rise for the same distance. It was quite impossible for the worst sailor to be ill under the circumstances, for there was not a speck of broken water to be seen anywhere, excepting the splashes made by the innumerable flying-fish leaping and falling into the sea. About noon we made out Cape Comorin far away to the northward—two slender peaks on the horizon standing out, beyond the possibility of being mistaken for clouds, against the serene blue sky. Some one who had once landed under them described the southernmost point of the Indian peninsula as being very wild and barren—great ranges of uninhabited bare mountains, towering one above the other, and below a broad beach, sloping into the water from the foot of the cliffs. This beach is said to present a curious appearance at a little distance, being banded very evenly with alternate black and yellow stripes of pulverized coal, of a coarse kind, and fine sand. Very beautiful and many rare shells are thickly scattered about, together with the famous "money-cowrie" and several sorts of valuable corals—all, of course, more or less broken up.

When my "boy" brought me the usual cup of coffee and biscuits the following morning, I roused myself and took a look round. We were still gliding at half-speed over a bright, sunlit sea, smooth as a mill-pond, without a ripple anywhere. The sun was but a very little way above the horizon, not high enough to dry up the heavy dew that hung thick and sparkling all over the ship. The sky was the pleasantest of pale-blues; so smooth and soft, it seemed it could never be black and frowning. But what riveted my attention at once was a long line of rugged blue mountains stretching along the eastern horizon, with a broad belt of green lowlands at their base, reaching down to the sea. That was Ceylon, the land of pearl and amethyst, of spices and palms—"where every prospect pleases, and only man is vile."

The word that there was land in sight soon brought an excited crowd with opera-glasses and telescopes to look at the new scenes. We divided our attention between watching for the town and harbour of Colombo, which lies low down on the coast, and admiring the ragged outline of Adam's Peak, which we made out very clearly far inland, although it is not usually seen at this time of year, the highest mountains being enveloped in the white sea-mist brought up by the south-west monsoon. From a religious point of view it is considered the holiest of holy spots, alike by Buddhists, Mohammedans, and Brahmans, for on the summit there is a huge footmark sunk deep into the hard rock, where it has been "since the world was made." This is ascribed by the Buddhists to the last incarnation of Buddha, the princely hermit Gautama—and certainly, if he lived up here he had plenty of time for thinking—while the Brahmans say it is the footstep of the holy Siva, and Mohammedans believe that Adam stood there for a few hundred years when he did penance after being expelled from the Garden of Eden. This holy print, or Sripada, is a depression in the face of the rock about five feet in length by some two and a half feet broad. Originally it bore only the very smallest resemblance to a human footmark, but the Buddhist priests who hold charge of it have ventured to touch it up with mortar, and, by marking the divisions of the toes and giving it a heel, have brought it now to a point of very passable resemblance to the left footprint of a vast giant. They have also erected a temple over it, to which many pilgrims go to say the comprehensive prayer, and from such pilgrims, who climb the great peak by a long succession of stone steps and bamboo ladders, the priests derive a handsome revenue.

Those great violet mountain ranges were grand and impressive, and had I gone no nearer I should have come away with a very high opinion of the beauty of Ceylon, but a closer acquaintance dispelled much of the pleasure of the first early morning glimpse we caught of the island. Sidney Smith said he had two illusions left—one was the Archbishop of Canterbury, and the other was raspberry-and-currant tart. I feel for him, as I had an illusion once, and it was Ceylon.

We neared the land very rapidly, although the sea was so smooth we could hardly believe we were moving. About thirty miles from the shore we ran through a fleet of trading vessels bound to the Maldive Islands with the money they had obtained by the sale of the fish, chank shells, and produce of the palm tree, which form the staple products of the locality. The cocoa-nut palm, in fact, is their staff of life, and nearly everything about the boats we saw was made from the palm-tree. The little boats looked very curious and picturesque, with flapping sails waiting for the morning breeze, as we made our way through them, and set each rocking astern of us; bearing as we did the proportion to the half-decked cockle shells that a well-fed pike does to a minnow. I would certainly rather be on board of them in a calm than in a monsoon storm, for they appear totally unfit for ocean trading; yet probably the wild-looking savages who form the crews understand the signs of the weather, and do not put out to sea unless they are sure of a fine run.

Still closer in to the land we passed through another fleet—this time of smaller boats—all busily engaged fishing with hand-line, on a long, low coral-bank that runs parallel with the coast, and has about fifteen fathoms of water on it, to supply the Colombo market with its daily supply of fish. It was a curious sight to note the naked brown figures of the fishermen in their uncouth boats, and hear their shouting and talking in unknown tongues, while they hauled up the glistening prey of all sorts and shapes, or threw overboard some refuse scraps of bait to the crowds of hungry gulls that wheeled around with discordant cries in the air overhead. None of them made room for us, however, though a few hundred years ago the appearance of such a ship as ours would have frightened their ancestors out of their wits; and we had to pick our way very carefully through the crowd, until we at last safely emerged on the inside of the fleet, without having done any greater harm than breaking a few lines and scaring the fish in the neighbourhood of our track. Then, as we slowly neared the land, the various details came forth one after another, and we made out tall feathery palms against the sky line, and then white houses, and lastly, a long, low, sandy beach, with a crowd of ships and boats of apparently every nation in the world, all peaceably at anchor under the guns of the white fort, from the summit of which the British flag fluttered gaily in the morning breeze.

It was only with the greatest reluctance we could tear ourselves away from the enchanting prospect, to turn our attention to such commonplace affairs as breakfast and packing up; but they both had to be transacted. However, we went below, and after a substantial meal and a little speech-making, in which our kind and attentive captain was suitably thanked by the spokesman of our party, we proceeded to put the finishing touches to our packing operations.

When I got on deck again, we were in the harbour of Colombo, which stretched round us in a deep crescent-shaped bay. To the right ran out a rocky promontory surrounded by a strongly built English fort, in the embrasures of which we could see, even at the distance of a mile, a large number of powerful cannons, ready to sweep the harbour if need be. Below it a long broken grey wall marked the battlements of the old fort built by the Portuguese when they held the island, but now fallen into decay, and deserted for the new and more powerful fortifications we have built. Behind the clean-looking fort we caught a glimpse of Government House, a fine four-storied white building, almost hidden in a dense mass of vivid green trees and palms, from the midst of which rose a tall flagstaff with the Union Jack fluttering out in the wind. Looking round the shores of the bay, first there was the English town of well-built white chunnam bungalows, all more than half buried in deep green foliage, and beyond the European town lay the native bazaar—a vast collection of picturesque little red-roofed huts, one storied, of course, and boasting only the simplest styles of architecture, reaching right down to the water's edge, where innumerable fishing-boats of strange forms and patterns were moored to piles or drawn up beyond the reach of the waves. These boats extended half round the great crescent-shaped bay, until the towering palms which were dotted about very numerously among the red-roofed mud dwellings gradually grew more and more numerous, and the outskirts of the town were reached, where an unbroken forest of splendid cocoa-nut palms swept right round the northern arm of the inlet. Above all, the brilliant sun was shining down on everything, and gave that tropical appearance to the view which must be seen to be understood.

CHAPTER IV.

CEYLON AND ITS PEOPLE.

AMONGST the ships in harbour were two or three of the crazy-looking two-masted Dutch barks, painted the usual green and white; and yet, somehow or other, these creep all over the world, and are to be found in every port and inlet whence merchandise can be shipped, no matter what the latitude or longitude. Here, if their crews have read modern history, they must feel a tinge of sorrow overspreading their minds as they look at the fertile island which was once their own. Besides these, there were vessels of several other countries in the harbour; but the English ships were much the most numerous, the best built, and the best ordered of all.

No sooner had our starboard anchor gone down with a great rattling of chain, and the ship swung into her berth, than we were stormed by the dusky crews of a dozen clumsy cargo boats that came alongside to take off our Colombo merchandise. Directly we were at rest these boats came bumping and pushing against the sides of the ship, until their crews, with a prodigious amount of shouting and fighting, had made them fast somehow or other, and then the bright-skinned Cingalese and Tamil boatmen seized the slack ropes hanging overboard, and scrambled up the sides of the ship, jumping down from the bulwarks. They were soon in apparent possession of the deck, though they happily confined themselves to the forward part of the vessel; one or two who ventured down towards the saloon, where the ladies were, being driven forward with but scant ceremony. Physically these men left very little to be desired. I had expected to find every one wearing a black skin in India on the verge of starvation, on account of the long famine that had existed for the last two years in the Madras Presidency and to the southward; and so I was pleased to see these coolies, at all events, remarkably well nourished, tall, and strongly made, many of them of good personal appearance. Although not particularly clean, they seemed to shave with great scrupulousness, never wearing the smallest vestige of hair about their faces; and when they took off the rag which was wound round their heads as a sort of apology for a turban, to mop up the perspiration which soaked their brows, I noticed that their scalps were also closely shaven. Whether their heads were newly shorn or not, all had left one long forelock just above the forehead, in order that the Angel of Death may, as has been said, take hold of it when he draws them up to heaven. The Red Indians leave just such a lock of hair growing, but with them it is not a religious form, being an act of courtesy to enable their enemies to "lift" their scalps with greater convenience when they kill them. This is very considerate!

While the swarm of black figures was hard at work unloading the fore-hold of the numerous English goods for the Colombo market, their ceaseless chatter and the fearful rattling of the energetic donkey-engine drove us half wild; but we completed our packing operations, tipped our special "boys" the usual ten rupees, and then, after a hasty meal, W—— and myself pushed off for the shore in a native canoe, after promising our friends to come back for one more dance that evening. The boat in which we embarked was a very remarkable structure, and about as uncomfortable as it was strange. As for "beam," it had none to speak of. It was constructed in this way. The bottom was formed of the trunk of a small palm-tree, hollowed out, rounded off at either end, and planed smooth below. The sides of the hollow were built upward with thin planks of teak bent together at the ends, and laced one to another with numberless strong fibres of coir, passing through small holes bored opposite each other in the planks. There is scarcely a nail about the boat, the cracks being caulked with coarse tow, and the lacing of fibres giving an elasticity and springiness which could not be obtained were the construction different, and proves of the greatest service in any rough weather. The top edge of the planks, about four feet out of the water, is roughly finished off by a lacing of small round bamboo, and the small seats are made of large split bamboos. The result is a canoe that would horrify an English boat-builder, but which is fully equal to a spell of rough weather. Although the length is eighteen or twenty feet, the beam is not more than a foot and a half, and the seats are between three and four inches above the water, so that the rowers, and the passengers too, if they like, can let their toes dangle in the waves on either side as they go along—a luxury which would, however, be dangerous on account of the sharks which abound along the coast. But this is not all; the most curious part of the canoe being two long light bamboo poles that pass across the boat, and, being lashed to the bulwarks on either side, project eight or nine feet over the water, having a long light log of palm or some other equally buoyant wood lashed to them. The purpose of this outrigger is to prevent the boat upsetting when struck by a sea, which duty it performs so well that these apparently fragile boats venture out in weather that would swamp an ordinary craft, while their speed over smooth water is only slightly diminished.

In a proa of this peculiar construction W—— and myself, whose fortunes were linked for the present, started for the shore at about 11.30 a.m., and had a fearfully hot row of three-quarters of an hour against a strong current and under a blazing sun. There was no awning to the boat, and though I had a white umbrella and a pith helmet, the latter boasted no puggaree, or linen flap hanging down behind, and the former was English made, so that the material, though all that could be desired as protection against English suns, let the fiery glare of the Indian orb through like water through a sieve. I was nearly roasted, and in much danger of sunstroke before we had threaded our way among the ships; but eventually we reached the stone steps of the landing-jetty.

To commence with, I had a very rude awakening from the ideal picture formed of Ceylon; for no sooner had we arrived within a hundred yards of the shore, than we were aware of a most fearful odour, which came to us on the hot land-wind that blows all day. This, getting worse as we approached, nearly completed the work of the roasting sun, and put us *hors de combat.* The cause was not far to seek, for on reaching the jetty we found the beach was a broad level of black putrid mud, on which the little waves of the harbour rolled over and over a dreadful collection of garbage, dead cats and dogs, and the general refuse of a large town. The only things that seemed anything but sickened in the neighbourhood were countless flocks of Indian crows, which hopped and cawed while they feasted royally on various carrion and acted as much-needed scavengers, though every now and then a big kite would come sailing along overhead, and, spying a choice morsel in the beak of some crow, would turn silently, by a motion of his long wings, and fall swooping down with the velocity of a crossbow bolt. Scattering the cawing black scavengers right and left, he would snatch up the

"HE WEARS THE LIVERY OF SIN WITHOUT A BLUSH."

tempting piece of offal, and flap slowly away to eat it in some neighbouring palm-tree or on the roof-ridge of a reed-thatched native hut. This was not a very promising beginning, but when once landed and on the shoreward side of the beach, things grew better, yet I shall not easily forget my first experience of the "spicy breezes" of Ceylon, though subsequently I experienced many that took the keen edge off the memory of the first.

At the bottom of the landing-jetty was a sandy yard with warehouse sheds and custom-house offices all round. Directly opposite to where we stood opened a fine gateway in the high brick wall of what had once been the outer barricade of the old Portuguese fort. This gateway had one tall central span for the bullock carts to pass through, and two narrow archways, one on either side, for the foot traffic; and it framed in very prettily a glimpse of the English town beyond, with its white houses standing amongst luxuriant green foliage.

But what struck me most were the white bullocks used for drawing the two-wheeled country carts. There were some fifty or sixty of them at the time lying or standing about the yard in all positions, some sleeping with half-closed eyes, some shaking their big ears from side to side and ruminating over the delights of inland pastures, while others stood in the shade shaking their heavy dewlaps and swinging their tails. All of them were sublimely idle; and so were the few native drivers who were to be seen curled up under the bandies, or chewing betel-nut in shady corners. Most of the bullocks were white, though some were grey, but whatever the colour, all stood adorned in a most extraordinary and fantastic manner by patterns and diagrams burnt into their hides with hot irons. One poor creature, who must have exercised a great deal of patience while his master was using him as a canvas for his artistic tastes, had a remarkable plant-like design starting from a point on his back, twisting and turning all over his body. There ran a couple of spiral tendrils down each leg, several things like full-blown sunflowers on either side, and every blank space left after the elaborate drawing had been finished was filled up with stars, moons, and circles. All these had been burnt into the hide long before, and probably gave the animal considerable suffering, to say the least of it; but it seems a very general custom, and is supposed to bring luck to the animals, some of which had even sentences from the holy books, and incantations, burnt into their skins in Tamil and Cingalese characters to keep off the evil eye and save them from disease. As far as beef-making went they certainly did not look much, having no points about them which would secure the favour of an English cattle judge; but they are very fairly fitted for beasts of draught in a land where no one ever hurries much, and where the travelling is done slowly over bad roads.

The bandies or country carts were also curious constructions, designed by simplicity itself, being nothing more than a narrow platform about seven or eight feet long and two feet wide, mounted on two high wooden wheels of country make, and consequently shaky and unreliable. To protect travellers from the glare of the sun, long bamboos in most cases were bent over from side to side, and coarse cocoa-nut matting or matting of split rattan canes placed upon this, laced down with coir fibres, thus forming a rude shelter open at both ends. The single pole to which the two bullocks are attached, one on each side, had at the further end a curved yoke, which goes just in front of the hump growing above the shoulders of all these cattle, and a single strap passing under the throat is the only thing that keeps the self-willed animals in their places. They thus have perfect freedom to turn round and stare the driver in the face, if they like, and occasionally do indulge in bad behaviour, but on the whole their conduct is very good, considering the treatment they

any real security against intruders; but in India one soon loses the English habit of locking and barring everything at sundown. The crows find their way in and make themselves quite at home. When the hotel servant first showed me my bedroom, there was a crow perched on the edge of the washing jug, regarding his shadow in the water beneath with Narcissus-like satisfaction which we rudely disturbed, sending him cawing and fluttering out to the sheds in the yard below.

Then, after a refreshing tub, always an important institution in India, I made my way down to the great cool *salle à manger*, and proceeded to take tiffin in solitary grandeur as the regular meal was over; but the chief result of this was that I had the whole set of waiters to myself. It was not an unalloyed pleasure, for there were six of them in immediate attendance on me, and sundry cooks and "cook boys" hanging about the room, or stealing glances at the latest arrival through the tatties. The punkah-wallah, when he saw me enter the room, sprang up from the shady corner, where he had been chewing betel-nut, and, spitting the juice at the lizard running along the gravel path outside, hurried to his post in the verandah and commenced to swing the long punkah waving over the table. The "boys" also put in an appearance from various quarters, shaking themselves together and setting their turbans straight, while I sat down and looked over the bill of fare. The food turned out to be, on the whole, good, commencing with a fish from the coral reefs outside the harbour, very much like salmon in appearance and taste, and then some ordinary courses, ending as usual with two or three sorts of curry and "Bombay ducks."

But, on the whole, I was rather glad when the "butler boy" brought me a finger glass with roses floating in it, and asked with a deep salaam if the sahib would smoke; and tiffin was over, for the half-dozen waiters—tall Cingalese in flowing white robes, worn like the old Roman toga, and tortoise-shell combs in their hair—who stood round the table in a circle, motionless as statues, and watched every action, were irksome.

The crows also became a nuisance. At first they were amusing, but there came twenty in attendance while I was at tiffin, and goodness only knows how many more about the hotel and the compound behind the house. They sat on the rafters overhead, on the top of each open door, on the venetian blinds, on the doorsteps, all along the edge of the verandah, and everywhere else. Once or twice, while the "boys" were out of the room, an extra bold bird flew in and deliberately perched on the back of a chair on the side of the table opposite to where I was sitting; thence, after a few caws, he pounced down on a piece of bread or meat, and bore it away in triumph through the window to a neighbouring roof-ridge. It was of no use trying to scare them away, as I soon found. At one time the cawing all round was so noisy that I seized a plantain out of a dish that stood near at hand, and hurled it at a black sinner flapping and squawking on the top of the door; but instead of moving on, he saw the action in a different light, and, pouncing down on the banana, invited all his friends, far and near, to join in the feast. The summons spread rapidly, and crows came trooping up from all parts, till there was scarcely standing room for them on the neighbouring tiles, and all the air was full of a horrible noise; so that the butler and his assistants had to rush forth, and shout and wave and throw stones, until the uproar had somewhat calmed down. Really a few of these crows ought to be taken up for "disorderly conduct," or suppressed by some means. I had read a great deal about them before, but they are much blacker in every way than any one who has not seen them would believe; in fact, these fowl were nearly the only thing that did not disappoint me on my first day in Ceylon.

The natives, of course, attracted a great deal of my attention during the first walk I took, and the Cingalese especially, who form by far the larger portion of the population—here in Colombo at all events. They are a very fine, muscular set, the thews and sinews of those that wore nothing but the cummerbund or waistcloth standing out very visibly from their dark limbs and forms. Most, however, were clothed in a single roll of white linen, twisted round the body and brought up over the left shoulder, leaving the right arm and part of the chest bare. Some of the richer classes wear embroidered shoes with turned-up toes, and all, rich or poor, fastened their hair behind with a high tortoise-shell comb, which, standing high above their heads, gave them a curious appearance. The hair of the men was remarkably long and thick, as long as that of the women, and it was a curious sight to see a fat old gentleman in a white toga, with yellow shoes, sitting on a stone under a shady tree and leisurely combing and twisting his long raven-black tresses, which hung down to the place where his waist used to be. I passed several thus employing their afternoon leisure.

The twilight deepened into night so rapidly that my first tour of exploration was brought to a close almost before it had begun, and I had some difficulty in finding the way back to the hotel, which, however, was reached just in time to dress for the *table d'hôte.* At this there sate a considerable gathering of English people, very few of whom lived in the hotel, but were bachelor citizens and officers who found the cooking more to their taste than such as they could get at their own bungalows or messes. The talk was very "shoppy"—nothing but "import and export duties," or kindred subjects; so, being both sleepy and tired after the day's exertions, I made my escape as soon as possible, and sought the seclusion of my loose-box-like bedroom; but not to sleep! I had somehow forgotten there were such things as mosquitoes, until reminded of the existence of those wretched creatures very effectually that evening. The first mosquito died; but there were hundreds more about, and before I could slip under the gauze curtains which hung round my bed, at least a dozen of the small assassins had made a blood-thirsty attempt on me. Even then two or three of the miscreants worked their way into the curtain at some unguarded hole, and persecuted me fearfully. If there is any truth in Buddhism, I wonder whose souls enter the bodies of these abominable little wretches?

About 1 a.m. I did drop off—probably because all the mosquitoes inside the curtains had supped heavily, and left me for a short time while they digested. But the respite was brief, for it soon began to rain, not in a civilized English drizzle, but a sudden outburst of water, as if all the reservoirs of heaven were broken. The rain came down in torrents, and rushed off the eaves on to the gravel below with a continuous clatter, so that it was impossible to sleep. Even the crows were disturbed, and two or three cawed wildly as they flapped about in the outside darkness trying to find shelter somewhere. The rain beat so violently on the tiles overhead as to wash two or three off; and I listened to the water coming down in my neighbour's room, and heard him, springing from the protection of his bed-curtains, call loudly for a "boy." Then there was considerable excitement amongst a family of little brown-striped squirrels, who perhaps had made their nest in the rain-water pipes under the eaves; at all events, something seemed to have gone wrong with them, as they set up a most prodigious chirrupping and squeaking, and rushed frantically backwards and forwards about the beams overhead, under the impression that the hours of the world were numbered, and Buddha was already destroying the six lower heavens, as is written in the sacred books that it shall be. So the night passed, with torrents of rain broken by bright flashes of lightning that gleamed through the bars of my venetian blinds every few minutes, and were followed by thunder, which sounded as though volcanic explosions were going off in rapid succession only a few feet above the roof. But at last the welcome dawn came, the rain stopped, and I must have seized this opportunity to snatch a brief slumber, for when I woke up the sun was shining brightly through the open windows, and my particular "boy," who had thrown them wide to wake me, was busy getting my bath-tub ready.

One thing strikes the new-comer on his very first day in an Indian house, and it is the lizards. Fancy the excitement there would be in a London drawing-room if even a single lacertan were to be observed stalking flies on the walls of the room, and yet here nothing is thought of a score of reptiles so engaged. Immediately it grows dusk and the palm-oil lamps are lit, they come from the crannies of the roof, where they have been dozing out the day, and commence a diligent search for food on the broad white expanse of their "happy hunting grounds." It does not seem to make the smallest difference to them what their position is, or whether their head or tail be uppermost —they lay their plans just as deeply if they are topsy-turvy as in any other attitude. When they espy a fly asleep on the horizon, they make tracks for him. I saw a smart little grey lizard start after a fly perched on the wall at the farthest corner of the room. The lizard at first approached his victim rapidly until the intervening space was very much reduced, and then he began to slacken his speed. Finding he was nearing the fly from a quarter whence he could be seen, he "fetched a compass" of a couple of feet, and got round to the rear of his victim. Then he began to approach more slowly still, and when only a few inches away, he proceeded with the utmost caution, placing first one paw down and then the other, until he came within an inch or two of the unconscious victim. There was a pause for a moment, a sudden spring forward, and the fly had gone, and the lizard was gulping something down his throat with every appearance of satisfaction. They rarely miss their aim, and, being most expert stalkers, the good which a score or two must do, feeding all night on the mosquitoes and flies, should be considerable.

While at Colombo I rose early one morning to walk over to the Museum and Botanical Gardens, which are well worth a visit. My way led me through the eastern portion of the native town, and getting lost for a time in a labyrinth of lanes, I saw a good deal of native modes of living and habits, which were occasionally more peculiar than pleasant; but the bright sun overhead, and the gay colours which glanced out from amongst the raggedest crowd, softened down the appearance of squalor and ennobled even dirt. There was the usual profusion of native fruits and vegetables in the bazaars, and the dry goods were nearly all of English manufacture; even the little native children were enjoying themselves in the hot dust with empty sardine-boxes, which they were towing about with string as miniature carts;

while Peak and Frean biscuit-cases were put to a multitude of domestic purposes.

Just outside the town there is a broad sheet of water with a palm-covered island in the centre. It cannot improve the health of the place, as it does not seem particularly clean; but there it stands, and is largely used by the natives for washing both themselves and the linen of the Europeans. A line of rails runs round this lake, and while walking along the road a curious accident happened. A dhoby, or washerman (all the washing is done out here by men), had been hard at work cleansing the linen of some English family, and, having got through early, had placed all the clean things in his basket, which he had deposited on the line of railway while he went away to chew betel-nut or something of the kind. No sooner had the luckless man gone out of sight behind some native huts, than an engine and tender came along at full speed, and dashed headlong into the basket, which was thrown into the air, discharging its "white confusion" like a bursting shell. The engine flew through the cloud of linen, and the next moment rushed by me with a variety of useful articles of attire streaming out in the air from the funnel and various parts to which they had stuck, while the remainder were torn to shreds amongst the wheels underneath.

I found myself at last in the gardens of the Museum, which were crowded with a variety of strange and new shrubs and plants, and alive with birds and butterflies. These gardens alone were amply sufficient for one morning's investigation, and afforded a regular "botanical debauch," as Mr. Grant Duff calls it in his charming "Notes on an Indian Journey." Here were growing together a vast collection of tropical plants brought from all corners of the island, but the chief places were given to those whose products were useful to humanity. Amongst them the cinnamon held a conspicuous rank. Close by was a cluster of the graceful cardamom plant, which is already affording profitable employment to planters in the jungles. There were cotton bushes, which grow the cotton of commerce, and towering cotton trees, in which the kites seem particularly fond of building their nests. A little further on rose a jungle of sugar-canes, with long rough leaves, and then a patch of tobacco plants in full bloom, receiving great attention from numerous black and red butterflies. There were bread-fruits and jack-fruits, calamanders, ebony, satin, rose, sappan, iron, jack, and innumerable others, but everywhere, the most useful of all, the omnipresent palm. Everybody appears to admire palms very much, but it seems to me they are over-praised. It is all very well to talk about their gracefulness, but they give little shade in a land where shade is a priceless luxury. Truly they are very useful commercially, but they do not come within a very long way of an old English oak or chestnut for beauty.

CHAPTER V.

A MOUNTAIN CITY.

On the following morning I was awakened by W——, who occupied the next room to mine, putting his head and shoulders over the partition which divided the rooms, and saying he had received orders last night from the Colombo agents of his company to proceed forthwith to the scene of his future labours, somewhere about forty miles to the north-west of Kandy, in the centre of the island, and was going to start by the first train. If I wanted to see the ancient capital of the island, now was my chance. After a moment's consideration his proposition was accepted, and a few minutes afterwards we were both seated in the dewan-khana, hard at work on coffee and eggs—very small ones these, by the way, four or five only making up the substance of one English egg—and then, getting through our chota hazri, we started off for the railway station.

When we reached the summit of a little eminence, from which a good view of the town and harbour was to be obtained, we both turned at once to take a last look at the *Almora*, but we looked in vain. There lay the green-and-white Dutchmen, and the Government frigate, and a score of other ships, but our vessel's berth was empty, and nothing left of her save a faint line of smoke on the southern horizon. We both felt that our last tie with England was gone, and, after watching the receding smoke for a few minutes, we smothered our feelings by setting off at a great pace for the station again. We took second-class tickets to Kandy, and got into what was labelled a second-class compartment, but in point of comfort it might have been a fourth or fifth class. It was open right through, with the hardest of hard wooden seats. We made a start about half-past seven, and at first the line ran through deep groves of palm trees and scattered native huts, in front of the doors of which there were always a collection of little brown children, dogs, and chickens, all living on terms of perfect equality, and apparently both very happy and very dirty. Beyond the palm groves, which only fringe the seacoast, the country became more open, and I saw rice growing again for the first time since I was a very small *chokra* and was out in India—about the time of the Mutiny.

The rice is called paddy by the natives, and the

English, adopting the word, call the places in which it is grown paddy-swamps; and they are real swamps. There are no hedges such as make the country so diverse and interesting in England, but each field is separated from the adjoining field by a high-mud bank, broad at the base and two or three feet wide at the top, which is from four to six feet above the level of the surrounding land. When the young rice is planted, the water is turned into the enclosure from some neighbouring stream or canal, and ploughed backwards and forwards by native ploughs drawn by white bullocks. The result is a fearful "Slough of Despond," the whole field becoming one sea of liquid mud, but that is the condition which the grain likes best. As we passed over the level country in the train, the young plants were just shooting above the soil in armies of tender green blades, and the recent rains having freshened things up a great deal, there seemed every prospect of a good harvest and an end of the famine. In some fields the rice had been sown earlier, and was a foot or more high, and here the paddy-birds—a very graceful species of white heron—seemed to be enjoying themselves along with two varieties of plovers.

After some fifteen or twenty miles of these paddy-swamps and scattered palm-groves, we approached the foot of the great inland mountains, and began to mount rapidly, the scenery and surroundings changing with every mile of our way, until we had left the lowlands and palm trees far below, and were climbing up amongst mountain valleys and gullies clad with thick forests of jack, fig, and many other trees. Every now and then we crossed a foaming mountain torrent by a light iron bridge, probably forged in Birmingham and brought out here piece by piece, or we rattled through dark tunnels pierced through the hearts of mountains too rough or too steep to be climbed.

We stopped at many stations, all of them very neatly kept, with clean white-looking offices and sheds, carefully cindered platforms, and generally a wonderful variety of flowers and shrubs rewarding attentions of the local coolies by luxuriant displays of foliage and blossoms. The name of every station was written up in black on a great white signboard, in three or four idioms, so as to be intelligible to the various races of her Britannic Majesty's subjects. First came the familiar English characters, and then a modified form of the classical Sanscrit, and then the twisting and twining Canarese letters, every one of which looks like a worm in convulsions. But, despite all these various ways of writing the name of the same place, the coolies, who filled several third-class compartments in another part of the train, did not seem to be much benefited. Probably most of them did not know a dot or letter of any of the five hundred languages of the world. At any rate, they grew very excited whenever we stopped at a station, and after a great deal of struggling and talking they usually ended by getting out with all their bundles and chattels, and wandering helplessly backwards and forwards until they were unceremoniously driven back to the train by the guards and porters, who appeared in some mysterious manner to know the exact destination of each man and woman.

At every stoppage there were men and women with plantains and cocoa-nuts to sell. The plantains were very good, and the price of a large bunch was only about a half-penny. In Covent Garden Market you would have to give four or five shillings for the same quantity, and then they would be nothing compared to these fresh-gathered fruits. The cocoa-nuts offered for sale were all unripe; there seemed to be no demand for the ripe fruit, it is, I believe, only used for flavouring curries, etc., in this country. The unripe cocoa-nut, from which the coarse outside husk had been peeled, was of a pale greenish colour and no harder than pulp. When a coolie bought one of these, the cocoa-nut man struck the top off with a blow from a small bill-hook he carried in his girdle for the purpose, and the coolie drank the milky contents up with every sign of satisfaction, though W—— persuaded me not to try any, as he said it was dangerous stuff at this time of the year.

The stationmasters on nearly all Indian lines of railway are either Europeans or Eurasians, and the engine-drivers are all Englishmen, who are found to be much more trustworthy and cool-headed, should danger arise, than the natives. The engine-drivers are remarkably well-to-do, much better off, in fact, than many hundreds of "gentlemen clerks" in London offices. On this line they only conduct two trains a day, one up and one down, which leaves them a good margin of time at their own disposal. I do not know what their pay is exactly, but it is very considerable, and they get besides the value of all the fuel saved each journey from a liberal allowance made for the working of the engine. Then they have an excellent bungalow at either end of the line, where they can live and sleep, and altogether their berth seems a very comfortable one.

As I had been making some inquiries about "Sensation Rock," which we were then approaching, an official asked if I would like to pass over it on the engine, as the Prince of Wales had done. I gladly accepted the offer, and at the next station we mounted up on the engine, and started for the far-famed rock. Probably many million people travel in trains for every one that has ever ridden on an engine. It is a most peculiar sensation. In a carriage you are held steady by the other carriages, fore and aft, but in the front of the train it is not so. The great iron horse is harnessed by nothing except the rear couplings, and leaps and bounds along, when going rapidly in a way that is decidedly startling at first. For a time I had to hold on to the railing until I got what we should call afloat my sea-legs. It was most exciting, while as for fresh air, we flew along so rapidly it was as much as one could do to breathe at all outside the shelter of the engine-shield.

From the tender, where my official friend and I established ourselves, there was twice as much to be seen as from the inside of a carriage, and we had the special advantage of knowing what we were coming to, which is not the case in ordinary travelling. At one point we saw a fine cobra asleep between the rails, and thought we should have run over him; but he felt the vibration of the coming danger, and crawled into the ditch on one side in time. However, we caught him up there, and had a good look at the snake as he turned to hiss defiance at us. K—— said he once saw a man bitten by one of these reptiles in the leg, and he died in three hours, in spite of all that could be done for him. There is no certain cure for the bite yet discovered, but perhaps the best remedy is ammonia poured into the wound, either pure, if the spirit is weak, or diluted with equal parts of water if strong. Sucking the puncture, and tying a ligature tight round the limb above it, is often useful, and helps to stop the spread of the poison.

Occasionally we passed the picturesque little bamboo hut of a line-watchman under the shelter of a spreading fig tree, and the man would come out and make a low salaam when he saw there were "burra sahibs" on the engine. At other times we rattled through long tunnels where the engine fires and the sparks from the funnel lit up the jagged granite roof above us, and looking back we saw the long string of carriages in our wake following and turning when we turned like a huge subterranean snake. Then again we were rushing through some deep cutting where the bushes and creepers nearly met overhead, leaving only one narrow streak of blue of all the sky, and rare and curious ferns of all shapes and sizes grew on the deep soil on either bank, while lizards and many different species of butterflies revelled in the flowers and dense undergrowth.

"Sensation Rock" is certainly a triumphant piece of engineering, and makes one giddy even from the safe point of view of the window of a railway carriage, but it is much more interesting from the platform of the engine. For some way the line has been running along the forest-clad side of a mountain, but eventually comes to a place where the sloping flanks are merged into the perpendicular face of a towering cliff. Along this the line is laid for a distance of a hundred yards or so on a sort of half bridge and half embankment. "Now," said K——, as we approached the precipice at thirty miles an hour, "if we go off the rails, it will be a 'long good night' to all of us, with no chance of escape;" and the next minute we were flying over the narrow causeway, with two hundred feet of towering precipice above us, and below nothing but sheer crag and air for something like a thousand feet. Leaning over the engine rail, we gazed far down into the valley below, where the green and brown paddy-fields were like the squares on a chess-board, and the men and oxen ploughing no bigger than the smallest dots, while here and there in the centre of dark-green patches of palms and bananas stood little Indian villages looking like brown smudges on the wide plain. Beyond, the hills rose ridge above ridge up to the sky, with dense forests and bright tracts of grass-land on their sides, and far away to the westward a streak of deeper blue showed where the sea lay.

At something like a thousand feet above the level of the plains we had an uninterrupted view of twenty miles to the southward over as rich a tract of forest-land as any in the world. What a museum of wonders there must have been hidden in that expanse—botanical, animal, and mineral! The wonderful armies of sylvan trees especially impressed me, clothing the hillsides with a covering that seemed as fine and close-fitting as velvet, and yet was made up of tens of thousands of forest giants, each an interesting study in itself. I always admired trees, and for a great forest I feel as much reverence as I do for a library.

But I was not half satisfied with gazing over the wide vista of mountain and plain, when it was abruptly hidden from us by the line entering another cutting, and "Sensation Rock" was nothing more than a memory. Even from below, probably, the cliff is a striking object, and it must open the eyes of the coolies ploughing in their ancestral paddy-swamps to look above and see far overhead, right up in the home of the kites and eagles, the iron horse of the "Feringees" toiling and panting along the face of the precipice where a few years ago not even the mountain sheep could have found a foothold!

A few miles further on we passed a tall stone pillar on the right-hand side, which K—— pointed out as marking the highest point of the railway, and then the freer running of the engine soon told us we were again on level ground. From here the scenery was less rugged and grand, as we had gained the top of the tableland, and were merely passing over an elevated plateau, differing from the low swamps of the seacoast in the drier soil and the different vegetation. The bamboos were still numerous—in fact, they grow at an elevation of 2500 feet, and our present altitude was not 1200—but they were not so prominent or luxuriant as below, and the rice crops had quite given place to various cereals. Here for the first time I saw coffee growing in its native soil. It had, however, obviously been suffering badly from leaf-disease, and the bushes were mere skeletons of their former selves, with meagre collections of limp yellow and green leaves and a few bunches of half-dried berries.

This leaf-disease long ago became a serious affair in Ceylon, where it firmly established itself, and has depreciated the value of a great many estates. It seems to be caused by a minute white fungus, which strikes its roots into the substance of the leaf from the under side and throws out numerous fine white thread-like fibres, which travel along the surface of the epidermis until they come to the pores of which the skin of every leaf is full, and here they send down a root and establish a fresh centre, wherefrom other fibres start out, until the whole under surface of the leaf is covered. What is the immediate cause of the mischief does not seem to be yet certainly known, some planters maintaining that it arises from exhaustion of the soil, others from wet seasons, bad aspects of the plantation, too much manure, and many other causes. The only thing about which all are agreed is that it is very harmful to the trees and greatly depreciates the value of the crop.

Just before reaching the terminus, W—— left me, to find his way up country, bound something like fifty miles away, and without knowing a word of any native language.

Our journey was finished about mid-day, when the train drew up in the large and clean station of Kandy, where myself and hand-bag were immediately besieged by a salaaming crowd of Tamils and Canarese, who seemed as pleased to see me as if they had been waiting and longing for this moment all the last six months. Entrusting my bag to a small boy who looked thin and in want of backshish, I told him to lead the way to the Quéen's Hotel, and followed him up a long dusty road under clumps of tulip trees and deep-shadowed figs, until we reached a long low white building at the corner of the two main thoroughfares of the town, which is dignified with the name of hotel. Here my belongings were deposited, and after a poor tiffin, the very worst cooked and served meal I had eaten since leaving England, I went for a stroll down the town, and of course directed my steps first of all to the far-famed temple of the "Light of Asia," Prince Buddha.

From the exterior it is rather like a Chinese pagoda, but has no very distinct form, on account of being surrounded with other buildings—priests' houses probably—and balconies with far-reaching eaves. I made my way up into one of these verandahs, and spent a long time admiring the extraordinary frescoes with which the walls were adorned. One would not think Buddhism was a very mild or gentle religion, if all one knew of it were gathered from these pictures, which are calculated to give a timid person bad dreams for a fortnight. They seemed to illustrate the various doings or misdoings of the demons who make it their special duty to torture poor sinners in the "lower regions." The men were all bright red in colour, and the demons sooty black. In the first fresco two devils were sitting on the chest of a somewhat stout gentleman, and tearing out his tongue with a large pair of red-hot pincers. Next came more imps, roasting another gentleman over a lively fire, the great white blisters on his skin and his uneasy expression being admirably given. Further on, there were more of the same kind, illustrating how some of us are to have our skin peeled off, or our eyes hooked out with sharp nails, some day; and the region depicted was so horrible, I felt sincerely sorry even for the little devils who had to live in it. I also penetrated a short way into the interior of the temple, which was only dimly lighted by a few palm-oil lamps. What was to be seen, however, was very rich and impressive in the mellow light, and at one end there was a sort of shrine, partly hidden by hanging curtains, and lit up inside by numerous small lamps. This was doubtless the abode of Buddha's tooth; and while I was standing admiring the surroundings, two priests in flowing yellow garments, with bare feet and closely shaven heads, came up to me and threw some handfuls of white flowers over me—a proceeding which I did not understand; and fearful that they would think I had come to be christened, or married, or something of the sort, I beat a retreat.

From the gaily painted temple of Buddha my wandering steps led me to a well-built and substantial English church, only a hundred yards away from the heathen pagoda. The size of this church and the number of pews showed the English residents up here to be numerous, and with the officers of the two or three British regiments quartered in the barracks close by they must form a pleasant little society.

The native streets of Kandy are very Oriental in appearance, and much brighter in colour and gayer than Colombo, where there is a great proportion of Government clerks and mercantile employés among the population, who affect European dress, or, if they wear their native costume, which becomes them much better, they confine themselves to white and black. Here in the principal streets there was a dense but ever-moving crowd and a tossing sea of coloured turbans, amongst which blue, red, yellow, and green were conspicuous, while the flowing yellow and saffron robes of Buddha's priests, the showy white of the Government "writers," and the many varied sarees of the women, filled up the main stream, and made as bright an everyday picture as could well be seen anywhere. The crowd, though thick, was very orderly, and but for the children and dogs, who were perpetually getting in one's way, there was no more scrimmaging or jostling than on a summer's afternoon in Hyde Park. To the English especially, either from reverence or fear, the natives were very deferential. For instance, I stopped to make a purchase at the counter of a worker in sandalwood, around which a group of well-to-do natives were talking and bargaining, and when I approached they at once discontinued talking and stepped aside. In the same way, when walking through the crowd in the thickest part of the bazaar, I always had plenty of elbow-room, and was not jostled once, the various groups dividing courteously to let me pass. At one place there were some little children sprawling all over the road directly in my path. They were so engaged making little mounds of dust and sticking feathers in them that they did not notice my approach; but just as I got up to them, a little girl of twelve or thirteen, in a sky-blue saree—clearly their guardian for the time—sprang up, and rushing to the group, said in a whisper, which I overheard, "Look! an Englishman!" while she seized one little brown imp, whose attire consisted of a piece of string and two glass bangles, by the top-knot, and dragged him out of my path with as much precipitation as though I had been an elephant.

I passed one real elephant, a giant, a great lumbering beast, towering high above the one-storied shops on either side of the street, but in spite of his vast size, which nearly blocked the whole road, stepping as softly and carefully along amongst the toes of the crowd as a young kid. A little further on two English officers came riding along, lifted high above the heads of the many-coloured throngs on their tall white chargers, and looking delightfully neat and cool in their becoming white-and-gold uniform. So rode the Roman legionaries amongst the wild Britons in England some sixteen or seventeen hundred years ago; and who shall say what changes such another period may bring about in the nations of the world? The Fijian may sketch the bittern-haunted ruins of Westminster Abbey, and moralize on the departed grandeur of the once great British nation, and the whole world may be ruled by new races.

There being no visitors at the Queen's Hotel, it was dull in the evening, and I had to amuse myself as best I might with an ancient newspaper. So, after a couple of cheroots smoked in the verandah, where a shower had made the air soft and cool, I determined to "turn in," and get back to Colombo as early the next morning as possible.

On the following morning, immediately after chota hazri, I "made tracks" for the station, and succeeded in catching the first down train for Colombo, to which place the run was uneventful, and by mid-day I was back in the Fort Hotel again.

It rained heavily during the afternoon, but I took a walk round by the fort and beach, which lines the peninsula on which it is built. There were vast numbers of crows all along the edge of the water, hopping and flapping about, or quarrelling over the bits of garbage thrown up by the surface. They are not particularly clean feeders—quantity rather than quality seems to be what they are set upon. They eat anything, vegetable or animal, and must really do a great deal of good as scavengers—carrion being better when fledged with black feathers than when lying open and ugly on the sand. It is curious how clean the birds keep themselves, in spite of their very objectionable tastes. Like the Syrian doves, which grovel all day in the odoriferous dust-heaps of the villages, and yet, when sunset comes, rise into the air and take their way homewards as bright and spotless as though they had done nothing but trim their feathers since morning, so these crows, no matter what they may have been feeding upon, are always glossy and neat. Their black feathers shine in the sunlight with almost as many tints of green and purple as a pigeon's neck, and their keen dark eyes are full of mischief and cunning. It must be to the fore-mentioned changing lights of the plumage of their neck that they owe their scientific name of *Corvus splendens;* they are certainly not splendid in any other respect. And yet, though they are abandoned wretches, given to all manner of wickedness, one cannot help liking them, they are so utterly indifferent to one's opinion of their proceedings; if they would only be a little less noisy, they might be quite estimable.

The beach was strewed with a variety of shells thrown up by the late storms, most of which, however, had been damaged against the rocks and boulders; but there were some new and curious specimens; amongst others three or four sorts of cowries, one of which was the money cowrie, used by the natives as small change. Very small change they are, as 5120 only equal the value of a rupee or two shillings.

The next morning, the 20th of September, I walked over the racecourse with M——, of the O. C. Bank, to see the club house, with which I was agreeably surprised. It is a very fair building for the town, and is well patronized. There had been a ball the night before, and consequently the place was in a great mess—heaps of empty soda-water and wine bottles in the courtyard, showing what hot work dancing had been. In the dining-room the crows were having a grand feast amongst the lobster-claws and chicken-bones under the table, while the squirrels were sitting on the beams overhead, and holding a hot argument about the extraordinary goings on of the strange beings below the previous night. Lastly, upstairs in the great dancing-saloon disorder reigned supreme, and the floor was littered with relics of the bygone gaiety. I picked up a programme of some much-dancing young lady, who had close on thirty names down for the evening's work. Close by was a crimson rosebud left on a chair, which I carried off, though doubtless it was not meant for me, and one might have made quite a collection of beads and tags of lace and ribbons, had one chosen.

The club house stands by itself, overlooking a fine grassy maidân, which is called the racecourse, and which is well suited for one save for the troublesome little land-crabs, who have pitted it far and near with their burrows, thus making the ground excessively dangerous for galloping. These mischievous crustacea come up from the sea close by and dig themselves homes in the soft soil, bringing out the sand in real armfuls, and, with a spring in the air, scattering it in a wide circle away from them. So continuous are their exertions, that though a staff of labourers is constantly at work filling up the holes, the war still goes on, and what the crabs dig in a night it takes the coolies all day to replace. These crabs, like Cæsar's ancient Britons, are equally ready to fight or fly. They possess wonderful swiftness of foot, and can run faster than a man can walk, so that it is not at all easy to cut them off from their burrows; but if they are circumvented, they at once throw themselves into a fighting position, and inflict severe injury on any one who seizes them rashly.

The Portuguese quarter of the town is interesting; the houses are (like the people who dwell in them) half native and half European. Some of the inhabitants are pure-blooded Portuguese, the remnants of the former owners of the island, but the majority have Indian blood in their veins, and associate more with their Asiatic relations than their European kinsmen. Their houses are better built than those of the Cingalese, and differ from them chiefly in having verandahs with blinds and steps leading to the doorways. The people themselves are a good-looking set, the women especially, having fair olive-coloured complexions, good eyes, and graceful carriage. They are not, unfortunately, particularly clean, the small children being much dirtier than native children. The chief street in this quarter is very steep, and goes by the suggestive name of Dam Street, which title is posted up on a very conspicuous board at the top of the hill. Certainly, as one toils up the slope, with a blazing sun overhead and a glaring white road underfoot, one does get rather ruffled, and perhaps it *is* a comfort to some people to have the feelings they scarcely like to utter exhibited in black and white when the summit is reached, and they pause to gain breath and mop up the perspiration.

CHAPTER VI.

UP THE COAST.

AFTER waiting more than a week at Colombo, and making daily pilgrimages to the British India Office to inquire "when on earth" the next steamer was coming (she was much overdue), she suddenly put in an appearance at the harbour mouth, and I forthwith packed up my shore-going kit, paid my bills, and went down to the custom-house docks to get my luggage out. About mid-day, I was once more afloat on "the sea—the fresh, the green, the ever free," following the cargo-boat in a light outrigger paddled by two sinewy natives.

The *Africa*, although a fine steamer, was not so smart and trim as the *Almora*, chiefly because she was merely a trading ship, and had been hard at work for the last few months carrying rice to all the ports of the Malabar and Coromandel coasts for the famine-stricken natives inland. She had, however, a good saloon, with any number of cabins and berths, of which I took my choice as there was only one passenger, besides myself, and he invariably slept on deck; in fact, I followed his example after one night spent below, when I was driven wild with cockroaches and stifled by the heat.

We spent the whole of the blazing hot day taking in cargo, principally jute and rice; and the noise of the donkey-engine, the dense volumes of smoke, and the close, sickly smell of the open holds, where hundreds of tons of rice were piled up as tight as it could be packed, made me long for the evening and the serang's shrill whistle for the crew to get up the anchor.

But though it was uncomfortable on deck, there were some "men and brothers" alongside infinitely more uncomfortable. These were a couple of hundred coolies going back to their homes in Madura and Malabar, after a year's work on the Ceylon plantations. They came off from the shore—men, women, and children, with all their small belongings, bundles and parcels of every shape and size—piled up in two cargo-boats, so tightly packed and squeezed together that it seemed impossible a baby could have been added to the load without turning some one out. Alas for them! there was a strong ground swell rolling into the harbour, which heaved the cargo-boats up and down, although the *Africa* sat as steady as a rock; and the result was that even before they reached her the coolies were abjectly sick, and they do not bear up well against adverse circumstances, so their sufferings were almost comical. They had left the shore sitting or standing in the boat as happy and trim as coolies ever can be, but when they got under our bows all were lying down at the bottom in one indistinguishable conglomerate of legs and arms.

The poor creatures looked more like a kettle of eels than anything else, and the rowers sitting on the seats above them only laughed at their miseries. Their sufferings, however, were only just beginning, for there was so much cargo and stealable property about on deck, that the first officer would not permit them to enter the ship until things had been got into better order on board. So there the miserable people lay, rolling and tossing about on the heavy ground swell, with a burning sun overhead, roasting them and adding to their miseries, while only a few feet away lay the great long ship as steady as dry ground, and doubtless a sort of heaven to their eyes. For three long hours they rolled about in the miseries of sea-sickness, from which they seemed to suffer as much as though they were Christians, until at length their sufferings were so intense I took pity on them. I went to the captain and begged him to be good enough to have them up as soon as might be, and he gave at once orders for the ship's ladder to be let down over the side, and the coolies proceeded to come on board. But this was not as easy as it might seem.

At one moment the ground swell brought the rice-boats up to within a few feet of our bulwarks, and the next, sinking rapidly, took the boat right down to the level of the orlop deck. The first coolie who made the attempt seized hold of the ladder with one hand when the boat was high, and when it sank back again the next moment was left kicking in the air, holding on by one hand and waving a dirty brown bundle with the other. He would inevitably have dropped off and been drowned or crushed, had not the lascars or native sailors sprung down to his rescue, and, seizing him by the top-knot and shoulders, pitched him headlong on deck, where he landed, sprawling like an octopus. Some of the men came up well, but the women and children were a great trouble, making fruitless attempts at the wrong time, and when a good opportunity occurred hanging back. Somehow or other they were at last all got on board. The worst cases were two Arab women done up in huge trousers and flowing robes, with yashmaks over their faces. They were so quiet and dignified amidst their sufferings that I felt for them under what, to them, must have been a fearful ordeal. Their dresses completely prevented them from doing anything in their behalf, and they were very loth to be touched by the hands of unbelieving giaours; so there they stood on the edge of the rice-boat, until the lascars lost patience, and, seizing them by anything they could get hold off, hoisted them on deck by main force.

At sunset the crows, who had been perched in lines on the rigging all day, took their departure to the shore with the kites and a fleet of empty cargo-boats; and the stopping of the donkey-engine left the vessel in peace while dinner was served in the saloon. It was not a particularly brilliant meal; the captain at the head of the table, MacB—— on one hand, and I on the other made up the whole company, with a flock of white-robed "boys" behind our chairs doing nothing but stare and listen to the stories by which the captain amused us during dinner; then, when he had said good night, we betook ourselves to our mattresses, and watched the bright stars overhead and shining globes of the jellyfish under water, until we sank into dreamland.

The next two or three days were remarkable for nothing but their tediousness. We first ran up to Tuticorin, in the Gulf of Manaar and close to Adam's Bridge—the ridge of sand and stones in many places just "awash," which connects Ceylon with India. This ridge is supposed by various signs to be rising slowly. Amongst others, a couple of Dutch ships, while being pursued by some Portuguese men-of-war, when Ceylon was in the possession of the latter, escaped by making a bold attempt to sail across the bar. In this they succeeded, while the Portugal ships, drawing more water, came to grief. As the Dutch ships could not get across now, this certainly goes some way to prove that the bank is higher than it was, but if rising at all it rises very gradually. Some day it may, perhaps, be dry land right across from the mainland to the island, but either such a bridge or a clear passage cut through for shipping would tell very heavily against the prosperity of Colombo, which would be left outside the new lines of traffic, and perhaps share the fate of Suez and Alexandria after the making of the Suez Canal.

Of Tuticorin I did not see much, as, owing to the shallowness of the water, we anchored some seven miles from the shore, and there was not time to row to land and return before nightfall. Immediately we let go our anchor we noted, with the help of our glasses, a fleet of flat-bottomed rice-boats putting off to us, and although, owing to the distance, we did not see them start, we were soon aware that the crows were coming too, and before we had well swung round to our anchor they arrived in a great flock, and took possession of the rigging and spars. Who shall say they are not enterprising and intelligent birds, when they make out a ship in the offing, and fly off seven miles to her for the chance of picking up a mutton bone or the leg of a chicken?

The natives in the heavy rice-boats took a much longer time to reach us, it being a two-hours' pull against the tide; but they were a muscular lot, and did not seem at all distressed when they reached the sides of the *Africa*. After they had had a grand quarrel for places, during which we were the centre of a wild pandemonium of voices, and the donkey engine had set to work, the rest of the day was steam, uproar, and the smell of damp rice. These natives are mostly Roman Catholics, and wear on their brown chests little crucifixes and medals, the symbols of their religion, which they occasionally take up and kiss in a rather demonstrative fashion. Probably the reason why the natives become converts to Roman Catholicism more readily than to Protestantism is that the forms and ceremonies of the former appeal more to their Oriental imaginations than the simpler Anglican worship, and perhaps also because the Catholic missionaries, who are numerous along this coast, obtain a greater hold over the natives by living amongst them and studying their habits and ways of life.

The dinner that evening was even more solitary than the last, since MacB—— had left us during the afternoon for Tuticorin, where he was to be famine correspondent to a London daily paper. So the captain and I dined in lonely state, and I had to listen to a score of wild tales about his adventures in various parts of the world. Amongst other things, we were talking of the sand ridge in the neighbourhood stretching across the gulf, and he said he believed it was entirely caused by the north-east and south-west monsoon, the former blowing for half the year and sweeping the sand in from the Bay of Bengal, and the latter driving the sand up the narrow channel from the Indian Ocean for the other six months. In this way the silt was banked up in a narrow ridge between the two seas, and the shallowness of the water off Tuticorin was due to the same cause. In fact, he thought both the Gulf of Manaar and Palk Strait were being slowly filled up with drifting deposit, the water being shallower off this harbour now than it was a few years ago, to his own knowledge. Our rice-loading operations being over by sunset, we steamed away to the southward during the course of the evening, and to my great regret passed Cape Comorin about midnight, when, as it was very dark and raining heavily, we could see nothing of the coast line.

In the morning I woke up to find we were anchored off Trevandrum on the Travancore coast, and were besieged by the usual swarms of cargo-boats and lightly clad natives, who had surrounded us and were shouting and struggling for first place.

All that can be seen of Trevandrum from the sea is a white flagstaff towering above the palms, and one white house on top of a steep rock. This may have been all there was of Trevandrum, but, as the name is printed large and thick in the maps, I am inclined to suspect there must have existed more "town" behind the palms inland. However, the rain came down in torrents shortly after daybreak, and hid even that solitary house from my sight.

All day the donkey-engines were at their monotonous work, hauling the fat rice-bags out of the close stuffy hold, and lowering them over the side of the ship, which the steam wrapped in white vapour from stem to stern, and, together with the driving rain, made it utterly impossible to keep dry anywhere on deck. So, after putting on every available pair of boots at hand, and getting them and all my clothes soaked through and through, I gave up the attempt, going about barefooted like the officers for the rest of the voyage. There were no ladies to mind how we were got up, and simply for want of something to do, I assisted the officers at tallying cargo, and even tried my hand at running the engines. But it was damp and uncomfortable work at best.

For two more days we rolled up the coast through the fag-end of the south-west monsoon, amidst an uninterrupted downpour of pelting rain, which did not leave me with as much as a dry handkerchief in my wardrobe. We stopped twice or even three times a day at different little waterside ports to disgorge the precious white grain, for lack of which the famine-stricken coolies were dying by thousands inland; but there was never anything to see on shore—nothing but a long flat coast, with an unbroken fringe of palms growing down to the water's edge, and the usual musterings of boatmen, kites, and crows.

Consequently I was glad when the morning of the 27th of September broke fine and sunny, and the captain pointed out to me, far ahead, a tiny white flagstaff towering above the palms, which he said was Cochin, the next port to Calicut, my destination.

We stayed at Cochin a few hours, and arrived finally off Calicut beach early in the afternoon.

From the sea, like all other ports along this low monotonous coast, there is not much to be said for the town. It consists of a line of open shanties on the beach, a white lighthouse, and the usual flagstaff, from which the Union Jack flutters gaily. The palm trees hide all the rest of the place, and fringe the coast northward and southward as far as the eye can reach. But inland the scene is enlivened by the misty blue outlines of what a Yankee would call "rising ground," and what is geographically known as the Western Ghauts—about the first hills I had seen since leaving Kandy. These hills form the western boundaries of the great coffee districts of Coorg and Mysore, perhaps the most productive in the world, and continue to characterize the coast in an almost unbroken line up to Bombay.

The boatmen, who soon came off from the shore, are slightly different in features and colour from those we had seen hitherto, but the most striking thing about them was their head-covering, which is the most extraordinary structure ever seen on a human head. Imagine a huge umbrella made of split bamboo and neatly covered with strips of fan-palm leaves; then remove the stick, and in its place substitute a cylinder, also of palm leaf, like an English silk hat minus the brim; and then place this edifice on the close-shaven head of a Tamil boatman, and you will understand their headgear, which serves the purpose of sun-hat or umbrella equally well, but is not adapted to carrying burdens in high winds. So broad are the hats, that when the first cargo-boat came off to us I saw nothing but the hull, twenty spoon-shaped paddles, and an undulating platform of things that looked at a distance like huge soup-plates turned upside down. In attire, or rather lack of it, these men were the same as their countrymen further down the coast, but the crosses and charms which hung on each brown chest in the neighbourhood of Tuticorin were not to be seen here, showing that the missionaries had not yet broached this part of the country, or had not been so successful.

I landed in the mail-boat by special favour of the postmaster-general of the district, a very pleasant Englishman, who gave me a complete and exhaustive account of the history of Calicut from the most remote period up to the present date, and threw in a supplement to his discourse about the future of the town, while we were being rowed ashore sitting on a sack of letters shortly to be distributed in the neighbourhood.

He mentioned, I remember, that the words "calico" and "Calicut" are one and the same, the former being the older form and the name of this town when it was a thriving and busy industrial centre and the chief manufactory of calico and cotton cloths. Since then it has gone down sadly in worldly prosperity, and is now nothing but a police station and the residence of some European coffee and mercantile agencies. That the place was once of great importance is certain for many reasons; amongst others, there is a colony of pale-skinned Jews to the southward of the town, who are supposed to be the direct descendants of the Jews whom Solomon the Magnificent sent to the "gorgeous East" to collect ivory and peacocks for his palaces. That they came here and established themselves shows the place must have had a wide-spreading trade, and have been well known at that period to the wandering Arabs and Persians, who were probably the earliest explorers that crossed any ocean in search of trade and commerce.

It is a hundred pities there is no harbour to the town, as were there one it might soon become a flourishing seaport again; but, indeed, there is scarcely a haven worthy of the name from Bombay in the north down to Colombo in the south, and when the monsoon blows in from the Arabian Sea the whole western coast of India becomes dangerous. Here especially, as there is not an atom of protection, the trading and passenger steamers have frequently to steam by with mails and passengers, and carry them on until they are able to get near the shore. Wrecks of native crafts are frequent here and at Cochin. They anchor near the shore during a lull in the monsoon, and perhaps while they are busy taking cargo a gale springs up; but, being dull, heavy tubs, they cannot get into the offing quick enough, and drive on shore, all hands being generally lost, and the beach strewn for miles with their freights of cocoa-nuts or palm-oil casks.

The strand, when we reached it, was a very animated scene: in the background long low lines of sheds for storing rice and merchandise, and a towering hedge of palm trees rising behind them, with the tall white lighthouse overtopping even the palms; coolies were hurrying to and fro between the cargo-boats and storehouses, bending under the weight of great rice-sacks; half-caste writers in white European garments, with white helmets on their heads, were standing at the doors, entering each bag in their day-books; native women, some gaily dressed in white calicoes with green or red sarees, and some not dressed at all, were running about with loads on their heads nearly as heavy as those carried by the men; scores of naked brown children, revelling and rioting in unlimited dirt and sand, were fighting with dozens of mangy dogs for bones and scraps of melon-peel; while above the busy crowd the cawing crows occupied every coign of advantage, and the kites swept round and in and out among the masts and palm trees in easy circles, every now and then coming down like meteors, and flapping away triumphantly with part of a dead dog, a fish's head, or some such tempting morsel. Above all the Indian sun flared down on the Christians and pagans, the "just and the unjust," and gave the scene that brilliant contrast of light and shadow which is seen nowhere except under a tropical sun.

After depositing my light effects with the agent of the British India Company, and sending off a special cargo-boat with a reis and twenty muscular rowers for my heavy baggage, which completely filled the cargo-boat and probably made the natives think the sahib had a remarkable supply of trousers and coats. I placed myself under the guidance of my friend of the mail-boat, and made my way to the English club house, where my name was entered as an honorary member, and under its hospitable roof I spent the rest of the day.

This club house is a very comfortable place, and much frequented by the English residents and stray planters, who come down from the hills, when fever-stricken, to see the doctor here, and imbibe the invigorating ozone of the sea-breezes. It boasts a capital reading-room, with a wide verandah, well stocked with the peculiar long-armed easy-chairs of the country, and opening directly on to the beach. Behind is a billiard-room, and across the courtyard there is a row of half a dozen comfortable bedrooms under a low thatched roof, with the inevitable verandah and punkah ropes hanging by every door-post. Then one passes down a long passage under a shady grove of palm trees, where the ripe nuts hang in great clusters at the top of the tapering stems, until the feeding department is reached, where I "tiffined" with two or three other Englishmen, one of whom subsequently turned out to be bound for the same part of the jungles as myself.

With tiffin, a game of billiards, and reading the latest English newspapers, I managed to get through the hotter hours of the day, until the crows began to fly homewards, and the little brown beings who had been playing in the hot white sand likewise "made tracks" for their mud huts, and there came a strong odour of burning cow-dung, the only fuel here, and of boiling rice. Then, waking up and stretching myself, I called out for a "boy," and ordered a buggy to be brought round. In this gilded pill-box I meandered down the various village streets and into the open country beyond, at a pace little above a walk. I did not understand then that, if you are in a buggy and want the bullocks to go faster, you have to beat the *driver*, who will then transmit the "walloping" to his "cattle." We soon pick up these things; but in my innocence, on that first day, after a couple of miles of dawdling, my usually serene temper was ruffled, and I got out and belaboured the sleepy white oxen with my big white umbrella—a proceeding which seemed to afford the "mild Hindoo" who was driving some gentle amusement, but did not take us on a bit faster. So I got inside again, and, lighting a cheroot, resigned myself to fate with the reflection that we must do at Rome as the Romans do.

After bumping and jolting along for several miles through village streets, under spreading fig trees and waving bamboo clumps, we turned suddenly to the left, thereby bringing my head into violent collision with the right side of the buggy, and, passing through an English-looking swing gate and white pillars, approached a large house, the residence of Mr. F——, of the firm of Messrs. H—— & Co., whose guest I was to be for the time.

The next morning I was up early, and after a refreshing tub went out into the compound until hazri should be announced. It had been raining in the night, and every leaf and spray was thickly hung with rain-drops, which glittered in the early sun like diamonds. The air itself was as fresh and sweet as possible, such as it often is on a May morning in some meadow-surrounded English country house. Here I first made the acquaintance of the gay little seven-sisters—a small kind of finch who keep in parties of that number, and play from bush to bush with a continual stream of chatter, as noisy as a convent of novices when the lady prioress has gone to bed. The little striped squirrels were in force too, cutting backwards and forwards across the path with their bushy tails held over their backs, or rushing up and down the trunks of the fig trees, occasionally stopping, often with their heads downwards, to have a gossip with a neighbour from the other end of the compound. From living long in security and unharmed, they have grown wonderfully tame, letting me stand within a couple of yards of them without manifesting the smallest uneasiness, simply keeping their bright eyes on me with an expression of interest rather than fear. But of the kites they seemed to have a wholesome dread, the appearance of one sailing above the tree-tops causing a great commotion, so that in less than a second every bushy tail had vanished into the tangled branches that formed their home and castle. They have other enemies besides the kites—among the worst the rat-snakes, who inhabit the roots of the mango and fig trees; for though these are commonly supposed to feed on the animal from which they take their name, they often vary their diet by a meal of young squirrels or fledglings. One of these rat-snakes crossed my path and escaped into the long grass on the other side of the road. Although perfectly harmless, he was an enormous reptile, nearly six feet long, glossy black and yellow in colour, his clean scale armour shining wet with the dew that had fallen upon him as he was making his way home from a night's freebooting.

Of butterflies when the sun got warm many kinds appeared, the commonest being the small saffron-coloured *Terias Hecate*, and the handsome black-and-crimson swallow-tail *Papilio pammon*, which seemed, by the way, to be the principal victims of the graceful green bee-eaters, a pair of which had their perches on the woodwork of a disused well, and every now and then made rapid darts at passing insects. They never missed their prey, and always brought their quarry back to the same spot to be diswinged before being swallowed, the ground under their watch-towers being thickly strewn with gaily painted shreds of unfortunate butterflies and bees. These meropes are delightful birds, with slim green bodies and pointed tails, but their chief charm lies in their ceaseless activity and the arrow-like certainty of their flight. Down by the same well where the bee-eaters had established themselves were many grey and pied wagtails, the exact prototypes of their English kindred in plumage, habits, and voice. These grey wagtails jerk their tails in the same way as their English relations, and their notes are exactly similar to those which may be heard any day by an English brook. Many of the butterflies, too, are cast in the same mould on both sides of the world; a "brimstone" which I caught in the compound had the peculiar red horns with a downward bend, and the same tuft of soft down at the base of each lower wing, which characterize the common English species. Have these creatures risen from the same stock, or have successive waves of immigration, each overlapping the other, diffused the same species and family likenesses all over the globe?

In the afternoon I made an expedition into the town on foot, not much caring about any more buggy-riding after yesterday's proceedings. The road was something like a Devonshire lane, with high red banks on either side, but the clumps of bamboos and palms spoil the comparison. Occasionally there were European bungalows standing back from the track in their compounds, where little white children were to be seen playing about, attended by ayahs and men-servants. Every now and then a string of women passed me, carrying enormous loads of grass on their heads and going at a quick trot. They did not seem particularly prepossessing according to our standard of female comeliness, and hard work and the life they lead spoil them very early. They wore only one garment—a long strip of cloth wound round and round their waists so as to form a short petticoat reaching to the knees; of this they bring the spare end up over their left shoulder, and let it hang down behind. The old women do not stand on ceremony in the matter of dress, and wear clothes only according to their means. Generally they are very poor.

Calicut seems to have a very varied trade, and the courtyard of the custom-house to which I went for my baggage was piled up with merchandise of every sort and variety waiting to be cleared, being meanwhile protected from the merciless beaks and claws of the crows and kites, with which the roof swarmed, by strong netting spread from one side of the courtyard to the other. It is a great pity, I repeat, no proper harbour can be made here; if there were one, it would be of immense importance to the "country side," and double the wealthy population of Mysore and Travancore. Probably some day the railway which now ends at Beypore will be brought on, and a breakwater erected to shelter the shipping when the south-west monsoon blows. At present the vessels lie in the open roads, and when a storm is seen to be coming on they have to up anchor and make for the open sea, for woe to the craft which puts off sailing too long, as she speedily comes under the palm trees fringing the beach!

After enjoying a game of billards at the club and reading the latest English newspapers, I started to walk back, thinking the cool of the evening would be refreshing and pleasant, but forgetting that darkness treads close on the heels of day out here. I had scarcely begun my walk when the sun went down, crimson and gold, behind the palm groves. For a little while there was a sort of bright reflected glow on everything, and then twilight deepened into darkness, and the owls and bats came out, till it was scarcely possible to see the road two yards ahead. Luckily it was a straight one, and though several times the outline of tall clumps of bamboos or deep shadowy fig trees made me fancy the way was lost, yet I kept on, and after a time smelt the peculiar and not easily forgotten scent of an Indian village at night —the odour of burning cow-dung and boiling ghee, and then saw the twinkling lights and the white-robed figures of the villagers standing out in the fire-light of the hamlet that lies halfway between Calicut and Plantation House. But the worst portion of the walk was yet to come; and the darkness increased until it was so dense that the only way of keeping the road was by feeling the hard surface underfoot. Several times I was brought to a sudden standstill by running into the hedge or colliding with the stem of a palm tree. Once, what seemed to be the glowing end of a cigar came down the road towards me, and, imagining there was an Englishman behind it, I waited until it showed close by, and then called out, "Who goes there?" But there was no answer; so, after a moment's pause, I called out again "Stop!" and the only answer was a sepulchral "stop" from an echo in the bamboo jungle at the side of the road. Thinking this very uncivil, and the cigar-end being close to my face, I put my hand where the smoker's shoulder ought to have been and yet felt nothing; so, without more ceremony, I made a grab at the light itself, which was bobbing round me in a very mysterious fashion, and seized—not a cigar, but a huge fire-fly, much larger than the common sort, who blazed for a moment, with a crimson glow of indignant surprise, and then put himself out and declined to light up again. My chief fear, however, was of snakes, which abound on all open spaces after dark, and indeed the English never go out without torch-bearers and thick sticks to guard themselves; but I had neither, and, as I was wearing low shoes and thin socks, it was with considerable relief that at last the long dark walk was finished and I saw the twinkling lights of F——'s hospitable mansion close in front of me.

At dinner that evening F—— said I had done a thing which his twenty years' experience of India would have made him extremely reluctant to imitate.

CHAPTER VII.

ON THE ROAD TO THE JUNGLE.

SUNDAY morning, the 30th, found me with kit packed and ready for a forward movement upon the jungle; so, after a comfortable breakfast I made my adieu to F—— and his pleasant family, tipped the butler and a great number of his satellites, who seemed fully accustomed to this habit of civilized countries, and eventually found myself *en route* for Beypore in a bullock-bandy with a considerable quantity of small packages, and the inevitable Indian tiffin basket, which is an absolute necessity when one travels.

I have mentioned before what a bullock-cart is like, so I will not repeat the description. It is, however, doubly trying to ride in one when bent on catching a train, and mine kept me in a fever of worry. It was ten miles from the house to the terminus of the railway, and as only one train went every day, and my luggage was going by that one, while bearers and all sorts of well-made arrangements awaited its arrival at my destination at Palghaut, the thought of missing it was distracting. And yet the placid white oxen in the shafts *would* not move faster than a walk. In vain

I got out and thumped them with my heavy umbrella, and equally in vain their driver twisted their long tails into knots (until one could almost hear the bones cracking) and heaped unmitigated abuse upon their female ancestors. Their tails proved as hard and senseless as their hides, and they seemed to consider that, their ancestors being long since departed to celestial pastures, it mattered little what calumny was heaped upon those unconscious heads. In brief, they won the fight and set their own pace, as doubtless they had done many times before, and I had to give in with the best grace possible, devoutly hoping something would happen to delay the departure of the train.

At Beypore there was a ferry-boat waiting apparently for me—for though the bows were laden with a miscellaneous collection of native passengers, a seat with a crimson cushion on it was reserved in the stern—so, stepping in, we put off at once, and, rowed by the sinewy arms of half a dozen bronze-skinned boatmen in the usual cool costume of broad hat and small handkerchief, we got to the other side in about twenty minutes. Here the boatmen first pushed the second-class passengers over into about two feet of water and let them get ashore how they could, and then turned the boat round and put a plank from the thwarts to the beach for myself. For this, however, I had to pay—my passage across, with its attendant luxuries, costing eight annas, while the coolies only paid two.

I was much surprised to find that the porter nuisance is as bad here as anywhere on the European continent. No sooner had I finished breakfast than my luggage was seized upon by a whole host of individuals, who had been squatting in the verandah for the special purpose ever since my arrival. It would not have seemed so bad if they had taken fair loads, but they took just as little as possible—one fellow pounced upon two bottles of lemonade and persisted in carrying them down to the train, which stood at the bottom of the single flight of stairs. I rewarded most of the others, but the lemonade gentleman was the last straw which overcame my generosity, and I told him to go; but he seemed to think he had earned a reward, and stood chattering and grinning at the window to the amusement of the other luggage-wallahs, so, after standing it for some time, I rolled up a newspaper and suddenly sprang out of the carriage. The fellow seemed to think his last hour had come, for he "scooted," as they say in America—fled down the platform, crossed the sandy beach and sprang into the nearest boat, and, I believe, would have cut the rope and put out to sea, only that, looking back, he saw that, contented with my bloodless victory, I had retired to the carriage again.

There was nothing of much interest or very new to be seen along the line. For some time we ran through the palm groves that fringe the seashore, with the huts of the fishermen scattered here and there among them. Once or twice we came to a very abrupt standstill, and, putting our heads out of the window, perceived that the obstruction was an old buffalo or cow, who was grazing leisurely between the rails, and sundry billets of wood had to be hurled before "Cyl" considered it advisable to move on. Afterwards we turned inland, and, leaving the palms behind, came to the regions of bamboos and paddy. Here the fields were green in places, and, like those of the neighbourhood of Colombo, simply swamps enclosed by mud embankments; in others the crops were nearly ready to cut, and little black fellows perched on muchâns, or platforms raised high in the air on four poles, kept up a continual rattle with split bamboos, to frighten away the swarming flocks of tiny birds that circled round and round overhead.

Small white egrets were numerous, and the air was full of kites and hawks, while the telegraph-wires were the roosting-places of bright green bee-eaters. Possibly there were quail and partridges among the paddy, for once or twice I saw foxes slinking along the sides of the embankments, doubtless searching for provisions. Every village that was not large enough to boast a tank had a well in the neighbourhood worked on the common Indian plan—very ancient, and, like most ancient things, inconvenient. The bucket-rope of these wells passes over a wooden wheel fixed on top, and an inclined roadway leads up to the summit of the wall which surrounds each well. Two oxen, generally superannuated and extremely "gharib," are harnessed to the rope, and when they move down the incline, up come the full buckets, which are emptied out into a sluice, and then the unfortunate animals have to lower the buckets again by laboriously backing up to the wheel. In this way, first going ahead and then veering astern, they spend their eventless existences.

But on the whole there was little of interest on the run up the line, though an enthusiastic traveller says, "The railway passes through the most glorious tropical scenery and luxuriant vegetation to be found south of Himalayas." But as I am not writing a guide-book, and consequently am not in artistic hysterics, the country must be described as flat paddy swamps, with a broad muddy river to the south—which, by the way, rolls down considerable quantities of gold to the sea, —and occasional clumps of bamboos or palms, hiding little villages of thatched huts with a thick population, principally dogs and children.

Arriving at the large comfortable station of Palghaut, I found four bandies or up-country carts waiting in the courtyard outside to take me and my multitudinous belongings to "Wheeler's bungalow," where supper was to be had and an English-speaking servant to be found, who would make arrangements for the other stages of the journey.

Here F——, whose acquaintance I had made coming up, proved of the greatest service to me, as he was an old Indian, knew the languages, and was going to his estate in the jungles, only a few miles from mine, so we had determined to travel together. What I should have done without his help it is difficult to say, as none of the bandy-wallahs knew a word of English or Hindustani, of which latter language I commanded a little. Fortunate indeed is the "griffin" who has his first journey up country made smooth for him by the friendly help of an experienced fellow-countryman; and if such help is not to be had, the next best thing is to secure the services of a native servant who speaks the languages of the district to which the traveller is going, and also the language of his master.

Such servants are always to be found in the large towns, and are not expensive luxuries, as they rarely get more than Rs. 15 a month, and, if of the right sort, save the Englishman a world of trouble. In F——, however, I had a pleasant companion as well as guide; and as soon as we had seen three of the bandies piled up with boxes, we climbed into the fourth, and, giving the signal to start, turned our backs on the station—our last link with civilization, and one which we knew we should not see again for many a long day—and so proceeded down the hot road to the English quarter of Palghaut, which lies three miles from the railway.

If travelling in the buggy of the Indian towns is uncomfortable, the unfortunate Englishman gets even more shaken up in these country bandies; and yet, in spite of the jolting, I liked them already—they are so delightfully primitive, and are so perfectly honest about the entire absence of springs or ornamentation of any sort. They do not pretend to be anything more than they are. When you first look at them you perceive a pair of big wheels supporting a muffin-traylike wooden platform, over which small bamboos have been arched from side to side, and bamboo matting lashed to this with finely split rattan creepers. In the shafts, or rather on either side of the pole, stand a pair of sleepy white or red oxen, having patterns burnt into their hides, and the curved yoke resting against the front of the strange-looking humps which grow up between their shoulder-blades. When you have taken in these things at a glance, you have seen all there is to be seen, and no matter how much you travel in bandies afterwards, you will find out nothing more about them except that what was very obvious to the eye will become equally obvious to the other senses. The traveller will learn that the straw which covers the body of the cart is but a poor remedy against lack of springs. Still, as one lies at full length in the dry paddy, with the pale yellow mats overhead to keep out the strong rays of the sun, the view goes gliding by the open ends of the cart, and the muttered exclamations of the driver perched on the pole sound dreamily on the ear, till there is a certain sense of comfort if one be not over tender-skinned. Then again, once up country no one is restrained by the conventionalities of society; one feels, as the Russians say in Transcaucasus, that "the heavens are high and the Czar far off;" and if one's coat and waistcoat are oppressive, it is easy and perfectly permissible to doff and sit on them by way of a cushion. So, on the whole, I would much rather journey in the unpretentious bandy than endure the cramping of a buggy.

We lumbered through the long Indian street with its usual crowd of natives, some gaily dressed in all the colours to be extracted from the multitudinous dyes of the country, and some perforce contented with their own brown skins and a small dhotee or waistcloth. One or two little children ran after the cart, and, thinking it was empty, proceeded to climb in behind, but shrank back very quickly when they saw there were two real live white sahibs inside. I was in constant fear we should kill somebody, as no one moved out of the roadway when we approached; but we got through in some wonderful manner without a mishap, and were presently winding amongst the fig and banian trees of the European quarter.

"And where," I said to F——, "may the shops be situated at which you buy whatever you want?" At which he laughed, and told me that there was only one shop which made any pretence of dealing with the Europeans of the town. Everything that could not be got there must be sent for from Madras or Bombay—a week off at the least. So to this single shop we made our way, and found it a curious little den kept by a spectacled Hindoo, who was profuse with his salaams, but kept everything except the articles wanted. The main stock of the establishment seemed to be wines, brandies, preserves, and tinned provisions of various kinds, while the walls all round were ornamented with pictures of Hindoo gods and goddesses, mostly in vermilion dresses against bright blue skies, alternating with engravings of English gleaners and the biscuit manufactories of Messrs. Peek, Frean, and Co. Having opened an account with the "mild" Hindoo, who seemed by the way to be very quick at figures, and ordering a supply of provisions to be sent up to the jungle, we got back to our bandies and proceeded to our destination for the evening. After twenty minutes more of creaking and crawling, we entered the compound of a pleasant little white bungalow. The heavy thatch roof coming nearly down to the ground and forming a wide and shady verandah all round, was very steeply "pitched," thereby showing that heavy rains are to be expected here. This was "Wheeler's bungalow," where, although the owner was away on the hills, I had received permission to sleep and make myself at home.

Half a dozen coolies were soon at work loading up the verandah with my baggage, and with a parting injunction to them to make haste and get it done before nightfall, F—— and I plunged into the house in search of supper and the servants. The cool way in which F—— made use of other people's property considerably astonished me. After shouting ourselves hoarse in vain endeavours to rouse up a "boy," we proceeded to the kitchen in the rear of the compound, where we captured a small *chokra*, with only a pair of boots and a necklace by way of clothing. Him we set to make a fire, and then F—— took down a frying-pan and proceeded to grease it before putting it on the stove. Seeing my look of astonishment, F—— asked me if I was hungry, and on my replying "certainly," said that in that case I had better set to work and help him get some supper, as we were now in a land where it does not do to rely upon providence. So I threw my white coat and helmet into one corner, and, rolling up my sleeves, was soon absorbed in poaching eggs and getting a refractory kettle to boil. When the cooking operations were nearly completed, we went to the dining-room to set the table, and without the slightest hesitation my friend dived into every cupboard and drawer in search of the necessary articles. At length we found them, together with a few tins of marmalade and preserves. These F—— set me to work to open, after solemnly assuring me he would be my bail if I was had up for housebreaking; and eventually we sat down to a capital meal, none the less palatable because it was earned by our own toil. Scarcely had we spread our napkins across our knees, when the heavy sound of a booted footfall was heard outside, and immediately after an Englishman entered and greeted F——, by whom I was at once introduced to the new-comer, S——, another of the half-dozen of coffee planters in the Annamully jungles. The latest arrival had brought a dozen of bottled beer with him, so we all sat down again and proceeded to make a feast of the meal, which S—— enlivened by some jungle stories and shooting adventures. The remainder of the evening we passed in the verandah, smoking long Trichinopoly cheroots and sipping iced brandy-pawnee, which one of the servants of the master of the bungalow, who had put in an appearance only when we had finished supper, concocted in a manner indicating a plentitude of practice.

Late in the evening we separated to get some sleep if possible, as our conveyances had been ordered for daybreak, and we had a long mountain-climb before us; but whatever F——'s fortunes may have been, mine were very bad, and I did not obtain even the theoretical "forty winks." First of all, the night was fearfully hot and close, and one by one I consigned every covering on the bed to the far corners of the room, but without relief. Then I fancied, in an evil moment, that it must be the close, heavy mosquito curtains which were so oppressive, and proceeded to roll them up and throw them over the bed-posts. But this was a fatal manœuvre, for scores of winged creatures rushed immediately to the attack, and proceeded to refresh themselves at my expense. It was too late to put the curtains down, as the enemy were already in possession, and I turned and tossed and tasted the torments of purgatory, until patience was worn out. Then, seeing that sleep was out of the question, I struck a light, and after taking vengeance on a dozen of mosquitoes, donned my habiliments and went out into the garden to smoke. There was no moon yet visible, but she was just rising and sending a subdued silvery moon-dawn before her, which, together with the gleam of a thousand beautiful stars, made everything look soft and fairy-like. I am a great lover of moonlight. To me it seems one of the most refined and beauteous of Nature's phases, and it was very pleasant wandering here in this Indian garden, with the graceful palms and sombre figs, half seen in the shadowy beams; through deep thickets of sweet-scented shrubs and great white-flowered convolvuli, all their blossoms turned toward the rising light, while the fireflies, with their small blue sparks, meandered about amongst the dark foliage; or to sit and meditate by a disused tank, where the sacred lotus flowers had it all their own way and covered the surface of the shining water with their half-closed fragrant flowers and broad leaves. Then, too, the air was full of strange sounds not heard during the day—the ceaseless chirruping of innumerable insects, giving voice to their feelings in a thousand tones, from the thick thatch of the bungalow to the tops of the cotton trees, and down again to the low flowering bushes and long grass. Far away the jackals were fighting over the bones of a newly dead buffalo, and the dogs of the nearest villages were barking enviously at them, apparently wishing they too were at the feast.

But at length my cheroot came to an end, and making my way back, I found a bandy with two sleepy white oxen standing in the moonlight by the verandah, lazily swinging their tufted tails to keep away the night insects. By the cart a dozen coolies were lying, or squatting on their heels, smoking and talking in low tones. These got up at once, and salaamed when I passed. Entering the house, I was nearly upset by F—— in his pyjamas, with a kettle in one hand and a saucepan in the other. He, as usual, was making himself useful, and we were soon snatching a hasty chota hazri, while some of our kit was being packed and stowed in the bandy in which my friend was to make the next stage, I going on ahead—to order breakfast—in a munchiel, or swing cot, with ten bearers—a mode of travelling which is much faster than being drawn by bullocks, and considered extremely aristocratic down here. The munchiel is a strong blue hammock, slung beneath a bamboo pole, and covered in by a broad flat palm-leaf mat which swings above the support. From either edge of the mat there are strings attached, which the traveller holds in his hands, being able consequently to tip the awning to either side, so as to keep off rain or sun. When arranged with a sufficiency of pillows and blankets, it is not at all an uncomfortable mode of travelling, and one gets a capital view of the scenery from it.

Our preparations being completed, we agreed to walk some way, as the moon was up and the early morning delightfully fresh and cool. Away we went down the road that leads to the southward, F—— with bare feet regardless of snakes, and the coolies jogging along behind us. At one time we were passing over paddy swamps, where the night wind played upon hundreds of acres of waving rice, and the moon shone down on pools and water-holes, making them as bright as silver, and apparently delighting the frogs, who were croaking, far and near, in hoarse choruses. At another time we were plunging into the black gloom of a banian grove, where it was too dark to see a couple of yards ahead, and the air was vibrating with the noise of myriads of insects amongst the foliage and fruit. After an hour's walking we passed a little roadside hut, and, the way abruptly sloping down, found ourselves on the margin of a broad rapid river. "Here," said F——, "we stand on British soil, but yonder black bank, with the tall palms, is the native territory of Cochin whither we are bound; and do you see those mountains far to the southward with rugged peaks standing out against the sky, and white clouds floating halfway up them? Those are the Annamullies, and above those clouds and in the hollows of those peaks lie the estates where we are to grow coffee for our stay-at-home countrymen and the rest of the world." Of course I was immensely interested at the sight of my future home, and could not take my eyes off the serrated range and the fleecy silver clouds, until the coolies came up and it became necessary to cross the river.

To see if this were practicable we first sent a man across, and on his safely reaching the other side—though the water once came up to his chest—I proceeded to get into my munchiel, which six men were supporting on their shoulders. But this was not so easy as might be supposed, the blue-cloth hammock going round and round in an extraordinary way directly any pressure was put upon it. Eventually I was in and comfortably tucked up, though as helpless as a tortoise if anything should happen; and all my men—five at either end of the pole—went down the slope and waded, waist-deep, into the shining water. At one part it was so deep that, to save me from a wetting, the bearers hoisted the bamboo pole on to their bare, smooth skulls, and I was conscious that a stumble of any one of them might plunge the whole party into the river. However, we reached the other side safely, and sat down to watch the passage of F—— in his cart. The bandy got along all right to nearly the middle of the stream, then the bullocks became frightened or sulky, and, in spite of the frantic yells of the bandy-wallah, tried to turn back, a feat which would have resulted in

A MOONLIGHT FORD.

F——'s getting a cold bath; but the munchiel bearers dashed into the stream, and, surrounding the cart and oxen, eventually brought the whole thing safe to shore, after which we proceeded on our journey—now on the "foreign soil" of Cochin.

In spite of not having had any rest the preceding evening, the scene was so novel and the mode of travelling so strange that I found it impossible to think of sleep. The heavy bandy was soon left far behind, and my bearers, going at a rapid trot, carried me along in excellent style. Besides the ten men, who now worked in relays, there was one old Tamil headman, with a smooth brown skin, neatly shaven head, and spotless white cloth wound loosely round his waist. He carried a native umbrella, made of palm-leaves, and at first I wondered why he held it up so persistently even in the darkest and stillest parts, but the truth was it would not shut, so he was forced to keep it open; and as he scudded along in front, with his white robes and his unclosable umbrella, he led a sort of rude chorus to keep the men in step and lighten their labours. At first it was, "Um bay! um bay! um bay!" continued for twenty minutes, till I was beginning to wonder what the next line would be, and then the old headman stopped for a second, but soon began again, "Ah hum! ah hum! ah hum!" and after a mile or two of this he went on with, "How hi! how hi! how hi!" The monotony very nearly sent me to sleep, but not quite; and I took note of all the features of the country in order to be able to find my way down to Palghaut, should I ever have occasion to travel alone.

At one time, as we were skimming rapidly through a moonlit grove between two topes of jungle, we rapidly approached something white lying on the road. At first I supposed it must be a heap of stones, but when we came up it took the shape of a man, and I saw it was a coolie—dead. The poor wretch was lying across the road, with his arms wide apart, his pale face and open eyes turned up to the moon, and nothing to cover him but his one tattered rag of cloth. It was my first "famine coolie." The munchiel-wallahs did not seem at all affected, never varying the evenness of their jog-trot. We swept right over him, and I could not note even a falter in the old Tamil's song, "How hi! how hi!" as he took the poor body in his stride. Half a mile further a jackal ran close by us—going, perhaps, to "bury" the dead coolie; it is probably the only sort of burial he will get, for this it must be remembered is native territory, and there are no sharp-eyed "collectors" here to inquire into the why and wherefore of every man's demise.

After this the moon went down, and the darkness became "Egyptian;" but we still sped along, and presently it began to grow very chilly, and a strange mysterious sort of light crept over the sky, near objects growing more and more distinct as the heavens in the east waxed paler and paler. The monotonous song of the bearers stopped, and the chirruping of the insects died away, so that for a time everything was silent and still, while the sky brightened and the heavy monsoon clouds showed first grey and silver, and then became fringed with pale saffron light. Gradually the golds and crimsons of sunrise climbed up into the sky, until at last it seemed all on fire from east to west, and then there was a bright glow in the horizon, and the sun rose splendid above the low grass hills; whereupon at once a new concert of sounds broke forth, and the green paroquets burst from the shelter of the fig trees, darting with glad screams through the air to proclaim the coming of another day.

I must have gone to sleep for a time, for, waking

up, I found myself apparently floating along in mid-air over extensive paddy-fields, with a little village a mile ahead, and beyond that low hills, rising gradually tier above tier into towering mountains whose top-most peaks were lost in the clouds. My coolies were, in fact, taking a short cut along the high mud walls which keep the irrigation streams inside the enclosures, and are very frequently used as footpaths by the natives. As these walls are five or six feet high and very narrow, I could see nothing of the ground from my hammock, and could not at first remember what sort of conveyance mine was; but recollections of the preceding evening soon came back, and, though the scenery was very beautiful, my thoughts wandered fondly to breakfast amid fervid hopes that nothing might have happened to F—— and the provisions. I had not long to wait, for getting amongst plots of ground cultivated with brinjals and sweet potatoes, the head man came up to my side, and with a salaam pointed to the village ahead, and said, "Wallenghay, sahib." Directly afterwards we forded a shallow stream only ankle-deep, and on the opposite side found ourselves amongst scattered huts and gardens, fenced in with light bamboo hedges. Turning sharp to the right, my men put on some extra pace—having "kept a trot for the avenue," as the Irish post-boys used to say—and we dashed down the little native bazaar, with its open booths on either side, the motley Hindoo crowd dividing and staring wonderingly at us, and the dogs barking and the chickens flying away in a ridiculous panic. Passing a broad banian tree at the head of the lane, round the stem of which a rude stone terrace had been erected as a location of the village gods—half a dozen strange elephant-headed idols smeared over with red and yellow paint, and surrounded with little offerings of flowers, rice, and glass bangles—

we, thirty yards further, pulled up in the clean-swept courtyard of a neat little native house, much used by the planters for breaking the journey between Palghaut and the hills.

My five hours in the munchiel had made me both stiff and hungry, and I could not help wondering at the much superior "condition" of the bearers, who had carried me all the way at a rapid trot, and yet seemed perfectly fresh—chatting with their acquaintances and chewing betel-nut without the least symptoms of fatigue. Having paid the old head man—for which purpose I called him to me, and he came bowing and holding out both hands edge to edge, as much as to say that the sahib's bounty was so munificent that it could not be contained in one hand—I dismissed them, and turned my thoughts to breakfast.

The neat little Hindoo lady who kept the house soon understood my signs and some half-forgotten Hindustani, and forthwith gave orders to a couple of brown young children to capture a promising young cockerel, who—luckless bird that he was—brought this fatal notice on himself by standing on the gate-post, and trying his very feeble voice at a crow in answer to a neighbouring rival. The boys attempted to stalk him, but he was too wide awake, and flew down at once, whereupon began a tremendous chase up and down and round about. The cock ran into the fireplace of a disused copper, and the children plunged after him. I thought his fate was sealed; but no, there was a loud cackle, and out he came from under the lid and set off round the yard, with his pursuers close after him. Over boxes and baskets they went, kicking up the dust and frightening the other fowls out of their small amount of wits. After ten minutes of this hot chase the boys were done up, and the widow had to come to their assistance, immediately effecting by strategy what could not be done by force. Getting a large sieve, she propped it up with a twig of bamboo from the hedge, and tied a long piece of cocoa-nut fibre to the centre, afterwards sprinkling some rice underneath. Down came the hens from the coigns of vantage whither they had fled during the chase, and set to work upon the grain. The youthful cock was obviously aware that there would soon be none left, so, keeping one bright eye on the brown urchins, who had retired some distance, and the other on the rice, he approached step by step. I had half a mind to intercede on behalf of so brave a bird, but while I watched with suspense he approached, walked once or twice round, and then ventured under the sieve. The string was pulled, both little savages gave a howl of delight at the same moment, and the betrayed victim was borne struggling into the kitchen.

While the breakfast was thus tragically preparing, I lit a cheroot, and took a stroll down the main and only street of the little village. The inhabitants seemed to know I was a stranger and bound for the jungles, for many were the nods and laying together of heads I saw from the corners of my eyes among the shopkeepers; indeed, I am sure I afforded an endless theme of conversation to some old women and children sitting under the village tree and expectorating bright red betel-nut juice all about them. What has always struck me about native markets is that almost all the stalls are devoted to food of some sort. One shop will be a pulse-vendor's, where many kinds of grain are exposed for sale in little wicker-work baskets, and the walls and roof are hidden by strings of queer-shaped nuts and bunches of chillies or bananas. Another shop is devoted to dried fish, which is hung up in festoons or piled on the same bench on which the proprietor sits cross-legged; and then there will be more seed shops and more fish merchants all down the bazaar. But where are the butchers, the bakers, the stationers, the linendrapers, and all the others which make a walk in London as good as a lecture on domestic economy? The truth is probably that the natives need none of them—they have not got so far along the path of civilization, and they have few needs beyond eating. As for furniture their houses boast little but the very simplest. I peeped into one or two of which the doors were open as I passed, and could see nothing but a hearth formed of three large stones, a miscellaneous collection of fire-blackened earthen chatties of all sizes, with a few mats made of the finely divided leaves of the fan-palm by way of couches. But these, of course, were the huts of the poorer classes; the houses of the rich natives in the English stations and towns are furnished much after the fashion of European dwellings. I certainly did expect to find both the booths of jewellers and sellers of linen and cloths in profusion, but neither were visible. The former, I fancy, have their little forges in their back yards, and in a place like this naturally do not keep much "stock," but content themselves with making bracelets and bangles when any one brings them the rough material in the shape of rupees; while for linen and clothing the inhabitants visit big weekly fairs in some part of the district, or trust to hawkers who wander from village to village with heavy packs.

Another thing missing was the monkeys. Hitherto I had not seen a single specimen, wild or tame, and yet all the books of Indian travel describe them as numerous everywhere—on the housetops and among the trees. But though monkeys may be absent, the kites and vultures are wonderfully numerous here. The sky is full of them all day, for ever wheeling round and round, each species seeming to keep to a certain stratum, the kites wheeling round the palm-tops lowest of all, while far away up under the blue dome the vultures and eagles are sailing round in mighty circles of ten miles' radius—overhead one moment and the next far away, searching the jungle, exploring the ravines and hollows, and then coming back across rivers and plains with scarcely a movement of the wings, ever gliding along with "supreme dominion" in their aerial voyages. Descending to the surface of the earth, there were many new and gorgeous butterflies to interest the naturalist—handsome swallowtails, with primrose-yellow and velvety black wings; great *Papilio Hectors*, rich-winged with crimson and brown, and many others, too varied to be mentioned, playing among the wayside herbage or hunting each other through the broad leaves of the ever-graceful bananas. A morning walk in India must always seem pleasant to a Western stranger, however dull an observer he may be under ordinary circumstances, for its life and surroundings are so new and different. He may have formed some ideas of the tropics which will be doomed to disappointment; but, taken as a whole, he cannot fail to be well satisfied. Perhaps the thing that struck me most was the lack of common flowers. I expected to find, on landing on Eastern soil, the whole country an almost endless show of blossoms, from the tops of the trees to the roots of the grass—a very extravagant idea, no doubt, but most people have some such when they arrive in India; whereas, in truth, there are not so many flowers visible—at this season, at least—as are to be seen in a summer walk in an English lane.

Coming back, I passed a curious Kindergarten school of small native children. Whether they were at work or play, it was difficult to tell, but they seemed to be enjoying themselves. There was a tall pole erected in the centre of the enclosed yard of a neat little hut, and round the staff thirty gay brown-skinned Tamil boys and girls were marching, with short sticks in either hand, with which they were beating time to a strange chorus of two or three words, repeated over and over again, in a sort of chant, by an extremely ugly old coolie woman in a blue saree, who appeared to be presiding over the performance. It was a pretty sight to see the children all absorbed in their occupation, the girls with their black hair, glossy with oil, waving in the wind, and the boys with their curious-looking shaven heads, as smooth as an ostrich-egg, with just one long tuft hanging over the forehead. In another spot was a village academy where a half circle of little naked scholars sate round a grey-headed schoolmaster, and worked sums with sticks on boards sprinkled with brick-dust.

Eventually a pair of white oxen and a bandy came meandering down the village street, and I was joined by F——, who was ravenously hungry and very sore with six hours' jolting in his waggon. So we got back to our comfortable little resting-house, and fell to work forthwith on some chicken curry, excellent, though I was unpleasantly conscious of whence the material came. Our hostess's crockery was not very numerous nor perfect. There was an old teapot which had lost both handle and lid in some past period, and had its spout broken short off; there were a couple of much-chipped dishes, two cracked teacups, and a saucer. With these, however, we managed to get on very comfortably. The furniture and decorations were about on a par with the china. There was a rickety charpoy, or native bedstead, of teak wood, doubtless very useful once, but not trustworthy now; a still more shaky table with treacherous legs, one chair without a back, and a wine-box, which we used as a stool. By way of decorations, the whitewashed walls were pasted over with indiscriminate cuttings from English illustrated papers, mixed up in the most odd manner, and not one of them horizontal or exactly perpendicular—natives never can or will see the beauty of straight lines or parallels; in fact, it takes an education to do so. Staring down on us from one wall were the carved heads of most grotesquely evil demons, with fierce red glass eyes, and wide-open mouths, showing long rows of snake fangs, while from their foreheads rose the pointed horns of the small hog-deer. Altogether, they were most hideous objects, but interesting, as showing the native ideas of the evil spirits of the jungle. Woodcarving seems to be very successfully practised in this village, for, as we sat in the broad chunamed verandah after breakfast, I noticed how skilfully all the heads of the pillars were ornamented, each with scrollwork and mythical symbols round the upper parts. The framing of the windows—needless to say they were glassless—were also carved with delicate leaves and flowers, the abundant and varied timber of the neighbourhood encouraging the art.

Then, with new munchiels, we were accompanied to the outskirts of the village by some of the native police; not that there was any need of their services, but they were sent as an act of courtesy to speed the parting guests, and ran by the sides of our hammocks until we had reached the open country when they salaamed low and left us to continue our journey. For some time it was extremely hot, and, despite the awning overhead, my blue swing-cot turned out to be uncomfortable, and liable to give cramps. I confided my feelings to F—— as we jogged along side by side, and, to comfort me, he narrated a story of how a fat and prosperous Englishman from Madras started one day to make a pilgrimage to these very jungles to see some coffee estate in which he was interested. The railway part of the journey he stood well enough, but coming on from the station to the traveller's bungalow at Palghaut in a bandy was fearfully trying, and his disgust reached a climax when he saw a munchiel for the first time, and learnt that was the best means of performing the next stage.

At first he could not be got to make the attempt, but eventually was persuaded to enter, and, once lying in the hammock, he was bound to finish the stage. What his sufferings were it is easy to imagine. He had never appreciated up-country travelling, and by the time he reached Wallenghay he had had quite enough of it, giving up all thoughts of visiting the coffee estate, and returning to Palghaut station the same day, whence he made his way back to his comfortable bungalow at Madras, considerably wiser and thinner than when he left. I felt myself losing weight rapidly, and was very glad of my experienced companion's assurances that we should be much cooler when we came to the Ghauts. So we stood it as well as we could, and watched the paddy-fields with the tall palms growing from the banks which divide them, and the wayside huts almost hidden in plantains and creeping plants, whence little children ran out to stare at our retinue as we trotted by; until presently we were aware of approaching a river, as the road began to slope down, and some oxen passed us with their hides still glossy and dripping from a recent bath. In another minute or two our bearers were splashing across a shallow stream, with overhanging trees on either bank, and the bed broken up with projecting slabs and pinnacles of grey rocks. Among these a party of native washermen were at work. All the washing seems to be done by men, although it would appear a naturally feminine employment. The *modus operandi* is the same as can be seen any day in the streams of Italy or Southern France, and consists of rolling the linen up into a wet "swab," and whacking it against a flat smooth stone. The more muscular the washermen, the quicker the linen is done, but it generally fares badly with the buttons. The style, however, was doubtless first invented for native garments, which rarely boast many such fastenings; but now all English clothing has to take its chance with sarees and cummerbunds.

Passing these semi-amphibious washers standing knee-deep in their own "tubs," we soon reached the commencement of the real ghaut road, and the vegetation became greener and more dense. Here, too, I saw more winged life than at any other point of my journey. The crow-pheasants were numerous—handsome birds, with black-and-chestnut bodies and long pheasant-like tails, of which they seemed both conscious and proud as they strutted sedately about amongst the low bushes. The ever-active mynahs were hard at work searching for worms and slugs, though they still kept a very keen look-out for hawks sailing overhead, and their sharp alarm notes sent all the small birds in the neighbourhood to cover when they were sounded. The paroquets also enlivened the scenery with their emerald-green bodies and long pointed tails. For some reason they can never fly without uttering a series of piercing shrieks, and as they go in flocks of ten or twenty, the noise where a party is disturbed is an experience not to be forgotten.

I was greatly impressed, as soon as the jungle was really entered, at the wonderful height and size of the forest trees, not so much in lateral spread as in loftiness and the distance from the ground to the nearest branches. There was one tree which was especially noticeable when we had mounted well above the plain; its trunk was smooth-barked and grey in colour, but as I ran my eyes up the mighty stems, I was astonished at their height. The first branches must have been from one hundred to one hundred and fifty feet above the road on which we travelled, and the head of the trees rose quite another fifty feet; in fact, the tree-tops became confused masses of green leaves, cloud-like and indefinite, and small birds amongst the highest branches were scarcely definable dots. The mightiest giants that adorn the parks and woodlands of England would seem but shrubs in comparison with these forest kings, and yet my companion pointed out, as I had already noticed myself, the curious fact that there are no trees in these jungles which have the aspect of any extreme old age. It may perhaps be partly due to the fact that the scarcely changing seasons make little mark on their outward appearance; but nevertheless, after travelling through miles of primeval forest, and being wonderstruck with the stature of the timber, I should not like to say I had seen anything more than a hundred years old.

But if the trees were wonderful, the undergrowth of smaller vegetation is insignificant. At first, as the broad, well-kept road approaches the foot of the ghaut, the trees and shrubs on either side combine the flora of both plain and mountain, and there the botanist can undoubtedly revel to his heart's content in grassy glades, with occasional dense patches of tangled creepers among herbaceous plants and thick-foliaged undergrowths. But when the real ascent is reached, and the road degenerates into a stony bridle-path winding backwards and forwards in sharp zigzags and abrupt curves, the temperature falls with every hundred feet of elevation, and while the forest trees become taller and more closely planted, their dense and high tops shut out the sunlight from the surface of the ground, and gradually supplant all the weaker vegetation, with the exception of mosses, ferns, and bamboos, the last of which monopolize whole hillsides to themselves, and attain astonishing dimensions in quiet and sheltered ravines.

The road ascended at a gradient of one in four or five feet in places, and was so steep that in many parts, being ahead of F——, I looked down upon his munchiel and bearers thirty or forty feet below me; and then his men would take a shorter cut than mine, whereupon I would catch a glimpse of them through the bamboo clumps a considerable distance above. In this way we went on all the afternoon, ascending the great Annamully range in a manner which was like nothing so much as going up a gigantic ladder, and taking the rungs first to the right and then to the left. About three o'clock we had reached an elevation of more than two thousand feet above the plain, and a sudden break in the roof of tree-tops gave us a brief but wonderful view of the lowlands through which we had travelled the night before, lying stretched out far to the northward like a gigantic map. Every one who has journeyed much in India has viewed such a scene. There lay the yellow paddy fields, with green patches of cultivated ground and sombre palm groves, through which wound the broad streams which we had forded in the moonlight, like meandering silver ribbons; and there were all the little villages along the high-road, up and down which tiny black dots marked the foot passengers and native carts carrying the produce of the fields to the bazaars of the neighbouring towns. Nearest of all, and looking in the clear mountain air to be within a stone's throw, though really far below us, was the palm-surrounded hamlet of Wallanghay, with the gay crowd still moving in its bazaar, and the path we had just taken clearly marked out among the gardens and cultivated plots that surrounded it. Only a few short hours ago I was envying the eagles up under the blue roof of heaven, and here I was feeling an eagle myself and seeing the world as they see it! When we have invented flying and can use our wings like the bird of Jove, it will matter little how the face of the country is disfigured with factory chimneys and big towns, for nothing could look commonplace from such an elevation as this.

After a brief halt to admire the splendid view, we had to continue our upward progress, and soon to content ourselves with remembrances of the scene below, for we had reached the level of the heavy monsoon clouds, which at this season float backwards and forwards along the face of the hills, and we became enveloped in dense white mist, which circled about, leaving us scarcely view enough to find the stony path that still continued ever upwards. In one place the pathway led by a smooth stage of bare rock, across the centre of which a single thread of water made its way, though this becomes, after a heavy rainfall, a dangerous foaming torrent. A little higher up the stream were six or seven deep circular holes, large enough for a man to get into, and at the bottom of several of them are heavy round stones of a harder rock. It is these stones that have scooped the great hollows when the winter rains have come rushing down and set them continually turning and joggling about; but considering the slowness with which the grinding process must go on, and the hardness of the bed of the nullah, the lapse of time which each hole represents must be enormous. Yet further up the track—which now had degenerated into a mere bridle-path—was cut across by a vein of gneiss, which the road-makers have found too hard for them to remove, and so have left it in its natural rugged condition. This obstacle alone would effectually cut off all carriage communication between the lowlands and jungle, without taking into consideration the roughness and steepness of the whole ascent. Getting out of the munchiels, a few more yards brought us to an open grassy plateau on the spur of a mountain, and here the bearers respectfully requested to be dismissed, as it was growing late, and they wanted to get back to the lowlands before nightfall, having a great dread of staying at such an elevation during darkness, believing these mountain woodlands to be the high place of fever and ill-willed spirits. So we paid them at the rate of twelve annas per man, equal to one shilling and twopence in English coinage, and, rolling up the hammocks and lashing them to their poles, they salaamed all round, and were soon lost in the mist and rain on the pathway below.

Left to ourselves, F—— and I looked about for a place wherein to make our frugal tiffin and to drink the beer we had brought up with us. This we soon lit upon in the shape of a circle of rough stones placed on the very extreme point of the spur, and overhanging a deep wooded ravine, along the bottom of which a mountain brook ran foaming and tumbling through the dark arcades of the jungle trees, till it was lost to sight far away in the direction of the plain. As the white mist came drifting round us and wetted our thin clothing through and through, and the wind moaned and sighed among the bare rocks and through the tree-tops, it was impossible not to feel the influence of the place, or quite to disbelieve it to be the home of departed spirits and of the inhabitants of another world. Apparently the natives living up here had felt the same uncanny sense, for the stones on which we sat down to lunch formed a *samee*, or worshipping place, of great sanctity. It was the abode of a spirit famous for effecting cures of all sorts, and the space enclosed by the stone ring was piled up thickly with rudely executed wooden carvings of every conceivable part of the human body. Legs and feet were, perhaps, the most common, but there were hands, arms, heads, and numberless other models in thick profusion. F——, who has often been here before, says he believes that when a Tamil coolie gets sick or hurts himself in any way, he sets to work and carves out of some soft wood as accurate an image of the afflicted part as he can. With this and a little rice in a pot, he comes, doubtless in fear and trembling, to the lonely mountain spur, and, having cooked and scattered the rice by way of offering, mutters some short prayers—as likely as not the name of some single deity—over and over again for a couple of hundred times, and then throws his model arm or leg into the enchanted circle by way of memorandum to the Unseen, afterwards going on his way convinced that he has done all that is possible. If the limb gets well, it is a proof of the efficiency of the samee place, and if it does not he comforts himself with the thought that perhaps the prayers were not long enough or the rice not sufficient in quantity, and hopes for better success on another occasion. It was a curious place, and I much wanted to carry away some of the carvings; but my companion, whom the white mist had made a little superstitious, persuaded me against it by assuring me if I did I should inherit some of the sicknesses.

Equally dividing the few effects we had brought up with us, we resumed our march through the gloomy, wet jungle for three miles, the road no longer ascending rapidly, but making its way along the sides of the hollows and round the shoulders of the hills, yet all the time overshadowed by mighty trees and heavy masses of bamboos, so that the ground was wet and sodden, and thickly carpeted with dead and dying leaves, which fall fast at this season, but never leave the trees quite bare, as new ones rapidly take their places.

It was here I first made the acquaintance of that abominable creature, the tropical leech. I was walking along over the soft matting of decaying vegetation, when I was suddenly aware of a pain in one instep, as though a carpenter's bradawl had been slowly thrust into my flesh, and naturally proceeded to investigate the cause. No sooner had I removed my leathern legging than out rolled a horrid blood-distended leech about the size and shape of a ripe black cherry, and there was a mark like a shot-hole above my foot from which the blood was slowly trickling, as it always does at first, owing to the depth of stab given by the creature's lancet. F—— pointed out to me other leeches that had "spotted" us, even while we halted, and were hurrying up from all quarters, getting over the ground at a wonderful rate by the simple process of seizing a convenient object in advance with the front suckers, and then looping the body up and placing the tail end just in rear of the head, when the latter part is moved forward again. When hungry—which, by the way, seems to be their chronic condition—they are of a light-brown colour, with a bright yellow line down either side, and numerous fine black points all over their skins. In length they are about an inch and a half—though they have a wonderful power of distending themselves to reach a convenient coign of vantage—and are about the thickness of a barley straw; but when they have succeeded in their fell ambition, and have drunk deeply of the blood of the white stranger, they become most loathsome and disgusting-looking red bags, with no perceptible difference at either extremity, and their utmost ability is then to roll into some nook or corner, and lie by until their appetite returns. It has always struck me as curious that they should entertain such bloodthirsty tastes when their natural and usual food must be simply decaying vegetation. For instance, this and every other lonely jungle path swarms with their flabby armies, and though the human passers-by must be very few and far between, the approach of any one sets them all stretching their ugly bodies and racing over the ground, in the hopes of reaching his feet and making their first and last meal on blood. Myriads of them must live and die on strictly vegetarian diet, and yet their descendants are as ready as ever to assault and drive their sharp beaks into the flesh of the first mortal who comes within their range!

After a long damp walk through the forest glades, my companion and I saw with satisfaction the sky showing through the tree-tops ahead, a sure sign that we were approaching open ground; and soon a sudden turn to the left brought us into daylight on the north-western edge of Polyampara, the oldest coffee estate on these hills, under the management of an energetic Cornishman, G. D——, who has been out here for some fifteen years, and may be considered the founder of the district. Here my entertaining and courteous companion shook hands with me, and, after exacting a promise that I would seize the first opportunity to visit his eyrie, "the highest and healthiest bungalow on the hills," he took his way through the jungles to his own estate, and left me to introduce myself to D——, who, he said, was sure to be delighted to put me up for the night. So, descrying a bungalow in the distance, I made for it, and speedily found the owner, who received me cordially, and, as I had been led to expect, invited me to stay the night.

Coffee planters are ever early birds, and on the morning after reaching the head of the ghaut, I was roused by an extraordinary sound, which at first seemed to be a thunderstorm, but on springing up and looking from the window of my room, I saw the noise came from D——'s head maistry, or overlooker, who was exerting all his strength in beating a great Chinese gong with a heavy hammer; so I proceeded to make a hasty toilet. By the time I had reached the verandah, the sun was just climbing over the tree-tops, and the thin white mists were falling back before him, but still resting in the deep hollows and behind every clump of forest where it was protected from the light morning breeze. Soon, lines of coolies of all ages and both sexes, grey-haired old men, women, and small children, with tools on their shoulders, were winding their way slowly and sleepily to various parts of the estate, while native maistries in white linen garments urged them on and directed their course. When the last of the men had left the group of sheds where they had been mustered, my host came towards the bungalow; and after due greetings made, and inquiries as to how I liked my first night on the hills, we proceeded to take our *chota hazri,* as the first morning meal is called. Having got through two or three rounds of toast and a cup of coffee—a light repast, on which, however, it is the fashion to do all the hard work of the morning—we drew on our heavy boots, and, donning pith helmets with streaming white puggarees behind, proceeded on a tour of inspection while the air was yet cool.

It is difficult to describe a coffee estate so that it may be clear to the imagination of one who has never seen that plant growing under cultivation, since it is little like any home production, and no part of England bears any resemblance to these jungle clearings. The first thing to be understood is that the land is a continual succession of hills and ravines. There is not such a thing anywhere in the district as a piece of ground, naturally level, of sufficient size to play a game of tennis on, but wherever you walk you are either slipping downhill or laboriously climbing upwards, except, of course, when you make use of the roads which run through the estates in two or three directions. But when working, that is the exception, and you have to force your way as the crow flies, over hill and dale. Another cause which renders the walking very hard work is the scattered logs of trees which cover the ground. On an old estate like Polyampara they are not a great inconvenience, as it is now fifteen years since they fell, and Nature, which in this land always exerts herself to get rid of dead matter as speedily as possible, has very nearly succeeded in crumbling them all back to dust. But on a newer estate matters are different, and a walk requires the nimbleness of a squirrel and strength of a professional gymnast. When it is first decided to open a garden, the Englishman comes up to the jungle, and, pitching his temporary encampment at a convenient spot near a stream, proceeds, with a dozen or two of coolies, to drive lanes through the tangled undergrowth to mark out the margins of his first "clearings." Perhaps his base line is twenty chains due south; then he works due east, north, and west, until he has completed the square; and all trees in that enclosure are doomed, so that the squirrels and monkeys had better remove their families as speedily as may be. For soon the sound of the axes is heard falling sharp and quick all day long, and one by one the forest monarchs snap and come rushing down to earth, breaking and bending all their neighbours, until the place is one wild scene of confusion—great tree trunks in all sorts of wonderful positions and angles, and ten feet deep of withering foliage and broken branches on the ground. During three long "hot months" of the year this lies drying under the fierce sun, a mournful wilderness of fallen grandeur, until the planter sees the sky clouding and knows the rains are coming, when he goes one windy morning and, with a single match, fires the mighty pile. Then the flames spread far and near, and the thick yellow smoke hides the sky, while the clearing burns night and day for a week or more. Meantime the planter has either made a "nursery," where he should have by this time a sufficient quantity of carefully tended and watered young coffee plants, about a foot high, or has to get his stock elsewhere. As soon as the clearing is burnt out, the assistant is sent on with bands of coolies, and "pits" the enclosure with long lines of square holes running from side to side of the plantation. Finally, when the rains come, the young plants are tenderly taken up, slipped into rough wicker baskets, and placed in the pits prepared for them, where each is carefully tucked up. There they grow into thick bushes, and the coffee planter spends the three years which must elapse before his first crop is ripe in opening more land, building pucka bungalows and coolie "lines" or sheds, and driving roads through the estate.

My friend D——'s place had reached this climax some years ago, and so showed how an estate ought to look when in full cultivation. I was much struck with the beautiful symmetry of the lines of coffee shrubs, which took their course undeviatingly over hills and down the steep sides of the nullahs from wherever we stood, right and left, to the very confines of the clearing. The advantages of this were obvious directly, for we soon came on a party of coolies hard at work weeding; and each man or woman having the space between two rows of bushes to himself or herself, we could tell at a glance if they were all working, and, walking behind the labourers, the maistries could plainly see if any work had been badly done, at once admonishing the offender. Armed with round baskets to hold the weeds, and with small implements of iron, shaped much like a mediæval battle-axe, with a spike on one side and a small hoe on the other, they were doing their feeble best at reducing the too-exuberant vegetation which a couple of days' rain had brought up. But they were a feeble set—the men thin and broken-down, wearing nothing but a dirty cummerbund, and the women equally miserably clad in a single grimy saree.

As we were walking along, one of the maistries called D——'s attention to a woman lying beneath a coffee bush, and trembling all over with fever. My companion beckoned her to come down to the road on which we were standing, and she got up and came slowly towards us, the whole line of coolies striking work and stopping to watch us. She was really a very pretty girl of about eighteen, with a fairer skin than usual among her kindred, and perhaps, in better times, before the famine, may have been noted in the village for her comeliness; but at present she was sadly down in the world. She had drawn the spare end of her thin green saree from her shoulders, and was carrying something rolled up in it. When she came and stood before us, she was trembling like an aspen with jungle fever, and D—— bid her hold out her hand to have her pulse felt. He rested his fingers on her wrist, and then told me to try it, upon which I found the pulsation very fast and feeble—nearly one hundred and ten beats a minute—doubtless partially due to her being frightened at being so near white sahibs. "What have you got here?" said D—— in Tamil, suddenly taking the end of the saree out of her hand, and down fell an armful of small weeds and the unripe berries of the coffee bush, which the girl had been collecting to eat for her supper. D—— scolded her, and asked her how she was to get well if she ate such stuff as that, and then ordered her to the "lines" and rest, where he would send her food and medicine; so she wrapped her green robe round her shivering body and went away to her hovel. My companion explained to me that she had but just come up from her native village, far away in Mysore, with some of her kindred; and he added, "These poor creatures want continual watching when they first arrive. They are so broken down and hopeless that they cannot understand that they are not going to be allowed to die. They eat any garbage or rubbish they can find, although they know the result will be fever immediate and heavy. They won't come for medicine, because they don't know what is the matter with them, and don't care; and, in fact, they are about as helpless and feeble as children of three or four years old. But I cannot afford to let them die, as it is a great trouble to bring them to the estates, and I find it cheaper to buy them food, feed them, and give them free board and lodging until they are fit to work. In this way nearly every English estate in the south of India is a 'relief camp,' and we do our best to help distress without saying anything about it."

To show me the sort of rough material which comes up from the famine-stricken lowlands, we went down to a large, roomy wooden building by a stream, which D—— called the "hospital shed," and here we found collected together a dozen of the most fearfully emaciated mortals it was ever my misfortune to behold. They were lying curled up on mats, or with their chins resting on their knees, and their bare fleshless limbs looking like withered branches. None of them moved when we entered; in fact, they were too far gone to do anything but moan and shiver under the cold fits of the ague and fever which always follows close behind starvation. But the most painful sight of all was at the end of the room, where a coarse cocoa-nut mat was thrown over something which I took to be firewood or rubbish. Judge, then, of my astonishment when D—— pushed it away with the point of his umbrella, and disclosed a poor little native child, about six months old, screwed up into a tight knot, with its thin limbs close to its body, and the knee and elbow joints bulging out from the dry, shrivelled skin. It was like nothing so much as the desiccated rats which are occasionally found in the crevices of old buildings; but, alas! it was alive, and kept rolling its great eyes about without seeming to see anything. All its remnant of life seemed in its eyes, and their only expression was one of wild suffering and pain. In reply to my asking if it could live long, D—— said, although perhaps it might live, it could never recover; so we covered it up, and went on with our walk.

It is curious under these circumstances to be told of the great difficulty that exists in getting labourers to accept work. One would think they would go anywhere sooner than starve, but it is not so. They cling to their districts and villages until they are almost too feeble to walk, and then only come up with great reluctance, and, needless to say, are worth little when they arrive. Besides the love of home, very strong within them, and a great distaste for being made to do a regular amount of work, which they know will be their fate up here, they have a vast dread of the silent and sombre jungle, peopled with all sorts of bad and malicious spirits and demons in their imaginations. Nor really can one blame them: the prospect of coming among the chilly airs and deadly mists of these regions, and probably being buried on some lonely hillside, with no kinsmen to perform the last friendly rites, is not pleasant; in fact, it needs a "Britisher's" pluck to do it willingly, and that is a quality of which these poor grain-fed people are almost wholly destitute.

CHAPTER VIII.

AT WORK.

After a very pleasant stroll round D——'s clearings, and imbibing much useful information, we finally got back to the bungalow; and, shaking hands with my courteous host, I set out for my own estate, under the guidance of a swarthy, short, curly-headed native, looking like an aboriginal Australian, who had been sent to show me the way to Pardagherry. We wound along by the side of a shallow stream for three or four miles; the road, well made and broad, running under continual avenues of trees, and crossing the bed of the stream once or twice by very solidly built bridges; until we came out into the open again, and a wide expanse of mature coffee lay before, with a clean white bungalow standing on a knoll nearly in the centre of the clearing, shadowed by two graceful palm trees—the only ones on these hills. As the road ran close by, I called upon the superintendent, and found him and his assistant hard at work over accounts. They were naturally astonished at the sudden appearance of a new "pale face," and it was necessary to explain who I was, when H——, the chik-doree, and W——, the superintendent, welcomed me cordially to the jungles. The assistant assured me that the vilest of Irish mud hovels was a paradise compared to the place I was going to, and painted the discomforts of jungle life in glowing terms, ending up with the ironical hope that I should be comfortable; so, with a promise to drop in at his bungalow some day and let him know what my quarters proved like, I marched forward again.

Another estate was passed, on a ridge of mountain

planted on both sides with coffee, and again we descended into a valley and left the cleared ground behind us. Here the vegetation appeared more dense and matted than farther to the north, great creepers swinging from tree to tree, while long rattan canes—a hundred springing from one root—climbed hither and thither, and overhung the road in festoons. Here, too, the pathway—for it was no longer a made road—ran along the top of a ridge, and although the valleys on either side were not discernible, the trees had clearly felt the influence of the wind; for there were many dead trunks lying about in all stages of decay, with green moss spreading a pall over them, and pale, scentless white orchids shooting up, fresh and beautiful, from the rotten wood.

After we had done a couple of miles along this road, a strange figure was seen coming down the path, and I was soon after confronted by R——, the superintendent of the company's estate where I was going to work. A very old hand himself at coffee planting, and a dweller all his life in wild regions, he had become a regular backwoodsman, and had discarded as superfluous many of the refinements of civilization. Imagine an old grey-headed man, his chin and cheeks long unacquainted with the razor, sharp black eyes long accustomed to look on nothing but obsequious natives, and a form bent with fever and hill-climbing, equipped in a loose and not particularly new suit of dark green cloth, white leather leggings, a broad-brimmed hat of coarse rice straw, and a heavy stick to lean upon. Such was my associate when he first presented himself to my sight, and, after making each other's acquaintance, he retraced his steps, and together we proceeded to the settlement. This we were not long in reaching, and the ideas I had formed of an encampment in embryo were rudely shaken. Dim notions had floated through my head of shady fig trees, with wide-spreading branches, and white tents under their shelter, with rows of neat native huts down by a neighbouring stream half hidden in verdant cool foliage, with horses and cattle grazing *ad libitum*, and laughing children and noisy dogs to welcome the traveller; but the reality was sadly otherwise.

The ridge along which we had been passing grew rapidly narrower, and began to slope downwards; while daylight and patches of blue sky showing through the trees on either side, indicated that we were passing along the centre of a narrow strip or belt of forest, which had been left when the clearings were made upon either side. As the pathway sloped more and more downwards, the soil had been washed off by the heavy rains rushing to the nearest watercourse, leaving the matted roots of the tall trees everywhere exposed, and making a wild entanglement which in places formed rude steps, of which we took advantage, and in others arches and lacework of timber, which it required care to thread without tripping. At the bottom of the hill we came suddenly in view of the "settlement." Totally different from what I had expected, it looked like nothing so much as a wild African village, such as Stanley has described and figured many times in his "Travels in the Dark Continent." The underwood had been cut down, together with a few of the most inconveniently placed trees, and in the rough clearing thus formed (all bristling with stumps and remains of bushes) half a dozen low reed-thatched hovels had grown up a little below an isolated residence, which, though of exactly the same construction as the others, seemed a trifle more carefully finished. This latter was our temporary home, and, arriving in the rudely built verandah, R—— bade me "welcome to the greenwood," and told me we should have to make ourselves as comfortable as circumstances would permit, until a slack time in the coffee planting gave us an opportunity to build pucka bungalows.

Certainly there was not very much to boast of in my new quarters. R——'s hut was about thirty feet long by about twelve broad, and was divided in two by a chinky partition of Palghaut mats. One half which abutted on the path by which we had approached was the dining-room, and for its sole furniture boasted a round table, a meat-safe with shelves and wire gauze to keep out flies and slugs, and a strong lock and key to keep out the "boys." The available space which these left was further diminished by a heavy iron safe, a stove with an exceedingly obtrusive chimney, and two or three chairs. The owner pointed out with great pride that the floor was not the actual surface of the soil, which had been smoothed and covered with rough-sawn boards laid side by side on it. He also begged me to notice that we had entered by glass folding-doors, which, though they would not close tightly, had been fixed up as a temporary arrangement, and he considered them extremely luxurious. The construction of the hut itself was very primitive, as I took in at a glance. Four strong forked poles had been driven in at the corners, and young saplings, roughly lopped and trimmed, had been placed on them. Upon these the roof had been constructed, with a very steep pitch to throw off the heavy monsoon rainfall, and had been thickly thatched with pale yellow lemon-grass from the neighbouring hillside. Yet though the roof was substantial enough, the sides of the hut were fragility itself. A few stout stakes had been driven in at equal distances, and to these Palghaut mats were fastened with split rattan creepers; yet, as there was only a single thickness of matting, daylight came in at a hundred places, and the green and yellow stains down the inside showed that they made no pretence of being watertight. Besides this, some one seemed to have been in a fidgety mode with the stove, which had been moved round and round the room—perhaps according to the changes of the wind—but wherever it went a hole had had to be cut in the side of the hut that the chimney might reach the outer air, and as the stove moved on these holes had been filled up with any material at hand—straw, sacking, or even brown paper.

Our sleeping quarters were even more cramped, there being three beds side by side across the division, and a washing-stand made out of an old box taking up all the remaining space. By way of decoration, the walls of the hut were hung with a wonderful collection of articles, guns, sword-bayonets, tin buckets, a side of bacon, several squirrel and monkey skins, dried fish, a few young coffee plants strung up by their roots, old clothes, hats, etc. Altogether, this sample of a coffee-planter's hut (the sort of thing every one who opens up a new estate for himself must put up with for a time) was most Robinson Crusoe-like and romantic to those who could look at it in such a light. Having somewhat shaken down and despatched a fair breakfast, at which curry made of goat's flesh was the chief dish, we were joined by R——'s son "Charlie," a pleasant English-looking boy of about sixteen, who had been out to shoot a pigeon with a long, heavy Snider smooth-bore, which, though rusty, has killed a fine bison lately.

We subsequently made a tour of inspection of that division of the property on which the settlement stands. The whole estate is divided into two portions, separated by a narrow stream. The most southerly consists of 1118 acres of virgin jungle, the home of the bison and elephant, untouched and unexplored since the world began, except by aboriginal tribes, to whom it is a veritable happy hunting-ground. The more northerly division consists of a thousand acres, and goes by the name of Pardagherry, meaning in Tamil the "New Rock," from some patches of bare stone which crop up in conspicuous places. On all the Government maps of a few years ago the site of our clearings was put down as "impenetrable jungle," and yet the soil was no sooner found suitable to coffee, than the "Britishers" broke through all barriers, laughed to scorn the "impenetrableness" of these unknown wilds, and made roads through the densest parts, establishing themselves firmly; so that probably, before many years, what was once the lonely home of the wild elephant will become a flourishing settled district.

Thus far, our part towards this end consists in having traced the "Top Entrance Road," as our survey names it, though it is more properly a bridle-path, but at present our only link with the other states and civilization. Besides this, during the two years he has been at work here, R—— has felled, cleared, and planted the best part of one hundred and thirty acres of land, and made and established two "nurseries" for rearing the young plants from the seeds. The ground already planted is, roughly speaking, in the shape of a parallelogram, its greatest length being from north to south. Through the centre runs a ridge with a belt of forest still standing along the top, and down this leads our main thoroughfare. The ground sloping away on the westward of the ridge is divided in two parts by another broad belt, which sweeps right down the slope to the margin of a mountain stream, about twenty feet wide, which we flatter with the name of the Manalora river. This stream curiously rises on the very brink of the precipices which overlook the great Palghaut plain, but instead of descending to the northward, a chance fall in the hillside leads its course to the southward, so that it winds its way through the jungle and passes our estate, and, after receiving many upland torrents, grows into a veritable river, and finally reaches the sea far to the southward in the neighbourhood of Cochin. On the other side of the rising ground which forms the backbone of the land already planted, the land trends down to the bed of a small nullah, and is cleared for a little distance up the opposite slope, when it is again bounded by primitive jungle and rises rapidly to a high ridge, called the "Poothapara Thund," on the far slope of which all is grass and an excellent place for bison and elephants. This side is also divided into two parts by a belt of about two chains in breadth. There are thus four separate clearings: No. 1 of fifty-six acres, No. 2 of twenty-two acres, both on the western side; No. 3 of thirty-six acres, and No. 4 of fourteen acres, on the eastern half. This arrangement will be found a very convenient one as a beginning of new estates.

With regard to the best size for clearings, there are many different opinions. One set of planters hold that large fields are much superior for many reasons. They maintain that if you have nothing less than fifty acres in extent, you enjoy freedom from the hosts of weeds which grow in the jungle, you are less troubled by harmful insects which love the shade and shelter of trees and undergrowth, and they think such clearings are more convenient and better managed. But the other side say that by making small plantations and leaving plenty of timber, you gain great shelter from high winds—a thing of considerable importance to coffee, especially in its young state—you have great stores of leaf mould within easy distance for using as manure, and they argue that, notwithstanding insects and weeds, the coffee thrives better than in the open. Probably the best size of clearing will vary with the conditions and aspect of the estate. On windy ridges such as this, where the young plants are liable to feel the full force of either monsoon, protection of some sort seems imperative, and none is so convenient and lasting as broad "belts" or strips of jungle, unfelled when the clearings are first made. These wind-shields should not be less than two chains through, or they will not answer their purpose; nor more, or they will take up too much valuable land. As it is, the strip along the top of our ridge and the two others running at right angles to it occupy thirty acres of our ground which might be bearing coffee, but it has been wisely devoted to its present purpose.

During a walk round the estate, undertaken after breakfast to show me the boundaries, we came upon a gang of forty coolies making a path through the north-easterly clearing for the greater convenience of weeding operations, which are in full swing about this time, and it was astonishing to see how quickly the work was done when there was some one by to keep the men up to the mark. When we scrambled down to them, the road had just got clear of the fallen timber of the enclosure, and was to take a slant upwards (the course having been previously set out with pegs by R——) until it penetrated through the jungle and ran into the "Top Entrance Road." Apparently the coolies had been taking it easily while the superintendent was away at his hut breakfasting, for he went down amongst them and began abusing them right and left in Tamil, supplementing his abuse by an occasional prod or two with his stick in the ribs of the most sleepy. There were about forty men present, and certainly under his eyes they progressed at a wonderful rate. In front of us was a dense clump of tall bamboos, the growth of many a year, and as this blocked up our way it had to come down. First, ten coolies with axes set to work on it, and one after another the green reed-like stems were cut through and brought low. Four minutes sufficed for this, and then the billhook and mamooty men, *i.e.* coolies with instruments like spades having the blade bent at right angles to the shaft, marched to the attack. In a couple of minutes the roots and stumps were hacked into bits and thrown aside, and another minute sufficed for the spademen to smooth the earth; and then the road went triumphantly forward across the place where but a short time before the bamboos had been masters. Next we came to a couple of small trees and a tangle of rattan creepers, which all followed the bamboos—the axe and bill men going first, slashing and hacking frantically, and the rest coming after. This is what we call a dug-out road; that is to say, the hillside being very steep, soil is shovelled away from the upper part and placed on the lower side till the road comes level. Thus there is a perpendicular wall on one hand and a steep scarp on the other, and being smoothed, the fresh red soil looks neat and nice, but requires some time to settle down. At first, owing to half the breadth being cut out of the solid, and half composed of loose soil, it is apt to sink on the outer side and has to be repaired. A little further on we came to a thicket of kewra bushes, where the hillside was so steep it was difficult to keep one's footing. These plants, which are a variety of those which grow in the lowlands, have a bare brown stem five and six feet long, and a crown of sabre-like leaves with edges sharp as knives and indented by numerous sawlike teeth. A thicket of such is practically impenetrable, and the coolies came to a stop on the outskirts, but the road had to go forward in spite of difficulties. So R—— took a bill and I took an axe, and led the attack. Being clothed, we got on better than our men, who were not; but my hands were considerably cut and full of thorns and prickles by the time we reached the other extremity of the barrier, while the poor coolies with bare legs and feet must have had a bad passage.

In this way we made rapid progress all the afternoon, until our watches told us it was past five o'clock, the usual hour for striking work, when we retraced our steps to the huts, and a great bell, suspended from two trees directly in front of our verandah, was rung, as the signal for the coolies to cease work all over the estate.

Presently they came trooping in, men, women, and children, in long lines from various points of the forest, with their tools across their shoulders, and their thin brown forms wrapped close in cumblies, the native shawls of the district; and as they arrived took up a position two deep on a patch of clear ground just below the bungalow. Here they formed a great hollow square, and after allowing time for stragglers to come in, R—— put a great day-book under his arm and marched into their midst, like the recording angel, to set down the day's work before the darkness fell. He proceeded to call over names, and each one who had been working all day was expected to answer "Here!" and, after depositing the tools he had been using, would be free to depart to the lines. The appellatives, Tamil, Canarese, Hindustani, and Malayalim, all mixed up and following each other in rapid succession, were wonderfully puzzling to pronounce, and I felt misgivings as to my success when this duty devolved upon my shoulders. R—— seemed perfectly at home amongst these outlandish designations, and rattled them off in a rapid manner, "Here!" "Here!" "Here!" following in rapid succession, and the circle getting thinner and thinner every moment. As each name in the book was called and answered to, a pencil mark was put down opposite it in another column, if the man or woman had worked a whole day; and by adding these up at the end of the week we could tell how much was due to each person.

Occasionally, however, the superintendent, who seemed to know nearly every coolie on the place by sight, came to one who had been lazy during the day, and either refused to put him down at all, thereby depriving him of a day's pay, or only entered him as having done six hours' work. Against this decision of the Englishman there was, of course, no appeal; so the responsibility was considerable, and all depended on the justice and accurate remembrance of the sahib. In one or two cases of poor creatures who got nothing, I fancied their fault was more owing to inability to toil than simply idleness; but it is always very hard to tell, and they must be kept up to the mark somehow or they would do no work. One or two of these latter hung about until roll-call was over, and then tried hard to move the decision of the superintendent, or get him to put them down for at least half a day, saying that in an unfortunate moment they had laid aside their mamooty or axe, and just then the sahib "whose generosity was boundless," had come up and fancied they had done nothing all day. But in most of these cases our generosity was limited by the stern necessity of making an example of some one occasionally, and the coolies had to go away without attaining their ends.

By this time the sun was going down, and its beams, which before had been so powerful, now came wandering through the forest, and tinged all the tree trunks rosy red, throwing a strange, unnatural glow on everything. Yet the day's work was not quite done, for we had to count a couple of hundred dirty axes and tools, and lay aside those that needed repairing, afterwards locking up the storehouse, which made one side of the square in which the coolies had mustered; and then returning to the bungalow to find half a dozen coolies squatting on their heels in the verandah. These were "medicine coolies," *i.e.* had come up to be doctored by R——, and in this very unpleasant work I assisted him. Half their maladies were directly due to want of cleanliness, and the remainder were owing to bad food or none at all. For instance, the first man drew off his cumbley at R——'s order, and showed his skin marked with the "itch" from head to foot—even while standing in front of us the poor fellow was in an agony of irritation—and we gave him some sulphur ointment in the top of a cocoanut shell which he had brought up for that purpose, and told him to rub it on, promising that he would be well in a couple of days; whereon he departed with a great sense of the sahib's wisdom. The next coolie had his legs tied up in multitudinous wrappings, and when he had unwound these, he showed us six or seven great sores which were eating into his flesh and totally prevented his walking. We gave him lint and clean bandages, and told him to wash himself clean, and then we would do something more. Another one was just recovering from smallpox, and seemed very weak and ill. Two more felt the fever coming on, and wanted to be dosed with quinine, and another man had his foot swollen up to the size of a pumpkin by some poisonous thorn which we spent twenty minutes in hunting for—an operation many times more unpleasant than simply washing the feet of beggars, which some saints have got credit for. Having done our best for them all, the day's work was at last over, and we went into the hut, struck a light, and proceeded to wash and brush ready for dinner.

Our chief illumination was a large paraffin lamp, which we slung from a rafter overhead in the "sitting-room," and under the cheerful influence of this the strange little dwelling did not look at all uncomfortable, with a red curtain across the glass door, and all other holes in the walls carefully stuffed up. We dined very contentedly, though my eyes were continually wandering to the bare grass roof, with its untrimmed rafters and long pendant cobwebs, and the mat walls with their strange collection of objects hung round them, and I could not help comparing it with the spacious silver-and-grey saloon of the *Almora,* in which I had so recently been dining. However, R—— assured me that when it began to rain again in a few days, as it would, we should find the place perfectly water-tight—with perhaps the exception of one or two places in the walls—and he told me this was a great deal to be thankful for on a new estate, *he* having lived many a day under little more than an umbrella and a blanket. On "turning in," my thoughts were again led to the *Almora,* for I remembered with fond regret that delightfully soft silk-cotton mattress which used to form my couch every evening on deck under the pleasant white awning. But here my resting-place was constructed of three boards placed side by side on the tops of two empty wine cases. This was not all. I could have put up with sleeping on boards, but it was unkind of Fate to let the planks be of unequal thicknesses, so that, whichever way they might be arranged, there was always a fearfully sharp-edged ridge running down the centre.

Above the bed-head there was a hanging string with a peg fastened to it, and after wondering what this could be for, I came to the conclusion it was a bell that communicated with a little shed outside in which our cooking was done, and which we honoured with the name of kitchen; so I was on the point of pulling it by way of experiment, when "Charlie" in the next cot to mine called out, "Pray, don't pull that; it is an elephant gun—four bore—loaded up to the muzzle with powder and ball, and fixed to one of the trees outside about ten yards from your head!" "You don't say so?" I inquired with considerable interest. "And which way does it point?" But on Charlie's assuring me it pointed towards the jungle, I agreed to draw down the peg if there should be an alarm of elephants during the night, and fell to sleep meditating on this infernal machine.

It has always surprised me how soon one gets into new habits, and under what various circumstances the human machine will work. For the first two or three days after my arrival it was only with the greatest difficulty I could rouse myself at the planter's hour of 5 a.m., but on the third or fourth day I woke up quite naturally some time before daybreak. One frequently reads that the early morning hours are the pleasantest of all in India; and so they may be down on the plains, where the midday sun is unbearably hot, but up here at this season they are decidedly raw and cold, with usually a thin drizzling mist or damp fog hanging about until the sun is up. Under such circumstances the planter turns out, and, after sounding the muster-call on his great bell or gong, makes a hasty toilet and partakes of the invigorating hot coffee and toast which his "cook boy" has prepared. Then, as soon as the coolies, all swaddled up to their chins in blankets, have sauntered up to the open ground by his hut, he takes his memorandum-book and goes down to divide them according to the work to be done. Twenty men, perhaps, under one maistry, are sent with axes and crowbars to cut and move the logs from the line of a new road; ten or twelve more to weed the "nursery;" so many women and children, under two or three overseers (they always want a lot of looking after), take baskets and hoes and depart to weed the coffee land already planted; some are sent to fetch grass, some to building, and so on.

As each party goes down to the store to get the necessary tools, the assistant has to see that each one takes the right thing and only the right thing, and the building is full of coolies pushing, fighting, and quarrelling, some taking the wrong implements, and some none at all, in spite of vigorous endeavours to get things straight. Even when all the natives present at muster have been told off and started with their tools, the day's troubles are only beginning; for no sooner are they clear of the settlement and winding along the narrow jungle paths, than they make all sorts of attempts and "dodges" to escape and get back to their huts, hoping, by being present at the morning muster and again at evening roll-call, that their absence during the day will not have been noticed, and so they may get a day's pay for doing no work.

On the second day after my arrival, I was told off to conduct fifty women and girls about half a mile away through the forest, to a new clearing that had just been made on the Poothopara Thund, and which we were planting with guinea-grass to be the feed of a future herd of cattle. I got my little convoy in order. After considerable trouble with one or two elderly females, who wanted to say their prayers under every fig tree we came to, and half a dozen coolie women with little children, who kept bolting into the jungle and had to be retrieved, we eventually reached our ground, and I forthwith arranged my workers in a long line and commenced operations. But although fifty had started, when I seized an opportunity of counting my forces I found there were only thirty-two present, and I had to go back to the settlement to find the remainder, and drive them before me. Getting back to the guinea-grass enclosure, which by the way was full of great crags of rock and huge fallen tree trunks, on counting the line, which had made very little progress since I left it, there were only twenty-nine women at work; so, hastily starting the contingent just brought up, I went in chase of the runaways, and after scrambling over rocks on hands and knees, and creeping in like position under tree trunks, I found and drove in nearly all of them, many being placidly asleep with their sarees thrown over their heads. Even when in line they are very troublesome. While I was at one side of the clearing showing some brown-skinned damsel the right way to work, every one would sit down and chew betel-nut at the far extremity, and by the time I had got over there and had wrathfully upbraided the transgressors, I would look round and see the coolies just left chatting or stretching themselves meditatively! All this under a hot Indian sun was very severe work, especially for one not accustomed to it, and yet it could not be avoided, though experience doubtless makes it easier.

Then, too, the women are much more troublesome than the men. It is a mistake to think they are easily managed; and before I had been on the estate many days, I sincerely wished they were all away at their native villages in Mysore and Madura, with their troublesome children and squealing babies. But it always falls to the "chik doree's" share to look after them when he first begins his experiences, as their occupations are usually the humble weeding and picking up sticks, while the men are engaged on more difficult tasks, which require skilled supervision. Our principal occupation for some time was clearing this guinea-grass enclosure of the loose sticks and as many of the branches as were movable, and fetching the grass roots from W——'s estate, where there was a flourishing plantation much patronized by the sambour and other deer of the neighbourhood. As this was three miles away or more, the work was very tedious, my share of it being continually driving long lines of women and children backwards and forwards. One way they were light-hearted enough, and probably laughed and joked at my expense, though my command of the language did not enable me to tell for certain. Perhaps that was as well; but coming home, each woman had a heavy load on her head, and each child a smaller one, and the path naturally seemed longer, while we were very much troubled by the leeches and flies. At the end of each double journey I really felt for my workers, who were weak and famine stricken; but there was no help for it, so the superintendent said, and three times every day we were expected to make the long gloomy walk, over hill and dale, through the wet jungle. It was bad enough for me, who was well shod, well fed, and marched both ways without a load; it must have been grievous to many of my poor followers, whose bare feet and legs were exposed to leech-bites and thorns, and who had to make half their journeys under great loads of the pale green grass, which, by hanging down in front and behind, nearly enveloped several of the smaller carriers.

It may be wondered how I got on with scanty knowledge of the language. In truth, it was very difficult work, as my Hindustani was of little or no good; and I should have been in greater difficulties, but for the assistance of the maistries, one or two of whom always accompanied the parties; and knowing by experience what had to be done, they were able to direct their more ignorant countrymen and women, I meanwhile standing by, looking as wise as might be. These maistries, or head workmen, are much superior to their compatriots in every way. First of all, they are always dressed somehow or other; one of them would no more appear in public in the piece of string and rag of a coolie than an Englishman would. In this respect they are very particular, and it gives them at once a great rise above the lower grades. In their homes they are small farmers, and have come up to the jungles when the land is burned like a brick from long-continued drought, and their bullocks have died from want of grass. Moreover, many of them are men who have been born and lived on coffee estates all their lives, and these are of course the most valuable, owing to their experience, and because they have grown to know the ways of the Englishmen, and often even their language; though, unfortunately for me, none of ours had arrived at that degree of excellence. There was a half-caste, however, on the estate who spoke both Tamil and English, and he was of considerable use from his knowledge of the operations and of the native methods. He lived in a small hut by himself, between our bungalow and the coolie settlement, so that he was always at hand when wanted; and whenever R—— had a more than usually unpleasant job to be done, somebody was always sent to fetch the unfortunate "clerk," who got considerably more "kicks than half-pence."

The position of these half-castes, who are very numerous all over the country, must be difficult to support with dignity. Born of native women, sometimes the wives of European soldiers, they live between the races in every respect. In colour they are a yellowish white, with poor physiques and the sloping shoulders of the native, with the same strangely formed hands and fingers. Unfortunately, while they inherit the weak points of both breeds, they do not seem to be particularly strong in the virtues of either. It may not be their fault; it may be want of education and training; but, as they stand at present, they are scorned by the pure-blooded natives, over whom they attempt to tyrannize (which the natives strongly resist, as they feel none of the respect for them which they do for the sahib), and looked down on by the Englishmen with even more hauteur than would be shown to a native of pure blood. They are thus placed "between the devil and the deep sea," and associate with neither, keeping to themselves, and coddling their wrongs—a great pity, as they and their descendants are becoming very numerous. Our particular clerk, who held a position just above the first native maistry, was, on the whole, a fair sample of his kindred. Dressing in thin, threadbare black clothes, cut on an English pattern (I fear his whole wardrobe), through all the worst of the wet monsoon, his poor battered white helmet and his thin-soled boots —which I fancy he kept on night and day, because he dared not take them off for fear of their coming to pieces—moved me to compassion. I have seen him, when the day's work was done, of which he had borne a big share with no chance of praise, steal away to his hut with the rain streaming down his clothes, and sit down to his miserable plate of boiled rice and fish; and in such a place! A low, miserable shed, having a mud floor, and walls of rotten mats that emitted a sickening smell night and day, and a thin thatch roof that harboured all sorts of unclean insects. Amid such surroundings—with no education, no knowledge, and very little hope here or hereafter; despised by his inferiors, and scorned by his superiors —who shall blame him much if he drank deep wherever and whenever he could? In fact, it was his great failing, poor fellow! R—— told me that he gets so wild on the subject, that if he cannot beg, borrow, or steal arrack or brandy from high or low, he will come up to hospital and declare he has a bad attack of cholera, in the hopes of getting hold of a bottle of chlorodyne; and, should he succeed, goes away triumphantly and drinks it, trying to think it is something stronger.

CHAPTER IX.

JUNGLE DAYS.

THE rain came down with very little intermission during my first week—not the warm drizzle of an English autumn, but a cold shower-bath, night and day. Again and again we all got wet through, and as nothing could be dried, owing to the saturated condition of the atmosphere, my whole wardrobe rapidly emerged from the packing-cases, and, becoming wet, was in turn hung up to take care of itself round our walls. I changed my hue like a chameleon, and at last began to look anxiously for a break in the clouds, in order that I might dry some things; otherwise I should be reduced to the necessity of going weeding in evening dress.

Every morning we rose at dawn, mustered the coolies in a downpour, worked all day under the same conditions, and when the evening came released our men, always a long and tedious affair, and gladly betook ourselves to the reeking hut, where we dined in a vapour-bath of moisture condensed by our lamp. Then, after a pipe and reading a little, we sought our bunks, and listened to the rain pattering overhead and the trees sighing with the wind that swept up the mountain gorges, until we dropped asleep.

One never knows what a man can stand until the time comes to make the trial. In England I should have thought this sort of life the height of misery, although well accustomed to "roughing it;" but here I had fallen quite naturally into the way, and regarded being drenched through and through, in spite of umbrellas and oil-skins, as of very slight importance. It told, however, on R——, who was "not so young as he was once," and, neglecting himself, he got worse and worse, putting duty after duty on my shoulders, until the 12th, when, coming home from work, he was clearly "run out." His dinner was pushed away untasted, and he insisted upon going to bed at once.

We helped the old coffee-planter to his cot; but he was stiff all over, and lay groaning and writhing long into the lonely hours of the night, while "Charlie" and I watched and tended him, and did what we could. But not even he himself had any idea what was the matter. About midnight nothing would satisfy him but starting at once for Palghaut, where there was a hospital with an intelligent native apothecary, who, he hoped, would be able to doctor him. In vain we tried to dissuade R—— from the long wet journey, for it was of no avail; so, while his son ran down to the lines to collect twenty of our strongest men, I set to work to construct a munchiel. This was rather difficult, as there were no bamboo clumps within a mile capable of affording a stem strong enough to support the burden down the rocky road to the plains. However, necessity is the mother of invention, and looking round, my eye lit upon the long poles, made of young sapling jack trees, which supported the division of our rooms; and seeing one could come away without bringing down everything in the neighbourhood, I was soon at work upon it with a clasp-knife, and, after being half choked with cobwebs and blinded with dust, got it safely down. But then there was the difficulty of the hammock. A blanket was lashed on, but wound itself into a robe, and was cut away as a failure. Then fortunately I bethought me of an Ashantee hammock which had been used on the voyage out, and this was tried and found a great success, though somewhat frail in appearance. About one o'clock in the morning, in the heavy silence which precedes the dawn and the dense black darkness, the coolies shouldered my roughly made munchiel, we helped R—— in, and telling him we hoped to see him back soon, the melancholy procession started, and the torches borne by two or three of the party gleamed fitfully upon the wet tree trunks as the path wound up the ridge, until the light, becoming fainter, finally died away altogether and left us in solitude.

The first pay day in the jungle is always a very difficult one for the new arrival, especially when he has to be his own paymaster to the forces, his cashier and clerk all rolled into one. The coinage is strange to him, and he is sure to get more or less mixed up in his pice, annas, and rupees, unless he has a head which is better fitted for a mercantile desk at home than the backwoods. Most of those who try coffee planting have souls above mathematics, and to them their first experience of paying a horde of coolies (who, like all natives, dote on disputation) will be long remembered as a *dies iræ.* Still it is a thing which has to be done, however unpleasant; but I feel for King James, "of sacred memory," who naïvely said, when receiving a petition to pay his Scotch bills, "Of all petitions this is the one which his majesty liketh the least."

Unfortunately for me, the next day after R——'s flight to the lowlands was Saturday, and all day long I was practising rapid reduction of rupees to the smallest coin of the empire, while striving to draw some consolation from the fact that the estate would have nothing to do with cowrie shells, 5120 of which go to the rupee. The thought of giving and counting out much small change of that sort would be distraction, four pice or cash to the anna being quite as much as I could stand with equanimity.

The day, like its predecessors, was miserably cold and dull, and, fearful of being overtaken by darkness before getting through the paying, the estate bell was rung an hour earlier than usual to recall the coolies to the mustering ground. They came trooping in from all parts in strong force, and apparently with considerable interest, to see what was going to take place. When they were all mustered, the crowd was thicker and denser than I had ever seen it before, everybody having turned out, even to the lame and sick who were too ill to go to work. When I entered the great circle of nearly two hundred men, women, and children, looking as solemn as might be, with the fateful day-book in one hand and a huge bag of copper and silver coins in the other, having the half-caste clerk at my elbow to interpret, I was conscious that all eyes were upon me, and my smallest motion was being watched, in deep silence, by the assembled coolies. Determined to get into practice as soon as possible, instead of letting the half-caste call over the names, I decided to do it myself, and, shooting out the bag of money into a glittering heap on the rough wooden table in front of me, plunged at once into the long columns of outlandish names, which filled ten or twelve folio pages of the day-book. Opposite to each name in our system of book-keeping, there were six rows of columns, one for each day of the week, and in each of these columns there was a whole mark, a half, or a blank, according as the coolie had worked—a whole day, a half-day, or none at all. Beyond these columns was one to record the total number of days worked out of the last six, and then another division to record the pay given out. At the end of the month the columns on each page were added up, both across and up and down, and, if exactly correct, the final reading in the bottom right-hand corner was exactly the same for both. Thus, it was impossible to make a mistake of even a pie without being able to discover it; but at the same time, among so many densely packed columns, it was difficult to avoid small errors, likely to show up large in the final result, and cause a vast amount of trouble in correcting.

I had to call each coolie's name first of all, and, if he had been working all day, put him down in the Saturday column with a mark; then add up his total work for the week—say, five and a half days—put this down in the space devoted to it, calculate five and a half days at five annas a day—the rate at which we pay our men—put down Rs. 1 11*a.* 2*p.* in the pay space, count it out of the heap of coinage at my elbow, give it to the man, and dismiss him. This may sound simple enough, but there were many little difficulties to be surmounted. When I began calling the fearful and wonderful Tamil and Canarese names, there was a general titter round the circle, and three or four men answered at once, my pronunciation being so shaky that they could not distinguish whose name it was. However, I suppressed the giggling, and, having obtained "silence in the court," forged slowly ahead, every now and then making some mistake which set the natives smiling, but getting slowly into the way, and running up the sums and counting out the change like a booking-clerk. Often a coolie would conclude he had not got the right amount, and open a discussion, which I had to cut very short; and fifty per cent. of them thought their rupees were bad, so that from all sides rose the sound of money being chinked upon the rock to test its ring. Each native as he came up salaamed and held out both his hands, edge to edge, to receive the overflowing bounty of the sahib. Poor people! the strongest man amongst them who had worked in the rain and sun all the week only took six times five annas—about equal to three shillings and fourpence—and on this, of course, many had to support a wife and children too ill or weak to toil. Then, again, the women—many of them mothers, with small brown fragments of humanity slung upon their backs—got three annas a day, and the most they could earn was little more than two shillings a week. Even the little children came up, ducked their small shaven heads in comical homage to the great white sahib, and held out very small brown hands for the price which those same hands were supposed to have earned, at the rate of a penny a day. Last of all, the maistries received pay at the rate of six or eight annas per diem, and then the horse-boys, cook, sweepers, and hangers-on of all sorts. When these were satisfied, there was still a small crowd of non-contents who came up and complained that their money was bad—would I change it? which I always did when possible, as if a poor fellow earned one rupee and chanced to get paid with a bad, unbarterable coin, there was nothing but starvation for him during the next week. Others thought there was a mistake somewhere—always to their disadvantage—and their names had to be hunted for, and the amount of money given compared with that entered in the book. It was hopeless to please them all, but on going over the accounts during the course of the next evening I was well satisfied to find there was only an error of a few annas—happily too much given out, not too little.

Muster and paying over, and the stores and outhouses locked up, the estate pony seen to, and his feed of grain measured out, there were the sick and ill clustered round the bungalow verandah to be attended to before being released for the day. With these I was much helped by R——'s son, who, having spent all his life in the south of India, knows the manners and habits of the natives. Between us we bandaged half a dozen ulcerated legs, sewed up a chopped finger, administered castor oil and Epsom salts—a horrible brew of "Charlie's" invention—to two babies, gave a dose of quinine to a young coolie girl who thought she had fever, and rubbed half a pot of sulphur ointment into two in-patients suffering from the itch. One old woman, who had recently had small-pox, came up for her daily allowance of cod-liver oil, but she had forgotten to bring the top of a cocoa-nut shell with her, that being the article which is usually produced to receive medicine. In this dilemma I was for sending her back to the lines to fetch the cocoa-nut, but my young friend solved the difficulty in a very simple manner. Telling the poor woman to sit down on the ground, and open her mouth as wide as possible, and keep her eyes shut, and not to move a muscle, he put the allowance of oil into a handleless teacup, in which we mixed all our medicines one after the other, and then poured the contents into the woman's open mouth, to her complete satisfaction.

After this we were free to enjoy a much-needed rest, and we dined in solitary grandeur, spending the last evening of my first week in the forest telling stories—"Charlie's" being about the jungle and the "Blue Mountains" of Bangalore, where he had passed all his sixteen years, and I discoursing on the wonders of civilization and the beauties of the home country, subjects of which neither of us ever tired.

With such a congenial companion, Sunday passed harmlessly away in unpacking and overhauling my belongings, and examining my four guns, with which my friend was delighted, his previous experience having been with heavy Snider rifles. We determined to take out the small "collecting gun" the next morning, to try it. Little did we think what an unfortunate resolve that was. A long eighteen-foot salmon rod, which I had brought in the expectation of getting some mahseer fishing, especially delighted "Charlie," who confessed he had never seen anything like it before, and persisted in practising fly-throwing with it all day. A more orthodox mode of spending the time was out of the question, as church was an unknown term here, and my book-box had not yet arrived, while R——'s library consisted of thirty copies of a pamphlet showing why he had suddenly left his last appointment, and "The Family Doctor," a useful though not romantic work.

For the next few days there was a most enjoyable break in the clouds, and we seized the opportunity to hang out our wardrobes on every available bush and rattan in the neighbourhood, that they might get dry after the last week's soaking. Like ants we also brought our stock of tinned provisions into the sunshine, and put our boots and bed-clothes in a heap in a sunny corner of the verandah. In fact, we had been so miserably saturated for many days and nights that we brought forth everything movable to dry; and much they needed it!

The daily work was gone on with, but an unfortunate accident which happened to my comrade spoiled our enjoyment, and took me away from the estate for a while. Seizing a spare half-hour at breakfast-time one morning, we went out, accompanied by a sporting maistry, named Timma, to try the powers of the small gun which had so taken "Charlie's" fancy. This was a sixteen-bore muzzle-loader, and, being only intended for securing specimens of birds, was loaded with a small charge. All went well, and we procured some finches and a thrush new to me, until we got to No. 3 clearing, where we rested for a time. I had previously noticed my friend was a little careless of the gun which he was carrying, and begged him to keep it at half-cock. He promised to do so, but while leaning against the trunk of a fallen tree in the young coffee, and listening to the grey pigeons in the jungle, he put the hammer up ready for a chance shot, and, resting the muzzle on the toe of his boot to keep it clean, began playing with the trigger while he talked. I was intent on watching for a pigeon, and did not notice this, but all of a sudden there was a report at my side, and, looking hastily round, I saw the gun fall to the ground and my companion stagger backwards. "What on earth is the matter?" I said. "Oh," said he, "my foot has gone!" But it was not quite so bad as that. When the smoke cleared away his foot was all right, but we saw an ugly sight. His boot was blackened with the burnt powder, and in the toe was a great ragged hole, out of which, as we looked, the blood slowly welled, and ran over upon the ground in a thick red stream. He behaved very pluckily, but would not let me take his boot off until we got home; so, there being no time to stand on ceremony or send for help, I threw the two guns to the maistry, and, taking my companion on my back, "made tracks" as fast as possible to the settlement, which was more than half a mile away. "Charlie" is a substantial fellow, and the day was hot, but the blood which trickled down continually kept me at my best pace, and in a few minutes we were safe in our hut and I was busy cutting away at the blood-sodden boot, every movement of which caused my unfortunate comrade a sharp pang. At last it began to come off, and I drew it away in fear and trembling, for I expected there would be two or three toes loose inside, but was delighted to see, when the foot was at length bare, that though the big toe and the next one were a powder-and-blood-stained mass, nothing had actually come away; and after washing them carefully in tepid water, I was able to assure the unfortunate fellow that, by a wonderful chance, the whole charge of shot had passed between the two toes. Thus, though both bones were visible and the flesh was hanging in shreds, no great harm was done. Patching the flesh up as well as might be, and sewing it together with white thread—silk being lacking—I finally wrapped all up in lint and rags, and there was my friend, disabled and looking like a gentleman with a bad attack of the gout. He had borne the whole thing with the most excellent fortitude, and when it was over was a good deal more cheerful than I was.

That night I ransacked my memory for thrilling accounts of adventures on English rivers and Norwegian fiords, and sat up late by the bedside of my damaged and wakeful comrade. But the next day, and the day after, his foot hurt him more and more; and he got an idea into his head that lockjaw was coming on, as the wound was looking rather green; and at last insisted upon going down to his father at Palghaut. So a second call was made upon my rough and ready carpentering abilities to make another munchiel, this of a young bamboo stem, supporting a strong blanket held open by short pieces of wood at either end, and covered in on top by a broad sheet of palm-leaf matting, strengthened by cross-bars. It was well I took the precaution to put a waterproof covering over the hammock, as the sky looked very threatening, and the thunder was rolling about like the chariot-wheels of Indra on the other side of the clouds.

Late in the afternoon of the 16th of October our preparations were complete; and having determined to take my friend down to the lowlands at his earnest request, as he was quite helpless by himself, and hoping to get back early the next morning, the munchiel and a dozen coolies, with a strong but bad-tempered old horse, the property of the estate, for myself, were all waiting outside. Scarcely had "Charlie" been safely stowed into the munchiel, than there was a bright flash of lightning and a roar of thunder directly overhead, which set my steed dancing and neighing with fright, and down came the rain, as if the floor of heaven had given way and a second deluge was coming on. Hastily giving the signal to start, I scrambled into the saddle, much to the disgust of the tattoo, who thought the stable more comfortable than the jungle paths on such an afternoon; and before we had gone a hundred yards every one of us but my friend in the hammock was saturated through and through. The rain was tremendous. Not content with coming down in drops like ordinary rain, it descended in blinding torrents. The thick roof of leaves overhead made no difference; every leaf was a small waterspout, and the tree-trunks were glossy with water pouring from them. The ground, which a few minutes before had been fairly dry and solid, was now a swamp in places, and on the steep parts was cut up by hundreds of rushing rivulets, which tore along, sweeping down sticks, stones, and rubbish to the nearest stream, in headlong cascades. I no longer wondered why the hill-tops of this region are bare and soilless. A few such storms would wash away anything except firmly fixed rocks. It is a wonder the trees themselves stood.

Through this cruel storm we made our way, scarcely seeing the bridle-track for the spray, the thunder rolling overhead and the trees swinging about and bending like reeds, threatening every moment to fall on us, or at least block our road; until, as darkness came on, we emerged into the estate of the Dewan of Cochin, from which, to the head of the ghaut, the road was "pucka," and there was less chance of missing it. Here, my horse being nervous and excited, I thought a gallop might do him good; so, leaving the munchiel behind, I made the best of my way through the tall coffee of this clearing, as fast as my steed liked to go, and never drew rein until on the borders of D——'s estate of Polyampara, where, after some time, the munchiel came up; thereon, holding a consultation with my friend and the maistry in charge, we determined to stay the night at D——'s bungalow, and go on the next morning to Palghaut. There was small chance of being able to cross the flooded rivers in the darkness and rain, leaving out of consideration the haunted samee place, which the coolies were loth to pass on such a night. So we betook ourselves to the friendly shelter, and were, as usual, hospitably received.

The journey down was concluded next day without any noteworthy incident, and R——, who was laid up in the hospital at Palghaut, received his son and news of the gun accident at the same time. Finding there was no hope of his being able to move for two or three days, and being anxious about the working of the coolies during my absence, I bade good-bye to two or three hospitable friends, picked up in the rapid way in which acquaintances are made at Indian stations, and early next morning turned my back on the pleasant little town—much more warm and genial than the gaunt, gloomy jungles. Riding hard, I reached Wallenghay in time for a late breakfast at Widow Vladimir's. Here I learnt that two Englishmen had gone the day before up to the jungles to shoot, and anxious to know who they were, I pressed on, fording the stream at the foot of the ghaut, and commenced the ascent.

Passing through the lowlands, the heat had seemed very great, in spite of the fact that my clothes were of the whitest and thinnest "duck;" but as I mounted into higher regions, the temperature fell very rapidly, and from the appearance of the clouds I feared there was another drenching in store for myself and horse.

Just as the bamboo region was reached, at an elevation of one thousand feet above the sea, the sky grew black as ink, and a wind came rushing out of the mountain gorges, bending the trees before it and bringing the mist in its wake; then the storm overhead broke and the rain came down in steaming torrents, turning a thousand rills into dashing streams and making the path a slippery cascade, in which my horse staggered hopelessly about. Between rain and steam I soon was in the condition of moist blotting-paper. But turning back was not to be thought of, and it was necessary to reach a torrent which crossed the road on ahead before it should be so flooded as to become impassable. This stream, which has been mentioned before as being noticeable for the six or seven round basins worn in its bed a little higher up, where the road cut it, has no well-defined course, but in dry weather trickles across a broad, flat shelf of rock, and falls with a musical tinkle into a beautiful fern-grown chasm on the far side. But now the scene was anything but promising. Instead of a rivulet meandering downwards, there was a foaming brown torrent racing over the ledge, carrying down great loose stones with it and falling with a loud roar far down into the unseen chasm below, while the road, which must be reached if I wanted any supper, was just discernible through the mist amongst the rocks on the far side.

My horse was frightened at the sight, and could not be brought to try the venture while I was on his back; so, seeing it was useless that way, and being already wet through, I jumped off and, dragging him after me, waded in. At first the water was only a foot deep, but it soon rose and filled my top-boots, and got higher and higher, until in mid-stream the rush was so severe, every moment I expected to lose my footing. The horse's hoofs clattered and slipped on the smooth rock, and he grew more and more nervous. In one place we were only a few yards from the edge where the stream broke into foam and went thundering down the gully, and a slip there would have sent us both to adventure in other worlds; but we got by and were almost safe, when a grey figure, that had been watching us unseen, sprang up among the misty rocks in front, and with a most sepulchral and mournful howl, such as none but evil-minded things could give, dashed back into the jungle. My horse reared right up and snorted, and I thought his last moment had come, but he regained his footing by a wonderful chance, and a moment after we were standing, dripping, safe on shore. The weird apparition that had startled us at so critical a moment was a hungry wolf on the look out for dead bodies. Probably he had seen us arrive on the opposite shore, and, with the cunning of his species, had fancied there was a bountiful supper in store for him, which, of course, must have been a very exciting prospect on so wet an afternoon. One can easily imagine with what eager interest, as he crouched among the rocks, the gaunt brute watched the Englishman and his horse; and his feelings can be understood when his supper *in futuro* passed the most dangerous place and had nearly reached safety. No wonder he howled!

Then into the saddle again, and ever upwards through the lonely and gloomy bamboo jungles—the chosen home of bison and tigers—where the rain half blinded me, and the tall stems on either side lashed about like reeds in the wind. The samee place was reached at dusk, and looked the very beau ideal of a haunt of ghosts, with the white mist eddying about the groaning trees, the dead leaves whirling in circles, and the great pile of wooden memorials of human suffering. Here, getting on to level ground, and consequently a better made road, it was possible to ride fast, and, galloping through the storm, we crossed Polyampara and the jungle beyond, passed the bungalow of C. H——, and skirted W——'s estate of Poothapara without stopping. I subsequently asked the latter if he had seen me, and he said he was smoking in his verandah and had noticed a horseman in white, on a "fiery black steed," passing along the high ground when the storm was at its worst, and had been sorely perplexed to think who could be out riding on such an evening. In fact, I let the horse make his own pace, and, his home being in front and his grain waiting, we did quick time for the rest of the way, and, just "saving daylight into harbour," cantered down into the settlement as darkness fell.

Persons of a sanguine temperament will find the first year on a new estate full of little difficulties and disappointments, and will often be severely tried if they are given to feeling lonely. Now, I had promised myself a comfortable dinner and a pleasant change into dry clothes after my long ride, but when the bungalow was reached, it was shut up and still, no cheerful light or promising smoke issuing from the chimney—everything was wet, cheerless, and dark. I shouted "Ghora-wallah!" till the jungle echoed, but no one came; so, vowing vengeance on the truant "horse boy," I took the horse to the stable, unsaddled him, wiped him down, fed him, and then got into my bungalow by the "office" window, as the door was locked.

It took ten minutes to find and rouse the "cook boy," who was stupefied with arrack, which he had been drinking to keep the damp and cold out; and, while he exerted his feeble intellect in making a fire in the store with a pile of wet logs, my clothes were changed; and, once more dry again and under shelter, my thoughts turned on dinner, my last "pucka" meal having been at the "Travellers' Bungalow" at Palghaut the evening before. So I asked the boy what he proposed to give me. He was still extremely foggy, and, after rubbing his eyes and thinking for a moment, said, "Nothing, sahib." My only reply was to direct him to open one of my tins of preserved soup, which I had brought up for such an occasion, and get it ready "juldie;" but, to my extreme disgust, he informed me, in confused sentences, that those two Englishmen had been up the day before, and had dropped in to see me, but finding I was away and, as the stupid "boy" told them, not expected back for some time, they breakfasted here, and seemed to have made free with the tinned provisions, after which they marched southward. A short note, which the servant produced from his turban, told me that their own provisions not having then come up, and hearing I should not be back for some time, they had looted what they had seen in the cupboard, and would replace them "with very many thanks before I returned." This was but cold comfort, and on examining what food there was left, I found that it consisted of a bottle of palm-brandy, two pounds of black pepper, and the remains of a piece of bacon which hung above my bed. The sole consolation was that my unknown guests had not been able to borrow my store of tobacco, which, under some benign influence, I had locked up before starting for the lowlands.

There was nothing to be done but to put the best face on the matter; so I was soon seated at the table, with the lamp burning dimly overhead in the dense opal-coloured smoke of the wood fire, which did not seem to care about going up the chimney in an orthodox manner, and several rashers of bacon in front, flanked by the arrack and huge pepper-tin. There was some comfort for the meagreness of the fare in making as much display as possible. After all, hunger is the best sauce for all kinds of food, and one can dine very fairly off bacon and plenty of pepper after a long wet ride, especially if there is nothing else to be had, while arrack punch is excellent when properly made.

There were, indeed, a few little extra inconveniences, such as the night insects, who seemed to be having a public meeting round the lamp and on the table, continually hopping into my plate or glass; and then again a musk-rat had been crawling over the bacon while it was suspended on the wall, and had left a remarkably strong taste behind him. This set me thinking on the many stories I had read of the skill of native servants in poisoning people in slow ways, so that they gradually languished and slid, without any vulgar symptons, into other worlds, and I fell to wondering whether my cook was to be trusted. He knew well there were several hundred rupees in the safe, the keys of which were in my pocket: what would be easier than for him to give me a sleeping draught or a dose of powdered glass, and a fortune lay at his command! And then what a shocking bad character he had! F—— had sent him down to me the first day of my arrival, with a note to the effect that he was sure I should be in want of a servant, and as the bearer was "the biggest rogue and greatest thief in the district," he could not keep him any longer, and hoped he might suit me until something better was to be had. His name was "Chokra" when he entered my service, but my young friend "Charlie" re-christened him "Sheitan" after a short acquaintance with his dusky form and darkling habits. Meditating in this vein, while the fire burnt low and the rain beat upon the thatch and the wind howled, something caused me to look over my shoulder, and there stood the object of my thoughts, with his arms folded on his chest, silent and motionless, scarcely anything of his evil face being visible in the gloom but his white teeth and rolling eyeballs. Thinking this might be a good opportunity to see what sort of a man he was, I proceeded to ask him a question or two. "Well, Sheitan," I said, "you told me the other day you had been to a native school; now, what did you learn there? Any geography?' This was rather a long word for him, but he said, "Yes;" so I continued, "That's right. Now, where do Englishmen come from?" Without moving a muscle he answered placidly, "Palghaut, sahib," and he obviously believed that was the rim of the world, his *Ultima Thule*, beyond which there was nothing but uncertainty. So I tried another track. "Are you a Christian, Sheitan?" I inquired. "Yes, sahib," he said. "That's right. Then of course you know where you will go when you die?" I inquired. He looked at me for a moment with his big gloomy eyes, and then, all solemn and motionless, said, "To hell, sahib." I thought, after this, I would not make any more inquiries as to his education, but bidding him pile up the fire and call me at daybreak, dismissed him for the night.

But at best it was not possible to spend a very cheerful evening. The rain beat down incessantly, and the wind sobbed amongst the tree-tops and rattled the long pendant creepers together in mournful tunes. Every now and then one of the stoppings of the holes in the sides of the hut, through which the stove-pipe had formerly passed, would be blown in, followed by a gust of wind and a torrent of rain, and the gap had to be hastily plugged up again with anything that came first to hand. Once or twice I heard big branches snap off from the trees in the jungle and fall crashing to earth, and any moment one might come through the roof of my hut.

Then the thoughts of the next day were not agreeable. A thousand acres of land on my hands, and a couple of hundred coolies to look after and control before I had been a week up here or knew a word of the language, and, last but not least, the grey mosquitoes drove me half wild, and the small beetles that would crawl down my back or up my sleeves just when I was comfortably smoking. As for fleas, they abound wherever coolies are, and I had grown indifferent to them and their bites—perhaps would have felt lonely without them. But there is a larger creature of the grasshopper tribe, which makes day and night hideous with its noise, and for this insect I entertained the most cordial hatred. The sound it makes is quite indescribable, but seems most like a couple of metal saws going through a plate of sheet iron. If I had any other feelings but wrath while this evil being is performing, they would be wonderment and admiration for the powers of so small a musician. Fancy a creature two inches long, who can cause himself to be heard half a mile away! What a blessing it is such powers are not given to human beings! An Irish member of Parliament with any such gift would upset our Constitution; but the thought is horrible. These terrible nuisances—the jungle crickets I mean —are supposed to make their fearful sounds by rubbing their legs over their wing-cases, and though their legs are certainly armed with a formidable row of sharp spines, they must work very hard to obtain such results.

One of them came into my bedroom on the evening of my return from Palghaut, just as I had put out the light and was falling asleep, and, settling on the rim of our washing-basin, deliberately tuned up and launched into a wild chorus of screeches. I listened for a moment, and then one of my boots flew in the direction of the sound, and knocked the basin to the ground. For a while the enemy was silenced, but just as I was falling asleep again he started afresh on the rafters overhead. Another boot dislodged him; but as fast as he was driven from one spot he turned up in another, and so, finding him irrepressible, I struck a light and, after a prolonged chase into every corner of the hut, succeeded in securing him, and magnanimously let him go through one of the holes in the sides of the bungalow. The last thing I heard before going to sleep was his detestable song from the roof-ridge of my shed, in return for this Buddhistic clemency.

CHAPTER X.

"UNDER THE SUN."

NATURALLY enough, the work that fell upon me after R——'s compulsory absence in hospital at Palghaut was very hard. At five o'clock each morning it was necessary to be up and have the great bell rung, and then came the mustering of the coolies, and the setting them their various tasks. This would have been nearly an impossibility, without a knowledge of Tamil and Canarese, but for the assistance of the half-caste, who interpreted my orders. Then, from 6 a.m. to 12.30 p.m. I was continually on the move, hurrying hither and thither, scrambling about the clearings, pushing through the jungles, and making myself as "numerous" as possible. For this sort of work it is, of course, hopeless to use a horse, as the ground is much too rough and obstructed, and riding in the jungle, except just in the beaten track, is out of the question, on account of the creepers and bamboos.

At half-past twelve there occurred a brief interval of rest for breakfast, during which our *tapal*, or running postman, from the plains, arrived, and some of the time had to be devoted to reading and answering letters, private and on business; and then, àll writing finished, and the necessary orders for food and the wants of the estate having been sent to the native agents in Palghaut and Wallenghay, the postman put his little wicker-basket on his head, and set out again for the lowlands.

The endurance of these men is something wonderful. We had four in our service, and every day one of them came up with our post, etc. They arranged that one man should start from Palghaut immediately on the arrival of the early morning mail, with letters, papers, butter, eggs, and occasionally clean clothes or something of the kind, all packed into a small basket, weighing perhaps five or six pounds, and carried on his head. He ran the whole eleven miles to Wallenghay by every short cut he knew of, and as fast as he could go. At Wallenghay he found another tapal waiting, and transferred the basket; whereupon the second man "made tracks" for the jungle, and his was the hardest stage, for he had to face the ghaut road, with its tiger-haunted glens and unholy places. Only stopping perhaps to drink and pray for a minute or two by some brook-side, he gained the mountain tops, and arrived at my bungalow about one o'clock. Then, as previously mentioned, while the man sat on his heels in the verandah and chewed a little betel-nut, I was writing the answers to the correspondence he had brought up, and when they were finished the basket was refilled with anything that had to be returned to the plains, and the tapal salaamed and started away again for the ghaut road. He generally managed to reach Wallenghay the same evening, whence my correspondence was taken to Palghaut in time for the early post to Madras and the rest of India the next morning. Thus the man who had Wallenghay to Pardagherry stage (and each of our four men took it regularly in turn) had to do sixteen miles uphill with a heavy weight on his head, and then sixteen miles downhill again, between ten in the morning and sunset. As might be expected, they were models of good training, without an ounce of superfluous fat anywhere about them; and, as their clothing consisted of a long strip of white cloth wound round and round the waist, and hanging down to the knees, it was possible to study the muscles of the human body, as shown forth under their smooth copper-coloured skin, to great advantage.

After the arrival and departure of the tapal—the event of the day in these lonely wilds—there was always another long spell of work to be done during the afternoon, and this was the hottest and most fatiguing part of the toil, made especially trying by the fact that the coolies were by this time nearly spent, and the greatest exertions were necessary, in our wilderness-like clearing, to get any work out of them. So by the hour the sun was sinking amongst the tree-tops in the west, and the great bell was tolling to recall every one, I was generally very glad to hear it. On getting back to the settlement, roll-call had to be gone through, the sick attended, the horse watched while he fed, in order that the ghora-wallah might not steal the grain, and the tools issued in the morning received back and counted, all of which made rest, and then dinner, very welcome.

The evenings that followed were oppressively solitary. No Englishman within five or six miles, and then only one, and he very taciturn. Riding to any of the estates was not to be thought of after a day's severe work in the sun, without taking into account the dark jungle paths reeking with fever-mist at night, tangled with roots, and the off-chance of meeting an elephant or bison. So there was nothing to do but smoke in silence, and turn in as early as might be.

I had a considerable amount of trouble with the boy "Sheitan." He would persist in washing himself and his clothes in my only saucepan, and kept my rice in an old stocking, while his kitchen, which abutted on the bungalow, was like nothing so much as a coal-hole, and had a great heap of refuse in one corner. Occasionally I looked into this place to keep the sanitary arrangements in some sort of control, and nearly always found my "boy" had company of some sort; in fact, I rather think there was a small relief camp on my premises under the cook's management for my rice went wonderfully fast, as did my other provisions. Once or twice I found a native woman nominally assisting at the cooking, and "Sheitan" always answered my inquiries by saying, "This is my mother, sahib, just come from Wallenghay"—apparently careless of the fact that he had said the same of quite another woman, and that it was not probable he had two or three mothers. Then, again, there was some difficulty in clothing him. When he first put in an appearance, he was in bathing costume, and, thinking such an important factotum should be respectably clad, I exercised my mind to find him some garments, but without success, until at last, calling him into the bungalow, I explained my views, and bade him look round and see if there was anything which might do; so in his solemn way he marched round and inspected all my belongings. He was dissatisfied with a shirt, and it must be confessed, when he was inside it, with the sleeves flapping helplessly over his hands and his head only just coming above the collar, he did not look very dignified or fit to wait at table. So he proceeded with his search, and, after a minute or two of hesitation over a pillow-case, finally chose a soiled linen-bag which was hanging on a peg, and expressed his opinion that, if he might have it, it would make a splendid pair of pyjamas. On receiving permission, he walked off with the bag, which was white, with large purple spots. I thought he intended to cut it up and make a jacket out of it, but in less than half an hour an animated bolster entered the hut, with a pair of brown legs below, and a head and arms on top. After having boasted of his tailoring skill, he had contented himself with laying the linen-bag on the floor, and, slicing off the two bottom corners with a knife, had roughly hemmed the edges, and then, getting into it, had put his feet through the holes and drawn the tapes at the mouth tight round his chest. He was perfectly serious, and afterwards continued to wear this ridiculous garment in all weathers, asleep and awake, for kitchen work and for waiting, during the next three weeks; and, as may be supposed, by that time it wanted washing.

On the estate, the work that had to be done was not very varied, but consisted in preparing the guinea-grass clearing, road-making, and utilizing the end of the monsoon for planting out a few thousand more coffee trees into one of the clearings, and filling up "failures" in others. The first work is simple enough, and when the grass is established, it needs no more attention, but in a good situation affords a continual cut of hay for cattle, without any trouble expended in return. In forming a field, the only thing necessary is to secure a wet week or ten days for the operation. The roots of the grass, having been brought into the clearing, which has been previously freed from weeds, stones, and branches so far as may be, are torn in parts, each of which should have about twelve stems. Coolies, armed with mamôties, then dig or scrape little holes in the ground, as much as possible in lines, and about eighteen inches apart. In these the second line of coolies, usually women or boys, place the roots, but instead of planting them upright, divide each bunch, and, when inserting them in the holes, bend half the stems one way and half the other—an arrangement which is supposed to make the plant spread more and cover the ground. In this way, when the field is completely planted, all care is over, for if the rain continues for a few days after the planting the roots will strike, and the young shoots, coming up with all the luxuriance of tropical vegetation, will soon hide rocks, fallen trees, and stones in a waving sea of green.

The road-making was harder work, and consisted in forcing a passage along the steep hillside in No. 4 clearing. This occupied a great number of our coolies, under the supervision of many of the maistries, and cost a very considerable amount above the usual allowance. Owing to the very heavy nature of the timber, and to the ground being on a steep hillside, all the trees in falling had gone one way, and had to be cut through; whereas on the level the trees take no particular direction, and frequently leave clear spaces of considerable magnitude. In the present case, however, we had not that advantage, and the three or four miles of road which R—— had requested me to open before his return constituted a formidable enterprise.

Every morning I marched out at the head of the attacking forces, consisting often of a hundred men armed with mamôties, crowbars, and axes, and every evening, as we wound our way homewards, the road had been a few yards further advanced. But we met obstacles which gave us a vast amount of trouble. Now and again it was the stump of a forest giant, that had been cut off five feet above the ground, which we had to draw, like a mighty tooth. One or two of these stumps took us four or five days' toil. The first day's would go in scratching away the soil and undermining the roots, and when those were laid bare we had the task of cutting through them, many being underground branches as thick as the stem of a small tree. When at last they were severed, all available hands were mustered, and, with crowbars and long levers, the stump was slowly hoisted out amongst the frantic cries of the maistries and shouts of the perspiring coolies, to be rolled down the hill-side, where it is to stay for twenty or thirty years, until sun and rain have resolved it into dust. The greater proportion of the trees were cut through in two places, and the intermediate portion was rolled away easily enough; but sometimes, in spite of my utmost engineering skill, the upper portion of the trunk would come rolling down the hill-slope, sending every one flying for his life, and blocking up the track again. A coolie was once overtaken by one of these, and only saved from being crushed out of all form by the log tilting up and sliding over that under which he crouched. But the most troublesome features of the road-making were the logs of ironwood, of which we had to remove three or four. Their name perfectly expresses their nature—they are literally vegetable iron; and I could tell, so soon as I entered the clearing, whether the coolies were at work upon one by the metal like ring the wood gave forth when struck by the axes. Standing close by, at every stroke that was made I saw the axes bound back as though struck against a steel block, and a very minute chip of wood was the only result; in fact, the axes often got the worst of the encounter, and had to be frequently changed. Rolling these logs was a work of immense labour, on account of their great density and weight. A few dynamite cartridges skilfully placed would have saved us a lot of trouble, but unfortunately we had none on the estate; but that is the way they dispose of tough tree-stumps in Australia, and it answers excellently.

The third of my chief occupations consisted in taking the young coffee plants up out of the "nursery," and removing them to the spots where they were finally to be planted. The "nursery," which was in the corner of No. 1, and in an angle formed by the Manalora river and a small stream which emptied itself into it, had been formed eighteen months before; in fact, it is always the first operation on a new estate after the planter and his coolies have been roughly hutted.

A suitable spot having been selected—and the great essentials are nearness to a stream, so that the young plants may be watered during the hot weather and immediately after they are planted, and that good shade-trees may overhang the "nursery;" a depth of rich earth, that of a brown colour is considered the best, with accessibility to all parts of the estate and to the jungle where the great stores of leaf-mould are. These things having been secured, the land is cleared of all weeds and shrubs, which are grubbed up and removed by hand, nothing in this case being burnt upon the spot; but the stuff removed is often formed into a hedge round the place to keep off the wild animals, which do a great deal of damage by roaming about at night and nibbling the young shoots of the coffee.

The next operation is to divide the ground with a broad path down the centre, and numerous parallel beds on either side, eighteen feet long by two broad. They should not be of any greater breadth, or it will be impossible to attend to the young plants, when they appear, without injuring some. When the beds have been deeply dug, the coffee seeds in the outer wrapper or "parchment" are planted in little holes drawn at right angles across the bed, each seed about four inches from its neighbours. A few weeks of warm, damp weather will bring the young plants to the surface, and they appear first with two cotyledons or seed leaves, after which the stem shoots rapidly up; and in from twelve to eighteen months the "nursery" will be in a flourishing condition, and the beds filled with luxuriant young plants with glossy dark green leaves about sixteen inches in height. At this stage of growth they require attention in the way of watering when the weather is exceptionally hot, and many planters collect dry leaves from the adjacent jungle, and spread them thickly between the rows in order to retain the moisture in the ground. We adopted this plan at the request of the company at home, and though the leaves were a decided advantage to the plants, they harboured an astonishing number of snakes, of which the coolies were very much frightened—without much cause, however, as the most common variety was a little grey-and-white reptile, about a foot long and quite harmless; though once or twice a very deadly snake, the tic-polonga, was seen making for the jungle, and was permitted to escape unmolested, every man taking to his heels in the opposite direction.

At last comes the important operation of "planting out," of which there are several modes. One is to scoop the young plant up by a complicated sort of trowel, made to remove the seedling with the earth round its roots, and then to convey it to the clearing, bedding the plant out, and filling up the hole with soil. But our way, which seems the most certain, though slightly more expensive, is to have great quantities of light wicker baskets manufactured at Palghaut and Wallenghay, of the size and shape of a flower-pot. These are made of split rattan cane, and, though they should be tough and elastic, it is essential that they should not be so closely woven as to prevent the roots of the plant piercing them and penetrating the surrounding soil. It is better to have them too loose than too well made. Into these a couple of handfuls of the best jungle leaf-mould is placed, and then the young coffee plants are carefully taken up with a short trowel, a small piece is cut off the tap-root to prevent it being bent, and they are placed one in each basket, where they may be safely left until it is convenient to move them into the clearings. It is curious that the centre fibre should be so sensitive, but if it gets at all bent it seems to impair the vitality of the top of the plant. Consequently, this part of the operation has to be very carefully watched, and only the maistries are intrusted with the pruning-knives. They go from coolie to coolie, and take off a few inches of each tap-root. One advantage of basket planting is that the plants can be left about for some time without danger. Thus, I had five thousand plants brought from the "nursery" into No. 3 clearing, and placed along the side of the road, where they awaited planting until more pressing work was over; and the rest of the time all the women and boys were filling up "failures," *i.e.* putting new plants in places where those formerly planted had died out from various causes, principally from having been placed in holes that have hard rock below, into which the roots cannot penetrate.

With such work as this, there was hardly time to feel lonely, as all my days were spent in continual activity, and the necessity of retiring early to rest, in order to be up the next morning at daybreak, cut the evening very short. Still, for two weeks I had not seen a single white face or spoken my own language, and at times it certainly was monotonous. My sole connection with civilization was the daily tapal, who brought me occasional and very welcome letters from "home," a chance paper from Madras, and advice from the hospital-bound superintendent at Palghaut. On Saturday mornings the same tapal brought up a couple of hundred rupees, more or less, in small coinage of copper and silver, for paying the coolies, and this had to be accurately counted before he left the plantation again. But the days at this season of the Indian year were very much alike—nearly all being characterized by pouring rain and cold mists in the early morning, and a wretched state of soppiness as to all my possessions; in fact, I never longed so eagerly for fine weather in an English February as I did while alone on the estate. Of course there are occasional breaks in the monsoon, when the sun is very powerful, and everything steams like a vapour-bath; but the usual state of affairs at the intermediate season is moist and cheerless beyond compare.

I had a slight attack of dysentery at one time, brought on probably by being so often wet through, and by the rapid changes of temperature. This made the work the harder; but after nursing myself for half a day, I found inaction was quite unbearable, and continued my usual occupations until the attack thought fit to slacken. In fact, there is so much hard work to be done on a new estate that getting ill is unpermissible.

On the last day of October the weather cleared up a little, and the bright sunshine brought out increased numbers of insects and butterflies, while the birds were more lively. They flew from tree to tree, chasing each other about and enjoying the warmth. The only striking species of birds I had noticed so far were a small colony of half a dozen golden orioles, who had their abode in a small patch of jungle in the bed of a nullah, and were chiefly remarkable for their discordant cries, ill becoming their beautiful orange plumage, and their extreme shyness. Another bird was somewhat like a magpie, of small and graceful proportions, with a black-and-white body, and a remarkable tail between one and two feet long. I first came across one of these birds when it was feeding amongst some low bushes, and it sprang up and ascended through the tops of the trees, dragging its long white tail behind like an animated rocket.

On the 1st of November R—— returned to resume the charge of affairs, and I was well satisfied to hear from him, after he had been round the estate, that the work done during his absence exceeded his expectations. Yet he was still feeble, and felt conscious of impaired energies, and he advised me to prepare myself to take charge of the estate again, as he felt very doubtful of being able to remain long away from the doctor's hands. In this way, the old planter advising and instructing often from his bed, where his weakness confined him most of the time, and I executing the instructions, working all day far and near, and of a necessity equally hard in rain and sunshine, and devoting the evenings to estate correspondence and accounts, we found ourselves at the end of the first week in November, with the dry season close at hand, and a great deal of interesting work to be done in the ensuing six months.

CHAPTER XI.

A FEEBLE FOLK.

FATE seemed determined that I should win experience single handed! I had not been on the estate ten days, when R—— was forced to go to the lowlands on account of sickness, and returned little improved in strength. After making a very plucky stand against his painful complaint for a week, and directing my labours from his couch, or feebly hobbling for short distances round the estate, leaning heavily on his stick, he broke down hopelessly again on the evening of the 7th, and begged me to get carriers and a hammock to take him away to the lowlands. So, deeply chagrined, I turned out, collected twenty coolies with a trustworthy maistry, and prepared the munchiel, at which experience had made me quite expert. It was a very dark night, with a fine drizzling rain, and the torches of split bamboo carried by the men threw fitful gleams around, making the tree-trunks look copper-coloured, and illuminating our little hut, but rendering the surrounding darkness even more dense by comparison. R—— was quite broken down, and as I helped him into the hammock he said, "Good-bye, Arnold; you will never see me again;" and with this cheerful remark the procession moved slowly off, and left me in the darkness and rain, to my not over-pleasing meditations.

There was nothing to do, however, but to "buckle to" again, and the next week my whole time was occupied with the usual work, and building a new set of temporary "lines" for some coolies expected from Madura. These were made of corrugated iron, the sheets being sent up from the agents at Calicut, and intended eventually for roofing the permanent buildings and bungalows. This iron costs a great deal for carriage, even from the lowlands, and much more must be added for transport from England, besides which it certainly does not make convenient coolie "lines;" and where there is much timber suited for roofing purposes, it seems hardly worth its cost.

The finishing touches were also put to a very small hut about fifteen yards from the one used hitherto, and just across the footpath, which was to be my abode for some time. It was not palatial in dimensions, being about twenty by fourteen feet, nor was the architecture impressive, or the decoration elaborate. It was simply a little band-box-like edifice, made of the usual "brown paper and touch-wood" sort of material which we used, *i.e.* stakes stuck into the ground and covered with Palghaut matting. It had, however, two advantages over the one I occupied before from a sanitary point of view: the floor was raised up and made of thick planks, resting on rough piles of stones fore and aft; and another advantage was that there were mats on both sides of the stakes instead of only on one, which made it drier. I had great trouble in getting the workmen to put these mats on straight. An accurate line is totally unappreciated by an ordinary native; again and again I showed them how the lines should run horizontal or perpendicular. They listened in silence, and seemed to understand perfectly, but the next two or three mats would point to every part of the compass, and cruelly ruffle my notions of order. The roof, which was made extra thick, with the eaves brought to within four feet of the ground to protect the sides, was made of the long sweet-scented lemon-grass, and there were three little glass windows, a door with a rough porch, and a wall of matting across the interior to divide the sleeping compartment from the day-room. Alogether it was a strange little place, pretty to look at while the materials were fresh and clean, but not good for hard use—the daylight streaming through the two thicknesses of matting in many places, and the wind coming in at every corner; while after a shower every part got damp, and, being entirely built of vegetable produce, there was a very strong odour of decaying matter—something between wet hay and bilge-water on a steamer. When dry, the lemon-grass had it all its own way, and the scent then was very pleasant.

While out one day in the clearings, the sun, which had been shining brightly a little while before, became rapidly overcast, and light shadows like falling leaves began to chase each other over the ground. Looking up to see what could be the explanation of this, I perceived a strange sight above. It was a mighty emigration of newly developed butterflies, seeking "fresh fields and pastures new." At first they came by ones and twos about fifty feet above the ground, borne very gently along with outspread pinions on a soft north-east breeze; but these were only the scouts of the main army, and soon they were passing by hundreds and thousands overhead, all apparently with one mind taking an undeviating course over hill and dale. Some object they must have had in view, but what it was would be very difficult to say, for nothing but lonely tracts of jungle lay in their path, and then the open sea. The wind was certainly not sufficiently strong to be sweeping them by, whether they wished it or not, and their steady flight and the way in which they seemed to be economizing their powers appeared to indicate a purpose to travel far before their destination was reached. Amongst others, there were large numbers of *Papilio erithonius* and *Papilio pammon*, and many *Pierides;* but the majority were too high to be recognized with any certainty. It was a wonderful sight, not easily forgotten, and during the two hours while the flight lasted, many hundreds of thousands must have passed over the spot where I stood, the whole column stretching far and wide.

One has little time, however, for studying natural history or anything of the sort on a new estate. The work is never ceasing, and the opportunities are nothing like those enjoyed by Englishmen in most other occupations. Then, too, my first season was exceptionally wet, for the rain stored up its forces and, after being much overdue, made up for lost time by descending in deluges. So copious a rainfall sent down the price of rice and grains in the markets of the low country, but it will be a long time before the coolies recover from the effects of the recent famines and agricultural ruin.

It is scarcely understood at what a low ebb, even in times of prosperity, the common people of India live. The natives of India subsist from hand to mouth, often in fact eating what they never earned, and running into debt. Not so very many years ago they were predial slaves, changing masters according as the land on which they lived changed owners; but the advent of British rule has amended this, and now the coolie gets the same wages as before, lives as he has lived for the last five hundred years, is free to wander where he likes,—and when hard times come, having no master, he is also free to take care of himself—in which he conspicuously fails. He is about as successful a free man as a child of six would be if released from the "barbarous trammels" of the nursery and told to enjoy the glorious privilege of fending for itself. Our friend the coolie, when he works for native ryots or cultivators of the soil, rarely takes his wages in coin of the realm, but is glad to receive as much coarse grain as will keep him and his household from day to day. He is a decided anti-Malthusian—marries early and rears large families, utterly heedless of to-morrow, his greatest windfalls the few rupees he receives as a present from his employer when the latter has a feast-day, and his highest ambition to buy his wife bangles and to outshine his humble neighbours at marriages and ceremonies. He never has any money, and, if he had, would not keep it a week. As long as food is cheap, he gets on fairly well, and even spares a little rice as an offering on the shrine of his household god, or goes to the extent of spending an anna in red ochre to ornament the *samee;* but when the Indian seasons go wrong, it fares very hard with the coolie.

The rain holds back when it ought to fall, or

THE SAMEE TREE.

descends in torrents when it is not wanted, and the harvest is bad. There is perhaps no grass, and then the cattle die of starvation far and wide. The coolie's labour grows worthless like himself, and as nobody has any capital invested in him, nobody cares what becomes of him, except perhaps the Government, and as there are probably no railways and few roads near his village, the Government may be said to be far off, wherever situated. He could save himself if he would move from the spot where all his life has been spent, but he clings to it wildly. He will not go to the relief works, where plenty of work and a little food is to be had. He will not confess himself a pauper and seek the famine camps; he will not even move up to the demon-haunted jungles, and enlist under the banners of the hardy Englishmen who are waging war against the fever-mists in these gloomy regions. So he wanders backwards and forwards, and picks the bones of his fellow-workmen, the buffaloes, along with the dogs and hyenas, and when those same ribs are clean and white, he turns herbivorous and chews the leaves of trees, small weeds, and the heart of the aloe; and if this does not kill him straight off by an attack of cholera or famine diarrhœa, he may at last crawl to the nearest relief camp or plantation. But by this time he is run out; his thread of life is spun too fine —he has no inside; continued starvation has dried it up, and he is nothing but an animate mummy, a skeleton wrapped in very dirty brown leather.

The extent of the last famine, and the difficulties of the Government in affording relief, may be better understood when it is remembered that in the Madras Presidency alone some three or four millions of natives find it hard enough to live in times of prosperity, when their food grains are selling at sixty to eighty pounds per rupee. When famine comes, and only from ten to fifteen pounds of the same food-stuff can be obtained for the same sum, as was the case during the last months of 1877, the nature of the distress and the task of the Government may be understood. It is not the fault of the natives, excepting in a negative way, inasmuch as they do very little to help themselves; and still less is it the fault of the landlords, who support their labourers as long as they can, but the stern laws of self-preservation compel them to be turned adrift at last. It is, first of all, due to the defective rainfall, and, secondly, to the fearful poverty and lack of resources of the cultivators. Both these causes can be modified to a great extent by a Government formed on the best of all principles, a mild despotism. If the Government would use a little compulsion on the native farmers in the matter of well-digging and tree-planting, great results might be attained. Nobody now doubts the benefits to be derived from these two works. Famines, alas! do not simply reduce the people to starvation and kill them off like flies, but they come attended by diseases of all sort, and leave behind them, when they pass away, a vast legacy of sickness and misery. Our own coolies on the estate bore only too clear a witness to what a long effort they had made before they had arrived there, showing in their wasted strength and attenuated forms how long the struggle would be to regain their former condition.

With such material the difficulty of working a new estate may be understood, especially by those who have had some experience of natives. My presence was essential, everywhere and all day, to get anything done, and even when on the spot the work accomplished by most of my coolies would have made an English navvy laugh. I once found three men engaged on the roots of a small jack tree which had to be removed. It was a mere sapling, but they had been squatting on their heels round it for half an hour, feebly picking at the soil with their mamôties; and probably they would have gone on for half an hour more, and eventually left it against another day; but happening to pass along, and being disgusted at their slowness, I laid hold of the small stem, twisted it once round, and pulled it out of the ground with a jerk, and, flinging it into a neighbouring nullah, left the coolies gazing blankly at the empty hole.

The women and children proved especially troublesome, since they were the very essence of feebleness and stupidity. It was necessary to get some work out of them, as they were drawing full wages, and yet, of course, it was impossible to speak so roughly to them as to the men. Still they seemed to stand in considerable awe of me, and did their best while I was actually watching; at a pace, however, which showed only too clearly it could not be maintained when my back was turned.

Another difficulty was doctoring the sick. Being totally inexperienced at this sort of duty, I was often in great perplexity, with no one to consult or ask advice of. But Nature, with some slight assistance, more or less adroit, from me, made a number of surprising cures. Many cases, however, were past the mending of any earthly doctor, and in one week fourteen coolies died in the "lines" within a stone's throw of my bungalow. Nearly every weekly report sent down to the agents at Palghaut contained the record of many deaths in brief totals, such as "died during the week—men, 5; women, 3; and children, 6," or whatever the numbers might be. They dropped out of the ranks to be buried in the nearest strip of jungle, and nobody knew whence they came or who they were. The most fatal disease was famine diarrhœa, which bears a great resemblance to common cholera; in fact, I do not know where the certain line can be drawn between them, except that the muscular cramps, which are so fearfully characteristic of the latter, are not present to any great extent in the malady brought on by famine and long privation. But there is little to choose between them in appearance, and the end often comes suddenly with both. In one case I was fetched to see a man who had been working in the clearing in the morning, but had been brought to the "lines" with all the symptoms of cholera morbus. He was obviously very far gone, and I went to the hut to get what medicine I could think of, but before it was mixed a maistry came up, salaamed, and said it was too late—the man was dead. This was by no means an isolated case. Every night (they had a peculiar habit of dying at night) one or more took the great plunge into the Unknown. Perhaps it was the chills of the evening killed them; at all events, the half-caste clerk was always wondering, when the day's work was over, who would die before sunrise. One night he was in my bungalow, standing at my elbow and explaining some entries made in the account-books before my arrival, when he suddenly paused in a long sum and said, "Hark, sahib!" The night was windy and wet, the rain was pelting against the matting, the wind was howling among the trees and finding its way into the hut at twenty holes, making my lamp flicker and the cobwebs wave about overhead. I listened, but nothing was to be heard for a time, except the continual sound of the monsoon storm; until, all of a sudden, there was a most ghostly hoot, and then a rattling laugh, from the trees on the neighbouring hillside about a hundred yards away. "Do you hear it, sahib?" said the half-caste. "It is the devil's messenger, and a coolie is dying, and the thing that makes that noise is waiting to take his spirit." Of course, I told him that was nonsense—probably it was some owl or nightjar disturbed from a snug retreat by a tree falling; but he was obviously unshaken in his barbarous belief, and all the multiplication and division were knocked clean out of his head, so that I had to give him some arrack punch and send him to his shed.

As I lay on my hard, badly jointed board cot, with the rain pelting against the single thickness of matting a few inches from my head, I listened intently to hear the unearthly sound again, but without success, and when I met the "writer" the next morning, asked him if any one had died to fulfil his prophecy. He said it was so—two coolies had died close together the evening before; so I had to pocket my scepticism and change the subject.

On another evening there was a new disturbance of a different kind. I had gone to bed, and everything was still and quiet, as it did not happen to be raining just then, although it was intensely dark; when, all of a sudden, there rose a sound like a loud blast on a brass trumpet from the direction of the coolie "lines," and the moment after "Sheitan" burst in and cried, "Sahib, sahib, the elephants are coming!" I sprang up, and, seizing a rifle and stuffing into it a cartridge, ran out in my flannel sleeping-suit and slippers. By the time I got down to the "lines" every single coolie in the place was howling and shouting at the top of his voice, while one or two were throwing lighted torches about, to the great danger of the thatches. There was nothing else to be seen, however, and as no elephant could stay in the neighbourhood of such a row, and as I did not care about a midnight hunt in slippers and sleeping-gear, I beat a retreat and turned in again. On investigation the following morning, it turned out that an old elephant, and a young one about eighteen months old, had come down the hillside, forded a small shallow stream at the bottom, and ascended into the coolie "lines." Probably they were all in amongst the huts before they knew whither they had strayed, though they ought to have been warned by the extremely powerful odour which pervaded the locality inhabited by my natives. There were their footmarks anyhow, all over the place, some of them twenty by eighteen inches across, and from this the size of the old elephant can be judged. In one place they had been within five yards of a hut occupied by two families of coolies, and had stepped upon and broken two large earthenware chatties left out overnight. A little further on, the fore foot of the larger animal had rested on the edge of a rough earth embankment forming a sort of raised causeway in front of a line of huts, and the ponderous weight had brought it down with a run. Every one of the coolies seemed to have been equally frightened, although only two or three had actually seen the animals.

CHAPTER XII.

BUILDING TABERNACLES.

For the next week or so my work was varied by very extensive lopping and burning operations on Bungalow Hill. This is a spur of the high range which bounds our land on the north-east, and was selected as a site for the "pucka" bungalow on account of standing centrally placed in the middle of the estate, and being some two hundred feet above the surrounding country, which should make it fairly healthy. The only hills which overtopped it were the high forest-clad cone of "Hootcha Mullah" to the eastward within this property, and to the north-west, across the Manalora stream (which was our boundary in that direction), the rocky grass-covered heights of the Pardagherry Mountain. On this same hill, and just visible from where I had been working lately, was a wonderful bare precipice, with a wall of rock some three hundred feet in height. Directly underneath, almost sheltered from the rain by the overhanging cliff above, with the help of a telescope it was possible to make out the picturesque little straw-thatched hut of another English planter, S——, who lived there by himself—the greatest hermit of us all.

The view was extensive whichever way one looked. To the right and left the high mountain just mentioned shut off the quarter of each monsoon, and looking southward down the winding valley of the Manalora, the eye ranged over long expanses of unclaimed jungle stretching right away to Cape Comorin. We were, in fact, the most southerly of all the estates in this direction, and beyond us was a wilderness, the home of the bison and elephant, all "impenetrable jungle." To the north-east we looked along the course of the road, which lead here, over half a dozen estates buried in deep frames of jungle, each with its little white bungalow and dusky coolie "lines;" and amid most of them one caught here and there the flashing of a pool or streamlet, the all-important water for turning the pulping machinery and supplying the coolies. Farther away the ghaut road began, and, the hills sloping down, nothing more was seen of the forest until the lowlands unrolled themselves, stretching far away like a wonderful fabric of green and silver cloth. At this distance the towns and villages could not be made out, but just where the great Southern Indian plain was melting away into indistinguishable distance, the great towering Neilgherry Mountains rose up again, ascending tier above tier into the sky.

Hither each morning I made my way, at the head of a long array of axe and bill men, threading the narrow path, while the mist still hung about, and every spider's web was beaded with a thousand glittering liquid diamonds. At the hill-top I generally stopped for a moment to admire the view, while the maistries got the coolies into working parties. But there was not much time for meditating on the beauties of nature, for much had to be done before any attempt could be made to build on this commanding spur. The forest which clothed it was cut down some six months before, and presented a scene of wild confusion; but, for some reason, when the three months of drying had been allowed and fire was applied, the "burn" proved a failure. The flames ran rapidly over the clearing, consuming all the leaves and lighter stuff without touching the heavier timber, which, of course, cannot be burnt as it lies, unless a great heat is obtained by the embers of the smaller materials. So it became necessary to lop up everything and burn it by instalments—a long job, and needing all the best labour on the estate. As soon as we arrived, the ashes of yesterday's fires were raked together and carefully nursed into a blaze by the skilful coolies, and then twelve or fifteen tiny columns of thin grey smoke curled up in the still morning air, and soon the ring of the axes was heard and the crackling of sticks, as the fires gained height and strength, and the coolies no longer enjoyed poking them, but threw on logs and branches from a respectful distance. By the time the sun came up we were encanopied in a dense curtain of yellow smoke, through which at first he shone only feebly, but when he got higher and stronger and glared on us from above, his rays, added to the heat of the now roaring bonfires, produced a result never to be forgotten. Nearly every day I was subjected to a temperature high enough, one could almost fancy, to cook a thick chop, and besides this I was continually choked with smoke, blinded with clouds of hot white ashes, and stifled with the fumes of hundreds of strange weeds and herbs. I went to work in the morning fresh, clean, and neat, in white linen jacket and trousers, with nicely polished top-boots and a snowy pith helmet, but when breakfast-time came nothing could present a more striking contrast than my appearance. My clothes were torn, soiled with earth, and marked from head to foot with charcoal. My hair was powdered thickly with white ashes, and my face and hands about the colour of a coolie's skin with smoke and dust. It was useless to wash until the day's work was done, so I usually breakfasted as I stood, and one of the planters, dropping in to see me one day at the midday meal, exclaimed as soon as he had dismounted and entered my hut, "Why, Arnold, what have you been doing? you look like a coal-heaver!" And I am afraid I did.

The coolies do not seem to find the heat too much for them; they possess the advantage of working entirely without clothes, and perspire freely, the moisture running down their bare bodies and cutting channels in the charcoal dust and ashes, until they make a most curious picture. But the superintendent is clothed, and has to be continually on the move amongst the fires, now crawling under charred logs on hands and knees, and now reaching a distant part of the clearing by walking along the tree-trunks and leaping from one to the other. While engaged in this latter way, I had a spill which might have resulted in serious consequences. Wishing to cross the crown of the hill, where the fires were burning fiercely, to see what a party of coolies on the opposite side were doing, I climbed up on a log of peepul wood lying across a lot of others, and, running and jumping from stem to stem, had nearly got through safely, but, being half blinded and choked with the dense yellow smoke and fearful heat, I dropped off one log, without due caution, on to another four feet below, thinking it was sound. But the fire had eaten along through the whole tree, leaving a glowing mass of burning embers and about half an inch of green bark all round. Directly my feet touched the trunk it gave way, and I came head over heels to the ground, amid a blinding storm of smoke, dust, and ashes. The only damage done was a few holes burnt in my clothes and one or two scorches on my hands, while, if it were possible, my clothes were grimier than ever.

It was impossible, however, to control the work successfully all over the estate for long with my limited knowledge of the language; and after a spell of hard uphill work, I wrote to Calicut to say that, as Mr. R—— would not probably be back for several months, the interests of the estate imperatively demanded there should be some one on it who had had more experience than had fallen to my share of the various operations. To this a reply was sent, allowing that the work was very hard for an unseasoned "*chickdoree*," and stating that as there was an unattached Englishman in the district—a brother of D——, of Polyampara—who had had considerable experience, he would soon be associated with me, if possible. Shortly afterwards my new acquaintance, E. D——, wrote to say he had accepted a temporary position on the estate, and would come over in heavy marching order the next day.

So I made a few preparations, rigged up another bunk, ordered an extra supply of provisions from Wallenghay; and while seated at breakfast one morning, I was aroused by the arrival of a long string of coolie women loaded with pots, pans, bedding, and general effects, and behind them marched an Englishman, whom I immediately recognized as one with whom I had tiffined on first landing at the club-house, Calicut. So we fraternized readily, and, having stowed the new arrival's kit, proceeded to breakfast, and then discussed future plans over our cheroots. My friend's build and stature—much like that of the robust Ghoorkhas of Northern India,—five feet nothing in height, by three feet broad—gave great promise of energy, which was not lessened by the fact that he was a Cornishman. He brought a servant with him, which was fortunate, as "Sheitan's" cooking was very poor and his habits deplorable. It was impossible to get any respect for cleanliness into that "boy's" head, and he had a most free and easy way with my property—breaking my small stock of china, cutting the stitches of the soles of my boots when he scraped the mud off, with many other offences, besides the expense which his numerous "mothers" caused me by eating my provisions.

One of the very few creatures which I had shot since reaching the estate was a specimen of the Malabar squirrel, *Sciurus maximus.* This extremely handsome animal is as large as a full-grown hare, with the richest soft-furred skin, mahogany colour on the back, striped with a broad black band on either side, and yellow underneath. The ears are ample and fringed with long hairs, the eyes large and hazel-coloured, while the face combines all the colours of the body in stripes. They utter a curious grunting sound when calling to each other, but are silent when alarmed, and glide from branch to branch, only betraying their presence by shaking the leaves and twigs as they spring. The first specimen I secured was feeding far up among the thick foliage of a jack tree, and might have been passed unnoticed, but for husks of broken seeds which kept falling to the ground as the squirrel unshelled the fruit. Even then it was no easy matter to make him out at the elevation.

I must also plead guilty to having shot two or three of the great black monkeys which abound in these jungles during the wet monsoon, but I always had a feeling of quasi-homicide when one was shot—they bear such wonderfully human faces, and they behave in much the same way as a human being might. Hearing some chattering in the tree-tops once, I went to the spot, and coming suddenly into view of one old monkey, he seemed to know that hiding was safer than flying under the circumstances, so, seizing hold of a leafy bough above, he drew it down until his head and shoulders were quite hidden; but it did not occur to him that all the rest of his body was exposed—his "untutored mind" fancied that if he could not see me, it followed naturally that he himself must be invisible,—much the same argument as those philosophers use who deny the existence of a spiritual world. The size of these monkeys is enormous when their arboreal life is taken into account. Many of them are as large as a retriever dog, and must weigh seventy or eighty pounds at the least. One that I shot was a monster, who taxed all my energies to get the carcass back half a mile to the bungalow, and when I threw him down in the verandah, I vowed he could be little under a hundred pounds. In colour they are jet black; the old males, however, carry a white frill round the neck and a white front. Their tails are long—as long as the body, but never used, as far as I have observed, for prehension; in fact, they are generally dragged behind their possessor in a careless sort of way, and when the monkey runs along a branch they wave to and fro in a very aimless manner. Their skins form excellent carriage rugs and mats, but are too coarse for wraps or cloaks. There is also a very considerable difficulty in preserving and drying them properly in the jungle, owing to the continual dampness of the atmosphere, which makes anything resembling leather very mouldy in a short time.

Monkeys are numbered amongst the foes of the coffee planter, as they make free with the sweet ripe berries, the stones of which are frequently found dry and clean, in lines, under branches and fallen trees, having passed uninjured through their digestive arrangements; and such seeds, old planters will tell you, make the very choicest coffee. The coolies eat monkey flesh quite freely—a sure proof their religion is not that of the Hindoos—and whenever my gun brought one down, there was a great deal of salaaming around me, and anxious inquiries as to how I intended to dispose of the body. Indeed, I tried the "devilled" leg of a young monkey myself at breakfast one morning, and it was not bad; probably a hungry man might enjoy it very much. The native superintendent of the Dewan of Cochin's estate, the next one to the north of ours, employed a boy to wander about in the jungles with a rusty musket, with which he shot the monkeys as they fed in the tree-tops, and got a small reward per skin. One day he came to my hut to know if I had any skins to sell him, but our commercial positions were reversed, as I bought all the fifteen which he had with him for a couple of rupees—considerably more than he would have obtained from the Dewan.

Another creature which only puts in an appearance when the days are growing brighter and hotter, is the gay little striped squirrel, a first cousin of the palm-squirrel of the plains, but rather darker in colour, and known to science by the name of *Sciurus trivittatus*. This does little harm to new estates, as it confines its attention, like the monkeys, to the ripe berries, and I was always glad to note their small lithe forms darting along the fallen timber, pulling up for half a moment to see what the enemy is doing, and then, with a flick of the bushy grey tail and a few sharp chirrups, vanishing into some hollow or broken bough. They make themselves wonderfully at home, especially on the outskirts of the clearings, where the timber is half overgrown by weeds and bushes; but curiously, though I have seen scores in such places, I never observed one climbing a standing tree—a sign they are not actually the same as the lowland squirrel, who spends all his time on the trunk and branches of his arboreal home.

Pardagherry Mountain, opposite to my hut, grew greener and greener every day of the Indian spring, as a vast expanse of mingled rocks and grass, with here a patch of jungle or reeds fringing some water-course, and there a sheer precipice of some hundred feet high, over which a foaming stream was for ever falling in a silver streak.

That same hill-top, though but seldom visited, has been on one of those rare occasions the scene of a sad event, which deprived the world of a brave English lady. Even her name is unknown to me, but, as I heard the story, she was the wife of a collector, or perhaps forest overseer, and with her husband and a few servants had ascended to the unknown wilds which overhang the estates of S——, about three miles from Pardagherry. As sunset was coming on one day, the Englishman rode on ahead to choose a camping-ground, leaving the lady, also mounted, to follow more leisurely. The former galloped up to a pleasant spot by a reedy stream, and was just congratulating himself on such a favoured locality, when a small herd of elephants at rest under the trees hard by saw him, and broke back as fast as they could go by the path hemmed in with rocks on either side, up which the lady was advancing. The panic-stricken herd charged down, and before any warning was given rushed upon the little party in the narrow path. The native servants, being on foot, escaped among the rocks; but the lady's horse shied, threw her, and fled before the elephants down the pass. The whole herd passed over the unfortunate Englishwoman, who had so pluckily followed her husband into these wild regions, and she died a few minutes after he came up; so the sylvan camping-place must have been sorrowful enough that night.

My friend "Charlie" returned from the lowlands after a time, having recovered from his gun accident, and began to open a small "nursery" for one of the planters on the other side of the Manalora stream, opposite to our territory. Besides him another young Englishman, L——, turned up and stayed on the estate for some time, until he could break more new land to the south of us for another company. Thus southward the course of civilization takes its way, and Pardagherry was no longer *Ultima Thule*, but was left behind by L——'s place, which, on account of the difficulty of access, its solitude, and deadly fever-mists, we named the "Bitter End." L——, however, was a plucky fellow. He readily left the Varlavachen Bungalow, the eyrie of F——, my acquaintance of Palghaut, perched upon the summit of a steep mountain, and descended to our low-lying hut, where no one could stay long without contracting jungle-fever.

Though he did not say so, it is obvious he thought very lightly of our style of life; and, in fact, the four of us were now packed about as tightly as could be in our little hut. We got on well enough during the day, as we were all employed in the jungles except just at meal times; but when night came and we turned in, it was a tight fit. Our four berths, placed side by side across the sleeping apartment, with the spaces occupied by the box which did duty for a washing-stand and one shaky chair, completely filled it up. We were always dreadfully tired after the day's work, and soon after dinner retired to our couches, though they were made of nothing softer than unplaned teak-boards supported on biscuit-boxes. Soon four forms might have been seen by the dim light of the lantern swinging overhead, each in a flannel sleeping-suit, and rolled up in grey blankets, with a long cheroot between each pair of lips. D—— had an accordion, which he generally brought to bed with him, and in the solemn stillness of the night, when the jungles were buried in darkness, and tigers and elephants roamed about as they listed, the strains of many songs went up in a fitful manner from our hut. If the coolies listened they must have had a poor opinion of us as a musical nation, for D—— was only a beginner on his instrument, and rarely got safely through more than two or three notes, when he recommenced, or broke off to tell us we were singing out of tune. It was the most mournful affair trying to follow him, for he had to go very slowly and think beforehand on each note; so as our cheroots burnt down he had things more and more his own way, till, finding us dozing, he generally attempted a lively "God save the Queen," by way of *finale*. A sleepy sort of idea that we ought to stand up and take our hats off pervaded us, but, on the whole, we did not think her Majesty would mind the omission, and soon silence settled down and suppressed even D——'s melancholy instrument.

I have mentioned one evening on which there was an alarm of elephants. On another, as we were all asleep, a great noise suddenly broke out in the coolie "lines," and we heard the natives shouting, "Hatti! hatti!"—"Elephants;" so we turned out as quickly as we could. I and L——, who were sleeping in neighbouring bunks, being only half awake, and no light burning, by some mischance seized upon the same pair of trousers. He monopolized one leg and I the other, and the natural result was that when we tried to get up we came a heavy cropper on the floor, which effectually woke us, and we sat facing each other for some moments, wondering what was the matter. At last we exclaimed together, "What are you doing with my trousers?" Meanwhile, D—— had taken down a rifle from the pegs, and had run out to get a shot if possible; but "Charlie" spoiled his chance by groping to the head of my bed, and, without a word of warning, pulling the string attached to the spring gun outside, which he had loaded the day before with a couple of handfuls of native powder and part of an old sock rammed tightly over the bullet. The result was a terrific explosion, which seemed to frighten both the elephants and the coolies equally, for all other sounds died away immediately afterwards, and we were left to finish the evening in peace.

But an undisturbed night was quite the exception. On one occasion a great cackling arose amongst some cocks and hens that we kept in a small shed, and, turning out with revolvers and sticks, we found an animal about the size of a large cat had broken in and killed three of our fowls, to the great consternation of the others. After a hunt, "Charlie" saw the beast escaping along a bough overhead, and brought him down with a shot from my revolver. We were also considerably troubled with rats, which played nocturnal games on our beds, and even nibbled us when they got the chance; so we borrowed a cat from Mrs. F—— of Varlavachen—a real English cat, who became a great pet—and it kept the rats somewhat in order. One night, as I was lying in my cot with the lamp dimly burning, a large rat came out, and, after wandering about the floor, jumped into a tin bucket. Just at that moment the cat came in, and, catching sight of the disappearing tail, proceeded to stalk the bucket in a very scientific style. Then some slight sound alarmed the rat, and I saw him jump out and run away on the off side. Meanwhile the cat, who felt sure of getting him, and had not observed this, crept to within a couple of paces, and then, gently lashing her tail from side to side and gathering her limbs under her, measured the distance, and with a single bound leapt right into the pail. Of course, there was nothing there, and I never saw a creature look so supremely astonished as she did. On windy nights our sleep was broken by the rubbing of the trees together, and by the long rattan creepers swinging to and fro and striking against each other, with the occasional falling of branches or trees—a danger to which we were exposed during the whole of the monsoon. If the elements were at rest, the insect world woke up and treated us to animated concerts of most mingled sounds; but fatigue is a good narcotic, and we paid at last very small attention to such things.

An occupation which now took up some of my time was fixing supports to the young coffee trees of two years old, which were growing into considerable bushes with thick heads of glossy dark green leaves. In spite of the belts of jungle left between the clearings, the plants feel the wind more or less, and when the ground is wet it swings them round and round, so that the stem works an opening in the soil just where it comes above ground. Then, if there should be any breeze on the next hot day, when the ground is baked hard by the sun, the plant chafes against this rim, cuts through its tender young bark, and very speedily dies. So we have to support it by driving in a three-foot stick, sloping towards the plant from the direction of the south-west monsoon, and firmly but gently tying them together with a thin rattan fibre, or the bark of a tree which grows wild in the jungles.

A considerable number of men were also employed, at various parts of the estate, cutting down young saplings of ten or twelve years' growth, chopping them into lengths of two feet, and then splitting the logs into light pegs, which were to be used for marking new pits when more clearings were opened. D—— says each man ought to make three hundred pegs a day, and the assistant superintendent ought to count them! Quite an impossibility! but this is the sort of thing one picks up by reading books on coffee planting; a little rough experience, however, takes the gloss off such book learning. My associate had some attacks of fever after arriving at the estate, which kept his liver in a chronic state of disturbance; in fact, he said no one can stay out in the jungle long without losing his liver altogether. I asked him if that was not rather serious, as the liver, with all its faults, is commonly supposed to be a useful part of one's internal arrangements; but he averred—and he ought to know—that one can get on quite comfortably without any. However, he seemed to part with his own reluctantly—it would have been a good thing, in fact, if he had had none left—for each attack irritated the little he believed there was remaining, and then everybody, from the "cook boy" to the smallest coolie, got into trouble.

CHAPTER XIII.

THE TRACKLESS WOODS.

I SPENT some spare hours in decorating the interior of my new hut, as much as circumstances would permit, with pictures, pipe-racks, guns, and all the paraphernalia of a sportsman. When this æsthetic effort suddenly burst upon the view of a new native servant whom I had engaged, he stood spell-bound; he clearly thought it was the most beautiful abode ever built, for he was only a "country servant," hailing from Wallenghay. The coolies too, when they were mustered in front of my open door in the morning, were silent with astonishment, and seemed to fancy it a sort of international exhibition. The pictures attracted the Tamils very much—they like anything coloured; so I at once gave them some vividly tinted English advertisements, with blue and white bills bearing the inscription "*Daily Telegraph,* Largest Circulation in the World," and these they forthwith hung up in their "lines." I also showed some of the maistries one or two of the full-page engravings in numbers of the *Graphic* and *Illustrated London News,* representing fights between Turks and Russians on the Danube. They were immensely interested, crowding round each picture in a dense circle of black faces, and nodding their heads and pointing to each incident in the picture with their dusky fingers. Only one of them, however, Jowra, the headman of the estate, had any idea of who the combatants really were; the others recognized some as "Inglish" by their pale faces, and the Turks were supposed to be outer barbarians of a distant country with whom the sahibs had some unknown quarrel. I put them on the straight track with the help of my new "boy," who spoke English well, besides his native Tamil, and they seemed to be much impressed.

My luggage and new furniture for the hut also now came up. It is usual for a company to supply the assistant superintendent with furniture and bedding, of which he has the free use, but such things are considered fixtures of the estate, and pass from successor to successor. It was a very welcome sight when the long string of coolies came winding down the jungle path with chairs, bedsteads, washing-stands, tables, etc., slung on poles, and upon their arrival there was a grand unpacking forthwith. Everything was made of the bright yellow jackwood, which is abundant, works well, and does not shrink; but the article which pleased me most was a silk-cotton mattress, which I thought a bed fit for an emperor, and thoroughly appreciated that night, after two months of sleeping on bare planks.

On the 12th of December we commenced a road to be carried from the southern slope of Bungalow Hill right away, without pause or turn, to the head of the ghaut. It had already been "traced" for some distance, and half formed through the jungle separating our estate from the next one to the northward. This bit, which follows the winding of the Manalora stream, was about the most picturesque spot in the neighbourhood, and best satisfied my idea of what a glade in the tropics ought to look like. Hitherto, I must confess, I had been considerably disappointed with the "gorgeous East," which had never seemed to me quite up to the mark; but this road presented a much richer variety of ferns and vegetation than almost any other spot yet visited. The way wound along the steep side of a "hanger," as Gilbert White would call it—a high ridge, on the crest of which, but completely hidden by the forest, is the old "Top Entrance Road," this new path being designated by the name of the "Lower Entrance Road." On the other side, a few feet below, our mountain river, like a Scotch torrent, went dashing and tumbling, now plunging into dense thickets of tangled herbage and feathery bamboos, where it was quite invisible, though it could be heard murmuring along, and then again sparkling out into the sunshine and breaking into twenty little streamlets among the rocks, only to reunite again and continue its progress among beds of waving reeds and tall grasses, beneath shady banks, where it ran more slowly under the graceful tree-ferns that swung their fronds over the water and, Narcissus-like, spent their existence in watching their own reflections. In one place a great tree had fallen across, dragging down to ruin with it three smaller ones, and together their leafless branches choked up the stream with a barrier impassable to anything larger than water-snakes; but the kingfishers found this a very convenient watch-tower, so that there were always a pair of them—lovely little sky-blue birds—perched among the twigs, their beautiful plumage contrasting well with the decaying branches. But they were shy and did not like visitors, dropping off their perches and skimming down the stream with lightning-like speed when any one approached. If I were a little fish, I thought as I watched them, I would rather be eaten by a bright bird than by a gormandizing old pike. The stream did not glide along in untroubled stillness, but its course was broken in many places by waterfalls of varying dimensions, all picturesque, and scores of little rivulets falling into the main stream on either side. These troubled us in an unromantic way when they were on our bank, as they washed away the soil and left deep hollows, which we had some difficulty in passing, as they were too small to be regularly bridged. We generally got over the difficulty by cutting down two trees, laying them across the gap, and crossing them with logs placed side by side, which did very well as a temporary arrangement.

Every day for two weeks I was busy on this work with a hundred and fifty men armed with mamôties and axes—a small army, which it took a great amount of exercise to thoroughly look after, as, owing to their being scattered in twos and threes at intervals of ten or fifteen paces, and out of sight of each other, it was necessary to be going constantly backwards and forwards. Even with this large force the road progressed slowly on the margins of the clearings, where the fallen trees were piled three or four deep, and each had to be cut in two places and rolled away—no light labour, as may be understood. In fact, on one occasion the whole force at my disposal, working from sunrise to sunset, only cleared fifty yards of ground eight feet wide; and as long as the "trace" ran through the felled ground, the pace remained very slow. After a time the unopened jungle on the borders of our plantation was reached, and, the trees here still standing, we got on better. But then arose new difficulties. First of all, the leeches swarmed amongst the dead leaves until these had been scraped away, and my socks were crimsoned with my own blood every day when I returned to breakfast, while the poor coolies spent half their time picking the vile creatures off their legs. Besides leeches, there lurked here numbers of snakes, for which the natives were constantly on the look out; but they were a matter of indifference to me, being in thick shooting-boots and leggings. The most deadly snakes, however, are said to be tree-climbers, occasionally dropping down on a person passing beneath—rather an unpleasant idea, the only remedy against which would be to keep an umbrella constantly up. But though one may have to look below and aloft at the same time for snakes, and it may not be agreeable to feel numerous holes bored in one's legs by bloodthirsty leeches, neither of these troubles are to be compared to the results of breaking into the nest of a thriving colony of large black ants, which was once my misfortune. We came upon them quite suddenly. One of my axemen pulled up a small bush by the roots, and disclosed a large hollow space, as big as a game-hamper, formed entirely by the industrious little people mentioned, and nearly filled with a great nest of papier-mâché-like material of a greyish colour, neatly arranged in terraces, one above the other, with corridors and numerous entrances to the inner parts. For one moment the sudden removal of the wall of their home showed the busy citizens stroking each other with their antennæ—some collected in groups round those, who may perhaps have been lecturing on domestic economy and kindred ant-subjects; while a few were walking up and down the passages with unhatched or imperfect baby ants in their jaws—clearly the nurses giving their charges a little fresh air. Others were putting things in order and executing a few necessary household repairs; while some seemed to be on guard at the mouths of the passages which led to the most secluded portions of the palace, perhaps the suite of rooms set apart for their much-loved queen. But after the first dazzling effect of the light had passed away, every citizen of the hitherto peaceful state boiled over with wrath. Clearly they had been working, like the ancient Jews, "with hammers in their hands and javelins by their sides." Never was army mobilized so quickly! While some hurried the young and feeble into the shelter of the citadel, and others ran to call up the troops from the rear and give the alarm through the rest of the city, the remainder, several thousands strong, poured forth to offer battle to the invaders, and, apparently without generals or captains, every warrior with the same object dashed at us, and, utterly regardless of life and limb, sought to fasten on our flesh and clothes. What a grand history would lie before the two-legged nation that could boast of such a people! Was ever any Roman braver than the ant who charged up my boot, and fixed his jaws so firmly into the calf of my leg, that when I pulled at him, he parted with his head rather than let go his hold? The small patriots, into whose town we had broken on this occasion, were certainly the stronger party, and I and my followers fled before them, ignominiously turning to work in another place, until, venturing back in half an hour, I found the whole colony had moved away with all the honours of war to the neighbouring jungle, where I sincerely hoped they were able to found a second city.

Another disadvantage of making a dug-out road through the jungle is the curious fact that the newly turned earth gives the coolies fever with great certainty. Man after man had to strike work and go back to the "lines" as we toiled each day. Perhaps it was owing to the chill which hangs about the moist fresh mould, or to the stores of decomposed vegetable gases which are set free. Certainly even I, who was yet too fresh from England to get actual fever, often felt very sick and uncomfortable as the work proceeded.

But, in spite of all these difficulties, we forged ahead gradually—every day adding a hundred yards or so of neatly smoothed road, fit for *bandy* traffic—by the side of the sparkling Manalora, with the thick forest trees of the upper bank arching over and shading us from the midday sun, and creepers and rattan canes hanging in graceful festoons from tree-top to tree-top. They never flower, these climbing plants, or not in a demonstrative way, and in this I was considerably disappointed, as "flowering creepers" formed one of the most important items in my old ideas of tropical vegetation.

One evening, when sunset came and relieved us from our toil, I congratulated myself on having added a hundred yards of roadway to the total. Truly it was somewhat soft, and, though as smoothly raked as a flower-bed, it would be necessary to let it settle and consolidate before it would be fit for heavy use. But fate was unkind, and on arriving next morning we found the whole of our work of the day before in a most terrible mess, broken away in places and full of great holes. A closer examination showed that two or three elephants had been down during the darkness to inspect the operations, which it is quite possible they had been watching during the daytime; and, finding the surface smooth and pleasant, had been promenading up and down, sinking their enormous feet deep into the fresh mould at every step, and in places bringing down the sides with a run. It was interesting, as showing the inquisitive and meddlesome nature of the animals, but woeful from a coffee planter's point of view.

On Sunday, the day being fine and hot, I and "Charlie" agreed to take our guns and call upon S——, of Nillacothy estate. So after breakfast we armed and booted ourselves, and walked over to Polyampara, shooting a couple of jungle fowl by the way, which we carried forward to replenish our friend's larder. Midway, after dropping in on W——, who was as usual smoking a big cheroot with his feet on the back of a neighbouring chair, we passed through the strong-grown ten-year-old coffee of his estate, and, gaining the jungle again, continued our walk down a rough "trace," or boundary line, made by lopping the underwood but leaving the big trees standing, until we came to a place where the stem of a huge fig tree, blown down in some previous monsoon and falling from bank to bank of the Manalora, formed a natural bridge. This we crossed with the help of some notches cut in the upper part to make it a little less slippery, and on the other side found ourselves in our friend's "nursery," and soon after met him in all the glory of clean Sunday clothes and newly blacked boots.

Of all the estates which I had seen, this one seemed to me most typical, and best to fulfil my ideas of what a coffee garden should look like. It was much more picturesquely situated than any of the others, the ground more broken and rocky, and the young plants, which were set out in beautifully even rows from jungle to jungle, were neither so old nor ragged as those of the more northerly plantations, nor so juvenile and straggling as our own. Then the "lines" were neatly built in two rows on the crown of a little hillock, with a "writer's" bungalow at one end, and looked many times more healthy and pleasant than those amongst which my lot was cast.

Crossing the estate, our host led us through the jungle, where, for the first time in India, I saw a real flowering forest tree, covered with white camellia-like blossoms, which the light breeze shook down on us, as we passed beneath, in a sweet-scented shower, and then a little further on we emerged into the open. After two months of the close dim jungle, and the small clearings walled in all round by dense belts of trees, it would be difficult to describe my feelings of joy on getting upon a wide grass plateau three thousand feet above the sea, with a cool wind waving the long lemon-grass and invigorating our enervated frames. The prospect was so delightful I sank down on a rock and expressed my intention of remaining there all day, but S—— assured us there were better things higher up; so we continued our climb till we scaled a steep bank, and reached the verandah of a neat little bungalow, with white chunam walls and thick thatch roof, standing close under the towering grey cliff which gives it its name. Here we breakfasted, and listened to our host's stories of the animals which roam at night round his lonely cabin.

He tells us there is a pool a hundred yards higher up, on the northward side of the mountain, which is a favourite place with the elephants, and many a night he has been unable to sleep for the noise they make bathing and trumpeting to each other. Sometimes a leopard comes down, and carries away chickens, or a goat, if there is one about. As for ibex and sambour deer, they are always plentiful, but wild. Our host had a dog with a touch of deerhound in him, and seeing the other day a sambour and its fawn feeding by the elephant pool, where there is some level grass, he slipped the dog at them, and witnessed an interesting spectacle. The old sambour could have escaped easily, but the young one could not go so fast, and the dog soon came up to them, and would have made short work of the little creature, but for the resolute way in which the mother kept off its attacks, walking round and round, and gradually edging towards the friendly shelter of the nearest jungle, which when once gained, they had it all their own way, and the dog came back crestfallen and beaten. Despite these splendid opportunities for sport, S—— does not hunt, for two good reasons—because he has no rifle, and because he says he is too near-sighted to shoot straight.

After tiffin, the prospect of a magnificent view over the plains tempted us to climb the lowest spur of the precipice, about two hundred feet above the bungalow; and with our guns slung on our backs, we scrambled up, getting a footing among the veins of quartz, which run at all angles in the face of the rock, and look as if they might hold gold; also grasping the roots of grasses, which occasionally gave way, and threatened to send us rolling back to the bungalow. But the highest possible point once gained, we were well repaid for our exertions. The Nillacothy Rock, the summit of which is four thousand feet above the sea, presents two perpendicular faces—one towards the upland valley of the coffee estates, which is, perhaps, three hundred and fifty feet above the Manalora stream, and forms a most conspicuous object from every part of the "district;" and the other face, looking due northward, is on the very edge of the ghaut, and has a sharp fall of between eight hundred and a thousand feet—a magnificent drop, which can be seen from the railway carriage windows far away on the Palghaut line. Standing as we did at the corner, we had a view such as the eagles only enjoy, and as extensive as the eye could take in. The lowlands stretched away beneath us in a vast chequered plain, mottled with tawny paddy-fields and palm clumps, every little village—and Wallenghay nearest of all—showing up a tiny grey patch with a framing of emerald green, which we knew to be the broad-leaved bananas in the gardens round the straw-thatched huts. The *tanks* caught the sunlight and sparkled, and where the streams were broken up and led among the growing rice by numerous channels, there was a fine lacework of silver threads. We might have seen Calicut on the Indian Ocean, and Madras itself on the Bay of Bengal, if our eyesight had been sufficient; but we could only look east and west till the plains mingled with the sky, and northward across the great Indian hollow to where the Wynnaad Ghauts and Neilgherries rose in lofty ridges at an elevation even greater than our own.

As we lay in the long grass, buried in silence and admiration, which life in our deep jungles made all the sincerer, there was a harsh cry, a rush of wings, and a black eagle came down like a thunderbolt from behind—perhaps to see if we were dead and fit to be eaten—but, shifting his course when within twenty yards of us, he went sailing away over the jungle below with widespread wings. The temptation was irresistible. My rifle was unslung, raised, and fired in a second, but the only result was one big pinion feather cut out of the eagle's wing, which came fluttering and twisting down to the ground, while the owner continued his course unmoved. Had I used the more accurate "express," instead of the short carbine that lay nearest to hand, the result might have been different, and the noble bird who now reigns supreme on those mountain-tops, the terror of all young deer and ibex kids, might surmount nothing higher than a hat-stand! Fate hangs on such little things!

We noticed in descending that the ground about a small nullah was pounded into clay by the feet of many animals who came there nightly to drink. There were the great plate-like "spoor" of the elephants, with the marks made all round the front edge by the hard horny toenails, the round cowlike prints of bison, and the finer pointed hoof-stamps of the sambour deer, of which S—— showed us how to make a guess at the ages by noting the spread of the heel and the size of the gap between the points of the hoof. There were also signs of the hill ibex in abundance, and the tiny little imprints made by hog-deer. When I first saw these—they are no larger than a dint made by the little finger of a man's hand—I passed them over, but my companion called attention to them, and, stooping down, I made out the clear impress of the tiny hoofs. Getting back down this much-spoored nullah was a regular scramble, in which we were continually falling over logs and masses of hidden rocks, or had to force our way by sheer strength through the tangled reeds and rushes. "Charlie," whose toe still pained him occasionally, being the shortest of the party, was quite hidden many times, and his whereabouts only to be guessed by the waving of the rank herbage. But though we beat right down the stream to where it runs by S——'s door, we put up no game, and only succeeded in making ourselves so thoroughly tired that we were glad to accept our host's pressing invitation to stay the night; and after dinner and the usual smoke, we rolled ourselves up in rugs till we looked like Egyptian mummies, and slept soundly on the floor till the first daylight appeared.

I had not been so cold as I was that next morning at daybreak for a long time. The rain was coming down after the Scotch fashion in thick drizzle, and light fleecy clouds were wandering about the hillside like flocks of masterless sheep. Some of these little clouds, which seemed to be the fragments of larger ones driven against the hillside and broken up, came floating across the grass outside and slipping amongst the trees almost as though they were animated creatures, and if I had possessed any feeling in my nose or my finger-tips, the scene would have been very enjoyable; but, as it was, my whole attention was given to helping S—— with a brew of coffee, which very interesting operation we performed ourselves, as the "boy" was stupefied by the temperature and quite useless. I asked our entertainer if the elevation of his bungalow—some 3500 feet above the sea level—did not make him secure against the attacks of jungle fever, but he said, "Nothing of the sort." Undoubtedly no fever could possibly be caught up here; but then, wherever the planter's bungalow may be, he must spend all the daytime in the valleys low down amongst the coffee, and he is sure to contract fever there, sooner or later, and bring it home with him. Of course a high-built bungalow is much better than a low one, as the air is purer, the planter is kept in better health and spirits, and his attacks of fever pass off sooner; but it is certainly not a complete safeguard. I pointed out to him that our mutual friend L—— had spent a year at Varlavachen, across the valley, at an elevation of three thousand feet, and had never had fever as long as he was up there; but this, S—— believed, was because he was fresh from England and did no work lower down. It was hard work and exposure to the sun and chills—necessities of a planter's life—which brought on fever, and he said the only thing to be done was to brave it out, and in course of time one would get rid of one's liver and become acclimatized—or find a quiet bed in the jungle, which would at least free you from the need of ever working again.

Breakfast over, we said good-bye and descended into the valley. The rain came down ceaselessly—heavier even in the coffee estates than on the open hillsides—and on getting back to Pardagherry bungalow I found there was no work being done, the wet keeping the coolies shivering in the "lines," whence thin jets of blue smoke wound upwards and hung under the thick roof of leaves. So the rest of the day was spent indoors, reading, writing, and smoking, huddled up in a woolly ulster, which I wore with as great satisfaction as I had done not many months before in the Scotch highlands.

The next day was much the same. We attempted to muster the coolies in a heavy downpour at half-past five in the morning, but none turned out except the maistries and two or three old women; so we gave these half pay and dismissed them to the "lines," getting on as best we could, till the evening relieved us from our desperate state of *ennui* and enabled us to turn in.

The succeeding day was brighter, and the coolies mustered in force, wishing to get something to their credit before pay-day came round. So I and D—— divided them as usual, he taking his lot to the southern jungle, where he was marking out some new clearings, and I proceeding to put the finishing touches to the new road, which had now got past the intervening forest and emerged into the Dewan's estate, through which we had made arrangements for carrying it.

Walking down through the mist, still thick under the trees, I suddenly came upon the marks of a very large old bison, probably a "rogue," the footmarks being five or six inches across, and so fresh that the water was still welling up into them. Having nothing with me but an umbrella, I proceeded cautiously along, expecting to see the great animal loom through the fog every minute, or to hear him snort and charge back on me; but he kept ahead, and after a few hundred yards went down to the river and forded it, the water being still disturbed and muddy when I got to the margin. That these animals are sometimes dangerous, more often, in fact, than any other creature in these jungles, there was sufficient proof even on the estate. As one came down the "Top Entrance Road" through the belt of trees on the way to the settlement, there was a gloomy spot, always damp and chilly in the brightest weather, where a road wound up from the Manalora side of the ridge and joined our main thoroughfare at right angles. This was called "Bison Gap," and one of the trees standing a little way back had a rough cross cut into the bark to mark the place of a bad accident. When R—— first opened the estate, some time before I joined, this was a very wild locality, in undisputed possession of the elephants and big game of all sorts. Especially there was one rogue bison of whom many stories were told. He was known by having uneven horns, one tending upwards and the other downwards, and this made him particularly bad tempered, so that the coolies were in constant dread of meeting him.

One misty evening they were streaming home after the day's work, with their tools on their shoulders and a maistry in front, when they came to this ill-omened spot, and there, in front of them and rubbing his horns, was the great terror of the jungle, his huge black body completely blocking the path and keeping the coolies from their homes. The natives threw down their loads and hid themselves behind trees, the maistry behind the trunk which now bears a cross; but as the bison did not move, and seemed sulkily determined to stay in the path, he came forward after a few minutes, and, waving his turban, tried to frighten the beast away. It was a fatal attempt, for the animal suddenly roused itself, and, resenting this familiarity, gave a deep snort and charged the unfortunate man. He fled to the shelter of the tree, but just as he was getting behind the bison rushed upon him and dashed him heavily against the trunk. It is to be hoped that this rendered him insensible, for the coolies from their surrounding| retreats saw the savage animal pound him against the stem of the tree and amongst the roots, till he bore no resemblance to the human form; and then the beast, with its forehead drenched with blood and shreds of torn clothing on its horns, turned and stalked away into the thickest of the jungle.

But the poor maistry was soon avenged. At that time R—— had as "cook boy" an old Madras shikarry, and the very next day the coolies brought him word that the same animal was standing under a clump of bamboo, just above what is now No. 3 clearing; so, borrowing the old long Snider—a percussion gun which forms R——'s whole battery—he loaded it with powder and two bullets, and then set out alone to interview the bison. He found him as the coolies had said, and, crawling for an hour and a half on his hands and knees, got close up to him. I believe that the bison brought his fate on himself by his sulky indifference to the presence of human beings as long as they did not molest him; for the shikarry seems to have crept within a dozen yards, when, resting the muzzle of the gun on a rock, he aimed at the broad heavy forehead of the bull, and when he pulled the trigger and the smoke cleared away, the bison was lying dead on the rocks. The company's agents at Calicut very properly gave him a reward of ten rupees for this plucky deed.

CHAPTER XIV.

JUNGLE SOCIETY.

WHEN the weather grew drier, we turned our attention in a new direction, and *pegging*, *lining*, and *pitting* (all very important operations in the coffee planter's list) took up the chief part of our time.

The first is an extremely tedious operation, and one which the new hand will find very difficult in thick jungle. It consists in marking out the exact spots where every coffee bush is to stand on a plot of woodland which has been only slightly cleared, and has been traced out by the trees, on what will eventually be the margin, having been notched, or the leaves and rubbish scraped away. Supposing the space thus enclosed is ten acres in extent, and putting the coffee at six feet apart in each direction, there will be room for about twenty-two thousand plants; and as the position of each has to be accurately noted with a peg stuck into the ground, the labour can be imagined.

The necessary number of pegs having been split some time before and piled in heaps along the future clearing, the planter goes to work with his men, and the first thing to be done is to strike a base line right across the ground. To do this, a "level" mounted on a pointed staff, and two men with other staffs painted red and white, are needed, besides trustworthy coolies, who have hold of the opposite ends of a long fifty-foot rope, divided into six-foot lengths by tags of tape or coloured rag, as well as numerous attendants with armfuls of pegs to mark the site of the holes to be dug. The Englishman then, starting from the edge of the future belt, directs the two line coolies to hold the rope taut in the direction which the instrument tells him is straight for the opposite side of the marked-out space, and as soon as this is satisfactorily accomplished the coolies stick in pegs directly under each six-foot mark. Then the line is taken forward again to the last peg, and another set measured off. This is all very well when the ground is clear and there are nothing but big trees to obstruct the view—a sure sign that the soil is good for coffee—but occasionally there are clumps of bamboo, thickets of thorny bushes, or, worst of all, deep nullahs; and these offer immense obstacles, not so much to the first or base line as to the subsequent ones, and if the planter's temper is at all quick, here is the work which will try it to the utmost. My companion, who was rather uncertain in that respect, gave himself several attacks of fever in trying to set the base lines out properly in the new clearings, and used to make it lively for the poor coolies, who were really not to be blamed, and had to get through places with bare legs which we ourselves did not much fancy, though heavily booted and clothed.

We came to one place, while working together, where the rocks, cropping up close to the surface, left not enough soil to support many large trees, though there was a dense patch of thicket upon it, the growth of centuries, all matted together into a wild tangle. It may perhaps be thought that it was useless to "peg" out such a place, as it could never be planted; but the truth is, every bit of a clearing must be measured off in order that the proportion between the succeeding lines shall be ascertained, and so a way had to be made through the thorny labyrinth at all costs. The billmen dived in, and by vigorous exertions cut out a sort of large rabbit-run; but when they were in the centre, it was not possible to keep them straight, and three or four times they diverged to the right or left, and their hard-won drives had to be abandoned. At last I called out for D—— and the compass, and he crawled in on hands and knees, making remarks about the thorns, at every yard, more noticeable for their emphasis than grace, and then we progressed better. Before we got through the thicket, D—— at one place was on his knees, bending over the instrument, and I close behind, when I saw a long grey snake, which I recognized at once as the broad-headed and very deadly tic-polonga—the worst reptile in these jungles —hanging down from a bush, with its ugly jaws within a short distance of the back of my companion's neck. He did not notice it, and the probabilities were it would strike him directly he made a move; so, taking a stick from a coolie, I crawled up, and, getting within striking distance, made a blow which killed the snake, and considerably astonished D——, who, however, expressed his gratitude very handsomely, considering his frame of mind, when he saw his dead enemy.

Another sort of obstruction which makes "lining" difficult in unfelled jungle are the deep and rocky watercourses or nullahs. It does not do to stretch the measuring line straight from bank to bank, as that would distort the position of subsequent lines, but it has to accurately follow the fall of the ground, which would be an easy matter with trained English labourers, but with such poor thick-headed natives as ours proved a matter of great difficulty, and took up much time. For my part, I never could understand the necessity of having the lines of coffee plants so exactly even that, from any point in the clearing, one can look up four neat roads only terminated by the belts of forest; but it is the custom, and is rigorously insisted upon in most estates, though probably it consumes more time and money than its few advantages repay.

At this work, with very little intermission or variety to enliven the monotony, the first two weeks of December were passed; and as the weather became hotter in the jungles every day, people at home were doubtless building up larger and larger fires, and making preparations for Christmas festivities. Although the English skies may be dull, and but little of the sun to be seen, yet even on the Indian hills we at this season were not in continual brightness, for the forests were often buried in mists and vapours all day, which made it decidedly cold and uncomfortable; or if the sun did come out, the wet jungle steamed like a damp blanket, and the heat was oppressive and unwholesome. In the morning I found it pleasant to go to work in a wrap of some kind, which was most welcome up to about ten o'clock, then the influence of the sun began to be felt, and the forests had nearly finished steaming for the day. After that hour an umbrella was more suitable in the clearings, or when superintending the work on new roads, etc. But the planter's toil is so varied and rough that he has to take things very much as he finds them, and adapt himself as he may to the most rapid changes, from cold moist shade to the burning glare of the midday sunshine.

Occasionally a little adventure would happen to

enliven the sameness of the work, and give us something to talk about at breakfast. For instance, one morning I was "pegging" in a fifteen-acre clearing on the side of a very steep hill, and had taken up my stand on the broken stump of a tree struck by lightning a few years before, in order to get a better view of some coolies who were working in a nullah below. After staying there some time and "pitching into" the coolies in the liveliest language I could think of, I got down and went higher up the hillside, to see what another gang were doing. It was a fresh morning, and a strong breeze, though we could feel nothing of it below, was obviously blowing up above, we could see, from the way in which the trees were swinging about. Hardly had I gone twenty yards up the hillside when a groan echoed through the aisles of the forest, and the coolies, who seemed to know what it meant, fled right and left. Then there was another and another such sound, and I saw a great tree, a hundred feet high, tottering. I was so close, I could hear the strong fibres in the stem snapping with a sound like pistol-shots, and then came a crack—the bark parted all round, and slowly the huge tree toppled over, bringing down another that was lashed to it with rattan creepers, and leaving a great gap in the forest roof, through which the sun shone brightly, the giant trunk falling with such a rush and thud to earth as made the ground vibrate. The stump on which I had been standing a few seconds before was cleft into three huge splinters by one of the branches; and all round, for a space of twenty yards, lay a mass of broken timber and leaves, affording us considerable occupation when it became necessary to continue the "pegging."

Besides trifling adventures of this sort, on Sundays we got an occasional chance of visiting our neighbours, as we called them, though the nearest was a long way off. On one occasion, Sunday being bright and fine, all the coolies away at a weekly bazaar at the head of the ghaut, and D—— and Charlie having gone to spend the day with C. H——, of Polyampara, I and L—— made up our minds—by no means an easy thing after a hard week's work—to call upon F—— and his wife in their bungalow, the only house in the district I had not yet visited. So, bestowing more care upon our "get up" than we had done for a long time, we shouldered our rifles and marched down the well-known "Sircar" road as far as W——'s estate. Then, following the guidance of L——, we crossed a belt of jungle, where he once shot a hog-deer at fifty yards with a charge of No. 6 shot, and saw F—— shortly afterwards kill a python, eighteen feet long, as it lay curled up on a branch overhead, we next passed through an abandoned nursery of coffee plants, some for which there had fallen no use, and, being planted very close together, they had run up to a height of twelve or fifteen feet. Beyond this our climb commenced, and as we threaded our way mile after mile through the trees, the path rose rapidly by zigzags, at times so steep that we mounted up natural steps of rocks until we had little strength left in us, and I was just making up my mind to call a halt, when L—— shouted to me to come on—"one struggle more and we are free." So, with a final effort we scrambled up a bush-grown bank, and, emerging from the shade of the trees on the top, perceived we were at our destination. It would be difficult to describe my delight, after two months and more of "roughing it," to find myself suddenly in a beautiful English-looking garden, full of roses and geraniums, and verdant with green lawns of short grass, the like of which I had not seen since leaving England. And then, too, there was an English lady—a rare species in the jungle—standing under the verandah, with some small children playing about, who looked astonishingly white and rosy to me after seeing so much of the chocolate-coloured coolie babies. We were cordially welcomed, and being joined soon after by F—— and S—— from the opposite side of the valley, we sat down to a real English meal, at a table with a cloth and silver teapots and sugar basins, all of which deeply impressed us, while we ate all sorts of forgotten luxuries brought up from Madras and Bombay by our charming hostess.

Such days in the planter's life were only too short. When we had looked over all the new English books and read the magazines, we went out and walked round the "terrace." The bungalow occupies an unusually commanding position, being perched upon the very summit of a rock which rises out of the forest as a volcanic island from a green sea. The forest trees come nearly to the verandah on the western side, but on every other face the ground slopes down, and is covered with a dense growth of lemon-grass, which waves in the wind like an autumn cornfield in delightful England. To lessen the danger to the bungalow of being surrounded and engulfed in one of the hill fires which consume the long grass every year, F—— has made a garden all round the house, and then cut a broad smooth road in a complete ring about his castle; so that, were the fire to come up the hill, he would make his first stand against it there, and believes he could keep it at bay until burnt out. The constant necessity of having this wide terrace perfectly free from weeds and vegetation makes it delightful to walk upon, and we spent half the time circumnavigating the bungalow and admiring the view—truly a magnificent one.

When we stood in front of the house we looked down on our coffee valley, with all its scattered plantations, seeing W——'s white bungalow, with its two palms in the courtyard, and the little Swiss château of S——, where we had spent the previous Sunday, and far away to the southward Ootcha Mulla and the clearings of our own estate. Then, wandering round to the other side of the hill, we looked down another slope of the ridge, upon a wide uninhabited valley stretching away as far as the eye could see to the east and southward—a wonderful stretch of unopened forest land where the white man has rarely been—the home of the bison and elephant who have things all their own way down there. The green of the forest here was broken by widespreading patches of yellow and brown vegetation formed by great expanses of bamboos, which, according to the custom of that curious plant, had seeded during the last twelve months for the first time in sixty years, and then died out. The old generation far and wide was withered and dead, and underneath them the ground was emerald with the shoots of young plants. Some of the stems in this valley, I heard, are of enormous size, sixty or seventy feet high, and a foot thick.

I should have much liked to have investigated these wonderful solitudes, but it was not possible that day; so, after lingering on the pleasant hill-tops as long as we could, and taking tea with our hostess, we were reluctantly obliged to make a start back for our own encampment just as dusk was coming on. By the time we had left the last estates behind us, and had entered the Ootcha Mulla jungle, darkness came down suddenly and enveloped everything, so that we had one of the roughest walks I can ever remember. The track, which in daylight is a mere beaten footpath, with dense forest on either side, and encumbered by fallen trees and short stumps sticking up at every step, in the gloom was terribly difficult to find. Fortunately both of us were clad in white from head to foot, and by keeping together we could just make out our respective forms. First, L—— came a "cropper" over a stump, and bruised himself considerably. Then my turn arrived, and, without any apparent reason, I found myself rolling over among the dead leaves and weeds, but was up again immediately and proceeding cautiously forward. It was very ridiculous, and my companion laughed uproariously every time I came in collision with a log or stump; while, if there were any tigers in the neighbourhood, they must have thought us the most light-hearted of benighted travellers. After innumerable tumbles, at last we saw the twinkling lights of the natives' watch-fires gleaming through the trees below us, and soon after were seated comfortably at supper in our tiny hut, which, however, seemed a palace of light after the dense darkness of the jungle. Before we turned in, we declared that it had been a jolly day, and that F——'s bungalow was worth a longer and even rougher walk.

Another occupation of the coffee planter on a new estate is "pitting," of which there are several methods. Our own was to pit each clearing before the forest is felled, and for this purpose I used to start out each morning at daybreak, with perhaps two hundred men following in Indian file at my heels, and proceed to the jungles, which had been already pegged and marked out. Each coolie brought with him a mammôty, an axe for cutting roots, and a long iron bar pointed at one end and flattened out into a spud at the other, chiefly used for removing heavy stones and loosening the soil. We then went to work, in a long straight line so far as was possible, but to get the hands into any sort of order in heavy jungle is much more easy to talk of than to effect, as it is not easy to see more than ten men at a time, and each man wants to work where the ground is softest and there are fewest roots. The daily task of each is supposed to be twenty-five pits of regulation size, and the superintendent has to see this properly done. Perhaps he places a mark where each man begins, at the last pit of yesterday's work, and then goes to the other end of the line, half a mile away. When he returns, he is surprised and pleased to find the first men have already finished half their tasks, but on investigating he sees the "mild Hindoos" have moved his pegs back so as to include ten or twelve of yesterday's pits, and then he grows wrathful, and perhaps, if his temper be hasty, "pitches into" the worst offenders. At another place a poor famine-stricken wretch, who has hardly strength to lift his mammôty, has scraped a few wretched holes scarcely big enough to plant a seed in, and much too small for a coffee bush, and the exertion having proved too great, he is lying shivering on the ground in the cold stage of fever.

What is the unhappy Englishman to do? If he maintains strict discipline and insists on the full task, the coolie cannot do it; or attempts it and dies, and is buried himself in a hole in the jungle. I am sure most planters would follow the more humane course, and deal gently with the sick and feeble, if they were working on their own land; but when working with the money of much-respected "shareholders," and with a vigilant agent on the look out to see where every anna goes, the superintendent is obliged by his official position to put humanity on one side and look at everything from a business point of view. Besides the coolies who scamp their allotted tasks from sickness, there are many others who give a vast amount of trouble by their stupidity in making pits out of the straight line, or just too small to pass muster—the regulation size being two feet deep by eighteen inches square, measured across from the level of the surface of the ground. The holes should have right-angled corners, as experienced planters believe that if a tree be set in a circular hole, the roots follow the limits of the soil which has been disturbed, and become as much "pot-bound" as though they grew in stone jars; but when the pit is square the roots grow into the angles, and, finding themselves faced by walls of earth, are obliged to penetrate them and spread into the surrounding soil.

This sort of work took up my whole attention during the week before Christmas, and it was impossible to call it enjoyable; in fact, it was dreadfully monotonous. By the time the pits began to be numbered by thousands, the ground also presented a curious aspect—something as if the jungle had been overrun by monstrous land-crabs, which had dug out their underground houses in every direction; but the walking was better than usual, owing to the pits being in straight lines and the timber still standing, instead of cumbering the ground, as it did in the planted clearings. I also found these holes were very productive traps for all sorts of strange creatures—beetles and lizards especially—though once or twice I have seen small snakes imprisoned in them. Early in the morning nearly every excavation is tenanted, often by insects and animals having natural antipathies to each other, and the results are fierce battles, in which all the combatants fight bravely, as they seem to know there is no escape for the vanquished. The lizards especially, whose wandering propensities often lead them down the crumbling sides of these pitfalls, contend like bull-dogs, and I have watched several well-sustained combats, in which the pugnacious creatures bit and kicked and shook each other with the greatest fury; but when either of the combatants was getting much the worst of it, I generally exercised my authority by suddenly seizing him by the tail and drawing him out of his arena, putting the little beast, to cool down and recover his senses, on the neighbouring moss.

Anything which breaks the current of such monotonous work as "pitting" is welcome, so it may be guessed with what satisfaction I received a pleasant note from Mrs. F——, to say that a picnic had been organized for Christmas Day at a waterfall close to S——'s bungalow.

When that day came, having started the coolies to work, I put on my full "war-paint," *i.e.* new white clothes, top-boots, and a sun helmet; and, mounting the estate pony, set off for W——'s. By the time I got there, there were several horses in the courtyard, being led about by their syces; and giving mine to the ghorawallah, who had been running behind me with my rifle, I joined the party in the verandah, which consisted of all the English settlers of the district (with the exception of D——), some eight gentlemen and one lady, and we soon made a move forward; the provisions, borne in baskets on the heads of coolies, leading the way, and we following more leisurely. Mrs. F—— was carried in a chair lashed to two strong bamboos and supported by four picked natives, who seemed very proud of their duty; indeed, their headman, an old Canarese maistry with clean shaven head and snowy waistcloth, nearly went frantic in his endeavours to make himself useful to the "mem sahib." He carried a small axe in his hand and ran on ahead, and whenever he saw a creeper or rattan cane likely to get in the way, hurled himself upon it and cut it into small pieces, and then salaamed and scudded on again. In this way we proceeded towards Nillacothy Rock, following the winding path down W——'s "trace," which, by the way, he had had cleared of leaves and sticks for the first time in five years, in order to make the journey smoother for the English lady. We crossed the Manalora by a fallen fig tree—

an undertaking which Mrs. F—— faced with great courage, though she could scarcely have felt comfortable in her swinging-chair so high above the water—and then, passing through the Nillacothy estate, took our way to a beautiful spot, where a mountain torrent came foaming down from the hills, and, after forming a deep still basin, went on down a shady avenue of forest trees, towards the valley. Here we found the cloth already spread, and several scarlet-turbaned servants busy boiling water in a kettle and making the food ready.

It was indeed a beautiful spot for this wild banquet of ours—a little tinkling waterfall above, the still deep pool at our side, and overhead tall, graceful, green tree-ferns, shading us from the sun and completely roofing in our dining-room. Lower down its quiet vista, the stream flowed amongst rocks and little sandy beaches, where a couple of grey-and-white stints were busy searching for insects among the stones, paying no more attention to us than if we had been a company of the elephants on whose haunts we were trespassing. But besides the little harmless birds and elephants, this was a noted spot for tigers; and as the sudden appearance of one of those striped brutes, as an unbidden guest, would have been worse than the proverbial wasp which puts in an unwelcome visit at English picnics, Mrs. F—— begged me to fire my rifle to frighten anything that might be in the neighbourhood, and the woods and rocks accordingly ran at the report with a hundred echoes. Then we sat down to a pleasant meal, booted and spurred as we were, and the stores of good things which inhedged our amiable hostess crumbled down and disappeared before our attacks; the last of all to vanish being a mountainous sponge-cake, with sugar ramparts and turrets, which we ate like schoolboys.

But the happiest hour must even end, and when

the gentlemen had smoked their cheroots and finished their last story, a move homeward was proposed just as it was growing dusk, and we walked slowly down the narrow path, followed by the servants, who had industriously finished off everything eatable and drinkable while we chatted, and so brought back with them nothing but china and empty bottles.

Darkness descended before we reached W——'s, and poor Mrs. F—— had a rough walk through the jungle and over the fallen trees, as her chair was useless, since the bearers could no longer keep together. Of course, we did what we could, but I fear we rather embarrassed her by the persistency with which we each tried to be useful. One helping hand is all very well in scrambling over a log, but seven or eight are too many.

The festivities, however, were not yet over, for W—— had prepared a big dinner for us, with a real turkey and a veritable tinned plum-pudding, of which we partook, and then sat up till late, drinking punch and champagne-cup in the verandah; so late, in fact, that it was "to-morrow" before we could think of separating. And then those amongst us who were furthest from their own places accepted W——'s and his assistant C. H——'s hospitality, and shook themselves down as best they might in hammocks and on sofas.

CHAPTER XV.

HARD AT WORK.

For the next few days I was entirely alone on the clearing, D—— being away picnicking at Palghaut, and L—— and "Charlie" visiting on other estates. It happened that at this time our pay-sheet contained the names of more men than had probably ever before been in these jungles since they first sprouted up, and certainly of the largest number under any one leader. My own personal coolies, living in the huts round me and within fifty yards, numbered a little over three hundred men, women, and children, and besides these there were two hundred "contract coolies" encamped in the middle of No. 1 clearing, making in all over five hundred natives under my orders. Such a condition of things is not usual on an estate of the size of ours, but we had been very desirous to force things on at a rapid pace, in order to get a large acreage planted during the season to tickle the imagination of the shareholders at home, and this accounts for the small army mentioned.

The "contract coolies" were not so much trouble to me as the others. They came up from Madura under their own maistries, and had been lodged in two parallel rows of huts among the coffee in the north-west clearing. Their chief headman was named Yaneta, a venerable, grey-bearded old patriarch, and every morning he stalked out with his flowing white garments and a long staff in his hand, to lead his men to the work, which he had contracted to finish by a certain date. The only concern which I had with this division was to visit them two or three times a day, and see that the operations—chiefly "pitting"—were conducted well and up to regulation standard. They also visited me in considerable numbers to be doctored every evening, and seemed to have considerable faith in my prescriptions, though I must confess these were more distinguished for simplicity than depth of medicinal knowledge.

But the coolies lodged around me, who belonged to the estate, were a great anxiety. First of all, they lived fearfully crowded—some three hundred human beings squeezed into five "lines" of low huts all close together, and only a few yards above the stream from which we got our drinking water. Inside, I am bound to say, the natives keep their huts very clean, and the constant pattering about of bare feet smooths and hardens the mud floors until they shine like marble; but, unfortunately, the tidiness ceases at their doorsteps, and beyond this their habits are horrible and knowledge of the plain rudiments of sanitation very slight. In fact, the "settlement" was in the most atrocious state of neglect. There had been no attempt at drainage or any necessary arrangements, and, having been inhabited by large numbers of the lowest orders of India for two years, its condition may be better imagined than described. I several times proposed to turn our attention for a spell to building better "lines" in a more elevated and healthy spot, but the reply was always to hurry forward the planting operations, and when those were completed to look after the coolies,—undoubtedly the right plan to follow when the first object is to get a dividend as big and as soon as possible. This is the worst of the best of "Corporations,"—they have no souls to be saved and no bodies to be kicked. So there we were still, and as the weather grew hotter, the danger of an epidemic became greater. Already there were five or six deaths every week, and the jungle round about was becoming thickly marked with the little hillocks which denoted the last resting-place of the poor wretches.

The coolies seemed to be very callous to suffering, and even to the death of their nearest relations. It may not be so in reality, but their conduct appeared such to an outsider like myself. For instance, one very hot day I appointed myself sanitary inspector, and went through the "lines" to see if anything might be done to render them more healthy. The coolies were at work, but from one hut rose a thin wisp of light blue smoke, not from a chimney, needless to say, but percolating through the thatch. Approaching to see who was inside, supposing it might be some sick person too ill to work, I went up to the low door, and, stooping down, looked in. There was a fearful odour about the place, and, accustomed as I had grown to strong smells, it was as much as I could do to keep my place. In the centre of the floor was a low stone fireplace, and a woman sat boiling rice in an earthen chatty over the embers. In the far corner lay something wrapped up in a coarse cumbley or shawl, and pushed as much out of the way as possible. Guessing this was the cause of the fearful taint, I asked, "What on earth have you got there?" "Oh," said the woman, as she squatted on her heels and leisurely stirred and tasted the conjee she was boiling, "that's my husband; he died five days ago." When I asked why she had not had him buried, instead of keeping him in such a shocking condition, she merely said she had been waiting for me to send men to do it. Half an hour afterwards, two men with mammôties were scraping a shallow hole in the jungle, under a sacred fig tree, and having made it about three feet deep, they rested from their work, when, after admiring the grave for a little time and rolling themselves a chew of betel-nut, they fetched the dead man and laid him in. The earth was replaced and trodden down, and there was an end of him; and when I read over his name at roll-call that evening and he did not answer, my pencil was drawn through it. So he had disappeared entirely—hopes, feelings, and ambitions (if he ever had any); Heaven only knows where all went to! Not even to his consort did his memory remain long green, for the same evening one of the men who had buried him seems to have hinted to her that there was room in his hut still vacant, and she moved across the next morning to his dwelling with all her worldly belongings—a palm-leaf mat to sleep upon, two clay chatties, some oil for her hair in an empty soda-water bottle, and two handsful of rice in an old piece of sackcloth. May her second matrimonial venture be more fortunate than her first!

And yet these coolies were undoubtedly honest, and very courteous and reverential towards their superiors. When I spoke to a maistry, very likely a venerable old grey-beard three times as old as I was, he listened in silence, and when I had done salaamed profoundly by placing both hands over his face and bowing down almost to the ground. At first this was rather overwhelming, but one soon gets accustomed to it, and it is undoubtedly agreeable to be bowed to. As Sancho Panza says, "It is good to know one's self master even though it be but of a flock of sheep." Then as to their honesty: my hut was always open—in fact, there was no fastening to the door at all, but a "bobbin;" and as my things must have seemed an immense wealth to so poor a people, they showed great forbearance in leaving them alone. Several times I returned from work and found my breakfast spread on the table, and three or four hungry and thin coolies crouched in my verandah—messengers from the other estates, or maistries—eyeing my provender and discussing the absent sahib's household arrangements, though no one ventured across the threshold. Perhaps my servant purloined a little that did not belong to him, but doubtless he looked upon all that as perquisites, and this habit is not entirely unknown in England.

As to heavier crimes and any violence towards myself or each other, it never seemed to enter the native head, as far as my limited experience went. Alone in the jungles, and surrounded by all these men, with a great number of rupees in the iron safe at my elbow, the keys of which hung at my belt, the wide woods around where any number of fugitives from justice might find safe and certain refuge, yet I slept every night as calmly and undisturbed as I might have done in the best guarded English town. Policemen or laws were practically unknown. Of course they existed, and I was still under the broad shield of English protection, but nothing was seen or heard of Government authority. Never since my arrival had I viewed an official of any kind, or paid "tribute" to any sircar.

Pleasant as it is to be thus "monarch of all you survey" for a time the novelty wears off by degrees, and then there comes a longing to speak one's own language and see white faces again, and one's thoughts wander away to the old home country, while the gorgeousness of the tropics grows dull and tedious, till one becomes regularly homesick—a state of mind very bad at the time, but in turn it passes off slowly.

On New Year's Eve, 1877, I was, I believe, the only Englishman in the district, every one else being away in the lowlands. Some day, when the Annamullies are a thriving corner of the Madras Presidency, with numerous English stations, good roads, and maybe a railway, it will hardly be believed that on the eve of that year of grace the sole representative of the dominant race was one "griffin," alone by himself in a "tooth-pick and brown paper" hut; and yet so it happened.

My attempts to commemorate the advent of the New Year were confined to making myself an extra good dinner—the usual way in which an Anglo-Saxon celebrates an anniversary of any sort. He does not discriminate, but banquets equally at the death of the old year or to hail the new one. In the evening he drinks to the departed, and in the morning the same bowl is full again to hail the new-comer. In Italy they would wave flags, or masquerade and march up and down the streets in gay throngs; the Frenchman would put on his best plumage and patronize the boulevards, supremely happy in staring and being stared at, and the American goes in for torchlight processions and visiting, but the Briton cannot get beyond dining. The red-letter days in his calendar ought to be marked with a saucepan and gridiron *saltire*-wise.

As may be supposed, I was scarcely sorry when my reign of undivided power came to an end on the return of the revellers from the lowlands. For to look after five hundred men and women in thick forest; to muster them, doctor them, and superintend everything; to be engineer, carpenter, cook, surveyor, horticulturist, doctor, accountant, and chief inspector of drainage in turn, with the thermometer varying from 40° to 90° every six hours, is exceptionally trying work.

Besides, we had at last finished "pitting" one clearing, and I was beginning to wonder what operations would come next, when D—— arrived, and, taking advantage of his superior experience, I consulted him. He at once said, that the next thing to be done, after having carefully dug these twenty-two thousand pits, was to fill them up again! At first, I naturally thought he must be joking, but the truth is the forest under which we had been so industriously scratching these holes for the last three weeks had now to be felled and burnt, and the sufficient reason for refilling the pits was that the valuable top soil, which contains the best nourishment, might be saved from the flames, which would bake it to a sort of brick—a result which should be avoided, if possible, yet which would assuredly happen if the "pitting" were delayed until after burning. So we set to work again, and with the same industry which we displayed before, filled up the holes far and wide, my chief care being to see that the top soil really went to the bottom of the pit, as the coolies are apt to scrape the soil in just as it lies. After the burn, we should be able to tell the position of each pit by the soil being a little higher over it than elsewhere.

Our larder had been replenished in a most satisfactory way by G. D——, of Polyampara. One night it happened that he was seated in the verandah of S——'s bungalow, meditating over an after-dinner cigar, when a sambour deer came out of the gloom of the woods by the stream, and, after sniffing the air, began to graze in the bright moonlight. D——, who is fond of venison and a good shot, stole into the house, and getting his rifle, reached a crag above the spot, unobserved; then, firing at his leisure at a hundred and fifty yards, the ball struck the sambour full between the horns, and it rolled over dead—a very creditable performance, as shooting by moonlight is much more difficult than in the daytime. The result of this shot was that for the next four or five days the whole district lived on venison, the animal being as large as a cow. I have tasted the best haunches of Scottish stags, the wild mouflon of Corsica, the thick-coated reindeer of Norway, and the sambour of the Indian jungles, and my choice is for the latter; but I say so with diffidence, as three months of the strong-fleshed Indian sheep had doubtless made me very ready to admire anything a wee bit more tender.

It is astonishing how little one sees of big game in these jungles, although their fresh footmarks everywhere show they are numerous and come forth regularly to feed in the open every evening. I fear a place like "the settlement," low down and surrounded by dense forest, was the worst situation that could be for a sportsman, as no view is obtained, and S—— on his wood-fringed grass plateau, or F—— on his hill-top, were in much better positions. Myself and L—— made a valiant attempt to climb the green Pardagherry

—the "hill of wonder"—one day in search of game with our rifles; but the jungle was absolutely impenetrable without billmen, and after reducing our clothes to a fearful condition, which cost us many hours of hard sewing to put right, we finally came to a standstill about half a mile from where the grass begins on top, and had to beat an ignominious retreat.

CHAPTER XVI.

BIRDS, BEASTS, AND SAVAGES.

WHEN the weather grew warmer in February, animal life became more varied in our jungles, and at our great elevation above the hot Indian plains there was much to remind me of the fauna and flora of England. Among the insects the most common was a small brown dragon-fly exactly resembling the English species. This was abundant everywhere in the openings of the forest and by every stream, but neither striking in colour nor peculiar to the country. Another familiar object was the bracken fern. On every estate more than two years old it grew in the greatest profusion. Poothpara, ten years old, was in parts hidden by it, and as I wandered through the dense ferns knee-deep, it was easy to imagine myself at home again on a Surrey hillside. The strange thing is, it never grows in the jungle or on the grass hills. There was not a root of it on our estate, or on the next youngest, Nillacothy; but on the others it was the most vigorous of weeds, and seemed to have risen by spontaneous generation, as it is almost impossible it should have been imported, and equally difficult to think the seeds or roots had lain dormant since the jungle first grew up.

Again, the commonest of our spring birds was a small species exactly resembling in habits and plumage the yellow wagtail so well known at home. I never passed along the stony bed of a nullah without disturbing two or three of these lively little birds, and they twittered as they flew, and jerked their slender tails in their search for insects and small beetles, after the fashion so familiar to any one who has given attention to English country sights and sounds.

Amongst the native butterflies, *Papilio polymnestor*, which was common during the damp weather at the close of the wet monsoon, almost disappeared when the dry weather came, and the very handsome black-and-gold *Papilio pompeius* took its place—an insect with wings five or six inches from tip to tip, looking more like a good-sized bird when flying than a simple butterfly. There is another beautiful species, known scientifically as *Hestia lynceus*, of even wider expanse of wing, and yielding in grace of flight and habits to none. I had left some specimens behind me amongst my collections in England, but what a poor idea they give of the insect in its native home! Truly in the "specimen" it is possible to admire their thin, semi-transparent, pearly white wings, marked out with numerous black velvet-like blotches, but "at home" the creature looked doubly beautiful. They are essentially water-loving, and the new road by the side of the Manalora was the best place to watch their love-play. Here the trees grow up in steep banks on either side, with the stream beneath and the blue sky overhead, and the *lynceus* revelled amongst the foliage on which their larvæ fed. Their habit was to lazily flap their wings while ascending to the tops of the trees, and then, keeping their wings spread out to the full on either side, they let themselves come slowly sailing down in wide circles, like large white blossoms, until just at the surface of the water, when they flutter over their own bright reflection for a moment, and again rise up to the tree-tops—a happy, lazy sort of way of spending existence, which I was generally reluctant to disturb, not being one of those naturalists so enthusiastic that they deem no creature has reached the goal of its existence until it has found a place in their cabinets.

It may be wondered how we obtained provisions and the necessaries of life, but the mode was really simple. Our ordinary everyday needs were supplied from Wallenghay, at the foot of the ghaut, and Palghaut on the railway. At each of these places we had a native agent, who received ten or twelve rupees a month, and sent up by estate-tapal or special coolie everything we ordered. Eggs were four for the value of an English penny—cheap, but very small; butter was also cheap, but, being made of buffalo milk, was white and tasteless. It came in little pats, wrapped up in banana leaves, in the tapal-basket from Wallenghay. Bread in small square loaves, mutton at twopence a pound, and vegetables, came from Palghaut. Sometimes, when there was a considerable demand, the butchers sent up an unfortunate brown sheep, which was slaughtered at one of the bungalows, and the meat distributed to "subscribers." No beef or pork could be had nearer than Ootocamund or Bangalore; and if we wanted any luxuries, such as cheese, sugar, tea, coffee, etc., we wrote down to the English stores, the price-lists of which we took care to have by us, at Madras or Calicut; and they were sent by train and coolie, which naturally made the cost heavy. It was possible to get wines and spirits from the native shopkeepers in the lowlands, but we sadly mistrusted them, and bought our beer, wine, and brandy from the coast. The bottled ale cost, by the time it reached my bungalow, about one and fourpence a bottle of the smallest size, and yet every one in the district drank it very freely. It is said that if the English left India to-morrow, all that would remain to mark their *raj* would be railways and mountains of empty bottles; and, though exaggerated, there is a good deal of truth in this. Even on our hills in every courtyard the beer-bottles stood in great heaps, and nobody utilized them except the wasps, which made nests in their necks. On the whole, the household expenses of the *chik-doree* are not heavy. If he spends more than usual for superfluities, he gets the necessities of life very cheaply. He pays no house-rent, as his bungalow almost always belongs to the estate. There are no taxes or licences; he dresses as he likes; and, as there are no shops, he cannot fritter away his income. There once lay a solitary rupee at the bottom of my pocket for three months; it was of no good to me, and I had overlooked its existence, and if it had not been for paying the coolies on Saturday evenings, I should have forgotten the very aspect of money, as all our transactions with the agents were settled every month by cheque. Living quite comfortably, with one servant, wines, beer, food, and everything else cost me between Rs. 100 and Rs. 125 per month; but one or two other assistants, who were more abstemious, did not smoke, and so on, kept their expenses within Rs. 100, which is less than £10 per month.

As the hot weather advanced and we began "to hate the sun," the grass hills dried and withered. Pardagherry especially changed its emerald livery for one of dusky brown, and we expected every day the junglemen would set fire to the grass, and then we should see a mountain in flames.

Some mention should be made of these Cardars, or forest-men. They seem to be allied to the Gonds of Central India and the Veddahs of Ceylon, but from what little I know of the three races, I think they are all slightly different in form and habits. These tribes are the wildest of the wild, and it is almost as hard to learn anything about their ways as to catch a leopard asleep. My first meeting with one of them happened when walking slowly down the new road; and my footsteps making no sound on the fresh earth, on turning a corner I suddenly came in sight of a small brown man fishing in the river below. He was sitting on his heels on a rock in the centre of the stream, with his back towards me, deeply intent upon watching a shoal of small fish playing about the line which hung from the long slender bamboo in his hand. He seemed to be of most diminutive size, not more than four feet six inches in height, and of the darkest brown colour, though well made and comfortably sleek of flesh; but the thing which gave him the most comical appearance was that his entire raiment consisted of a Scotch cap, which, there could be no doubt, had once hung in the shop-window of a booth in "Auld Reekie." How he came by it is difficult to say. It may have been dropped in the jungle, or found its way to him through some native bazaar, but there it was on the curly head of this otherwise entirely unclad savage. For a minute or so I admired him unobserved; but when I moved he caught the sound of my footfall, and, hastily springing up, gave one look at me; and, though I called out to him in Tamil and Hindustani to stop, he sprang lightly from rock to rock, and disappeared in the jungle on the far side. On another occasion, walking down this same road and turning a corner abruptly, I met three jungle-men face to face. They were very much frightened; but, as there was a steep bank on one side and a drop on the other, they had to walk by me. The tallest of them was not five feet high, so I towered over him by twelve inches. They were all as black as charcoal, with woolly heads and thick noses of a negroid type. They bore no weapons with them, but were carrying some sort of fruit, wrapped up in banana leaves, on their heads.

In the jungles we sometimes came upon traces of them, such as holes where they had been digging up the ginger roots, or their little sheep-like tracks over the dead leaves and in and out of the tree stems—the highways of this small, shy people! In one spot, under a wild fig tree, in the hot weather, I found the remains of one of their villages, consisting of three huts made by slanting sticks together and thatching them with boughs and grass; but the poor little structures had been almost destroyed by wind and rain, and no other traces of the builders existed except a few fire-blackened stones. But the relics of their work which impressed me most, were the wonderful ladders they made and left behind them when raiding the nests of the wild bees. Let us suppose a jungle-man, wandering about, finds a nest with a swarm in it high up, perhaps a hundred feet above the ground, on the branch of a forest tree.

He forthwith sets to work, and out of the stem of full-grown bamboos cuts himself several hundred pegs, wedge-shaped at one end and slightly notched at the other, taking care that the nodes of the bamboo shall be at the notched end of the peg, so that they shall be less liable to split when hammered. Then he waits until nightfall, when he proceeds, with some clansmen, to the tree and commences his dangerous climb. Numerous young saplings, of the thickness of a man's thumb, are cut down and trimmed from twigs, and some rattan canes split into thin fibres, and the party set to work. With a rude wooden mallet the first bamboo peg is driven into the tree-trunk, about two feet from the ground, and the butt of the first sapling is lashed to it with fibres. Then the "junglewallah" mounts on to this peg, which does not stick out from the tree more than four inches, and drives another in at about the height of his chest, and again fastens the slender sapling to it. Then, holding pegs, mallet, and fibres in his mouth or slung on his back, he again steps upwards in some marvellous manner, and another peg is driven, until the end of the first sapling is reached, when another is passed to him from below, and the wonderful ladder carried on. It must be remembered all this is done at the dead of night, for not even a Cardar could look down from so great a height as he presently reaches and so slender a perch without becoming giddy; and darkness is essential to prevent him seeing below. But it must also hinder his view of his work, and to my idea there could scarcely be a more uncomfortable position than standing on a clothes'-peg, with one's nose to the smooth trunk of a tree, a hundred feet or more above the ground on a dark and perhaps windy night, and, worst of all, nothing to hold to! But these little men do not seem to mind it much, and they generally reach the first branch in safety. After that it is comparatively plain sailing, though very often the ladders have to be continued again and again. When the nest is reached, the bees are driven out by smoke, and a rich reward then awaits the adventurer, who slings the honeycomb on his back and perhaps eats a little by way of refreshment, of which he must stand much in need, retracing his steps slowly downwards, feeling for each peg and holding on to the slight sticks lashed to them. Let us hope the bees permit him to descend in peace, and that he regains his friends and *terra firma* with ample spoil and no bones broken. Truly a fair booty makes a brave thief!

Work went on much as usual during this pleasant season, and by the time we got home each evening we cared to do little but sit still and smoke. Occasionally, however, we had some shooting, for which it was not necessary to go further than the verandah; for above our hut grew a far-spreading fig tree, the fruit of which seemed to be ripe about March. Then, every evening, flocks of a beautiful pigeon, with claret-coloured back and wings and yellow-green body, repaired to roost and sup amongst the figs. So we brought out our guns, and made as much noise as if we were at a warm corner of a covert on the 1st of October; but the tree being high, and the birds very small, we did little damage. It was wonderful how difficult it became to see the pigeons when once they had perched. Their under parts, being pale yellow, matched almost exactly with the slender fig-leaves; and sometimes, although there were a hundred of them in the tree, none of us could make out a single bird, until they began to move and feed, and send the figs rattling to the ground.

When darkness settled down, and we lay silent in our armchairs, with our cheroots gleaming and the guns idle at our sides, the flying foxes (squirrels they really are) sallied forth, and skimmed, with wide-spread limbs, from tree to tree. We watched for them, and when one crossed a patch of sky above, some one fired, and the silent forest re-echoed with the sound. But that was generally the only result, for the light in the evening was so misleading, I believe we often fired at the shadows of the animals. Yet, though dark at first, when the moon came out, and the silver light streamed down through the tree-tops and illuminated some things and threw others into deep shadow, the effect was most soft and beautiful. But, alas! we could not safely enjoy it, for with the moon rose the fever-mist, a death-cloud; it could be seen, a thin white web of transparent light, down among the rocks that lined the bed of the nullah; and we knew that behind that glistening veil hid the face of the fever and ague. So we retired to the poor protection of our hut, and lit the lamp and drew a red curtain over the doorway, in order, as well as might be, to shut out foreboding thought and make the best of the present.

For my part, although I had almost given up hopes of any really good shooting, yet, one day when work was slack, I arranged with L—— to start at daybreak the next morning, and explore the far side of the ridge at the end of which lies the Varlavachen bungalow. So at dawn he was in my hut and asking what we were going to look for. I proposed elephants, and it was agreed, although only my express rifle was serviceable, as there was no ammunition for the other guns. However, L——, who was a desperate smoker, took a tin of "bird's-eye" in one pocket, some sandwiches in the other, his beloved meerschaum in his mouth, and a revolver and hunting-knife in his belt, and declared he was ready to go anywhere. I was equally ready, and we started just as the sun was rising. But the sun gets up very quickly in India, and by the time we had threaded our way through the rocky clearing, now green with the guinea grass we planted two months ago, it was beginning to be very hot, and we were glad of the friendly shelter of a belt of jungle, through which we picked our way, noticing the hoof-prints of sambour and hog-deer everywhere, and the marks of a leopard or young tiger who had been out for a constitutional just before us. We were considerably startled by a troop of twenty large black monkeys, who fled from branch to branch at our approach, and made the forest resound with their cries.

Then into the sun again; and we were on the far side of the ridge, our view wandering over the wonderful Poothpara Thund. A most extensive view! It was impossible to look over this region without a feeling of satisfaction, in these days of dense populations, that there was still so much land to spare, and unopened even, for the myriads of India. For my part, I do not think we are within measurable distance of the time when the whole world will be a town—an idea dreadful to think of. Population undoubtedly increases to an alarming extent in every quarter of the globe, but an industrious calculator tells us the whole human race could still find standing room on the Isle of Wight, and while there are such tracts as these Indian hills to be opened and cultivated, we cannot call ourselves cramped for room.

Right away from our feet the great valley stretched as far as we could see, a vast expanse of undulating forest, as smooth and close as velvet, but formed in reality of countless thousands of mighty trees and labyrinths of creepers. One small hill—which looked so close, in comparison to the wide expanse, that it seemed one might walk to it in half an hour—my friend told me, was two days' journey away on horseback; so how far must it have been to the great wall of rocks which rose above the ocean of green jungle on the horizon to the south and westward? Even there our view did not stop, for those remote cliffs were crowned with wide fields of waving grass and darker patches of jungle and trees. I think I never saw a scene which impressed me more with its vastness and its silent, deep loneliness; for our glance passed over no habitation of men, only the fastnesses of the jungle-wallahs and the haunts of elephants.

It was a long time before we could continue our walk, so enchanting was the scene; and when we did, it was to talk of what effect the newly rediscovered gold mines of the Palghaut river would have on this district, and to speculate as to whether there was any gold up here. L—— feared the gold mining operations would be very bad for the plantations by drawing away all the labour and making everything too expensive; and, so chatting, we made our way along the side of the ridge.

But it was by no means easy progress. The tall dry grass grew up to our shoulders, and we looked more as if we were swimming than walking on hard ground. Nothing was to be seen of my companion but his face, his helmet, and his hand occasionally, making desperate efforts to part the grass stems in front, and at every few steps he suddenly disappeared altogether, having stumbled over a stone, in which I frequently kept him company. The broken limestone rocks were scattered everywhere amongst the grass roots, so that our way was as unpleasant as going a pilgrimage with unboiled peas in one's shoes, until we, by good luck, hit upon a new elephant trail, and then, the grass being trampled flat by the huge beasts, we could at least see where we were stepping. The trail we followed seemed to have been made by fifteen or twenty elephants marching in single file the night before, and L—— was all hot to catch them up and get a shot with the rifle I carried; so we made the best pace we could, pushing through thickets of dwarf date-palm—which, by the way, only grow on these open hillsides—scrambling often on hands and knees over bare ledges of rocks, where the heat of the mid-day sun above and the radiation from the hard surface nearly roasted us. My companion would give me no rest, but led me on, in and out of nullahs, over rocks, through thickets, until the trail entered the jungle on top of the ridge, and a few minutes' more hard scrambling brought us to a beautiful bit of green-sward under a patriarchal fig tree, from which many creepers hung down in graceful festoons, and gay little butterflies hovered about in the stray gleams of sun-shine which found their way through the thick green roof of foliage. It was one of those pleasant spots always associated with woodland countries, but which, when found in India, artists sketch and take home to the old country with them, and say, "Behold the tropics!" whereat the stay-at-home "Britisher" is much edified, and concludes every part of India is as pleasant.

Here the elephants had been taking their noonday rest, for the ground was trampled down and many branches broken, etc. In fact, it may have been our own footsteps which frightened them away; they certainly had not been gone long. But it was useless and dangerous to follow them into the thick jungle; so we let ourselves cool down, and then regained the grassy hillside and continued our swimming walk. At last we found the work was too hard under such a powerful sun; so we camped a little after midday by the side of a tree-grown watercourse, and proceeded to make our modest tiffin. The spot was a very likely one for tigers—just the kind of place they choose to spend the hot hours in—and hardly had we sat down, and I was spreading some mustard with scientific accuracy on a mutton sandwich, when my companion called out suddenly, "Look sharp!" Down went the sandwich into the dust, and I sprang up, gun in hand. Some big animal undoubtedly broke away from the nullah, and came up through the long grass at us, for we saw the grass wave and part before it like water under the bows of a ship in full sail, though we could not see the beast itself. But when it was within thirty yards of us, L—— suddenly raised the revolver he carried, and fired, and the animal forthwith changed its course and gained the jungle without showing the colour of its hide. Perhaps it was fortunate for us it did so, as there was no open ground in front, and consequently a snap shot would have been all I could have got.

Very little proper shooting can be done in this way. We started too late in the day. Had we been by this nullah and up a tree at daybreak, we should have stood a good chance of a shot or two; but all the big game—more careful of themselves than such reckless young Englishmen as we—creep into the cool jungle when the sun grows hot, and leave the hillsides to the lizards. We saw, however, plenty of traces of game; the most numerous being the little holes scraped by bears when searching for roots and, as I expect, the nests of honey-making ground bees; and also the places where sambour deer had been lying out under the willow-like wild gooseberry tree, the fruit of which is their special delight. At the margins of the nullahs, bison, wild dog, and elephant "spoor" of all ages was numerous; so the country was clearly "gamey."

We finished our repast in peace, and took a delightful siesta, lying at full length under the shade of the trees, and gazing over the mighty forests, through the curling blue smoke of our pipes—a "bird's-eye" view, perhaps I might dare to say,—till the sun began to fall low in the sky, and then we gathered up our traps, and proceeded to retrace our steps through the long grass—a most toilsome and tedious process, which set us thinking how it might be overcome. In a little time a bright idea occurred to me, and calling out to L——, who was up to his eyes in dry herbage, I proposed, as there did not seem to be anybody but ourselves on the hills, to set fire to the grass. No sooner said than done. My companion was on his knees in a moment with a box of matches, and as soon as he had put a light into the grass, a bright crimson flame shot high into the air, and we turned and ran for our lives to windward. I never saw anything burn as that hill did. In half a minute the fire was twenty yards wide and utterly beyond human control. In a minute it was a seething mass of flame, stretching far to the right and left;

and then, under the influence of a fresh breeze, it advanced leaping and crackling up the hillside, like the long line of an army, beneath a dense canopy of smoke. Nothing could resist it! Before it lay the long yellow grass that had been drying for a month under a fierce Indian sun, and as the fire roared up the mountain, the herbage burst into yellow flame; the rocks split with dull thuds amongst showers of sparks; tall bamboos struggled for a moment while the flame twined round them like a bright-flowered creeper, and then came crashing down; until at last the jungle on top of the ridge was reached, and the flames surged against the dense green barrier, leaping to the tops of the trees and frightening out scores of bewildered birds, while the bushes and stems, too green to burn, snapped and withered. Just as the waves during a gale rush on a rock-bound coast, and leap up and burst in spray against the unshaken wall of cliff, so the long array of flame hurled itself in sheets on the face of the forest, and then, finding all its endeavours useless, made a few final spurts, and died away as suddenly as it had risen.

The measure was most successful as far as we were concerned, for the hillside, which had been such toilsome walking in the morning, was now as bare as the clean-shaven head of a Hindoo; and instead of swimming in long grass, we marched along over a light layer of charcoal, and, seeing the rocks and stones, were enabled to save ourselves from many tumbles.

One curious thing was that, although we had walked all the early part of the day without noticing more than two or three hawks far up in the sky, no sooner was the wide black flag of the smoke unfurled over the hill, than birds of prey of all sizes appeared on every side of us, and commenced hawking along the line in rear of the fire. Who shall say they have no reason? They must have benefited by many other jungle fires, and treasured their knowledge like any human beings; for when the smoke rose, they gathered from all parts, by tens and scores, to pick up the snakes and lizards. It really seemed as though they were born of the smoke, for they came shooting down through it, where none had been visible before. Thus our walk ended; and though our bag was *nil*, owing to the late start, the noble country and pleasant mountain air will not easily be forgotten by either of us.

CHAPTER XVII.

THE FEVER-FIEND.

WHEN anything unpleasant is in store for me, I like to face it as soon as possible; and consequently, as there was no hope of escaping altogether from the jungle fever, I had been rather impatient for the first attack. On the 14th of February it came on, and I was able to say my curiosity was thoroughly satisfied. The first symptoms showed about breakfast-time, when a bad headache was rapidly succeeded by a fit of ague, which set me shivering until it was scarcely possible to stand up, and quite impossible to do any work while it lasted, which was about two hours. Then succeeded the hot stage, with sharp pains in every limb and joint, accompanied by a fierce throbbing headache and a terrible thirst, which no amount of drink could allay. In fact, from twelve o'clock to midnight I was too ill to speak; but then the attack passed off, and by five the next morning, though still weak, I was able to get to work.

Unfortunately this work was particularly trying,

and taxed my endurance to the utmost. Our contract coolies had some time before felled half a dozen small clearings on the far side of Bungalow Hill, and about a mile from the settlement. These it was now necessary to lop and burn ; but the latter operation, when it had been attempted, proved a decided failure, owing to the wood not having been sufficiently dried, so the former duty became doubly laborious. Every morning the weary pilgrimage had to be made up the slope of Bungalow Hill, over its shoulder, and down the winding rocky path on the far side to the new land close by the Manalora, our *Ultima Thule.* For a little while after our arrival things were well enough, since the dew hung about, and the sun coming above the trees just warmed us with its early beams, while the thin columns of blue smoke from yesterday's fires mounted straight up into the air, telling us how little wind there was and how hot it would be presently. And, truly, the place soon became a Pandemonium. The ground lay six inches deep in hot white ashes, and littered with still smouldering logs of wood. At midday thirty or forty fires were roaring all round us, enveloping everything in dense yellow smoke, while overhead the sun blazed down as he only can in India. The coolies, gleaming with perspiration and white with ashes, piled up wood on the fires, appearing and disappearing through the smoke, while they shouted to each other in their uncouth tongues, like imps of darkness. *They* did not seem to mind it much; but to me, roasted from above, below, and on all sides, it was purgatorial. My head used to spin, and everything danced before my eyes; but there was no help, since I could never bring myself to stand in the shade while my men worked in the open. Thus the long morning had to be got through, and afterwards came the heavy tramp home to breakfast, the fording of the settlement stream, and the climb through the evil-smelling coolie "lines" to my own small bungalow on top. Then the scarcely tasted breakfast was pushed away and a fresh start made, another long walk and another good roasting, and so back again to muster; and at last the day ended.

On top of all this, and perhaps resulting from it, I had fever three or four times, and began to feel my strength ebbing fast. Generally a sense of oppression about the head and pains in every limb heralded the approach of an attack, when I sought the shelter of the hut, and lay shivering or burning all through the long hours of the hot midday, while the creepers swung monotonously to and fro, and the jungle cicadæ set the forest vibrating with their horrid music. But once I was caught by my enemy when out at work, and felt the full force of his power in a way not easily forgotten. I had risen at dawn as usual, and, in particularly good spirits, accompanied the coolies to our daily purgatory; but experience was beginning to teach me that "whistling before breakfast means crying before supper," and a light heart in the morning was the certain sign of a heavy head at bedtime. The sun had scarcely topped the trees when I felt the fever coming on again, and had to make tracks for my bungalow; but too late. I took a short cut through the jungle and over some newly burnt clearings, where the coolies were not yet at work; but as I went the fever increased, my head throbbed and swam, and my teeth began to chatter, though there was a burning sky overhead. Still I pushed on, crawling under some logs and scrambling over others; but the two miles were more than I could manage, and in the middle of a big clearing my strength ran out, and I sank down by a log, sensible only that for all the riches which Crœsus ever owned, I could not move another step.

Then came the cold fit, and the midday sun glared

down on me for a couple of hours without for a moment checking the "shivers," which shook me from head to foot. This was again succeeded by the hot stage, when I felt my blood throbbing backwards and forwards like molten lead, and a consuming thirst drove me half mad; but there was not a drop of water to be had anywhere, and not a living thing in sight—nothing but the hot, glaring white ashes on which I was lying; and the last thing I remembered was sitting up and shouting out for water at the top of my voice. I must have fallen asleep after this, for when I roused myself the sun was low down behind the trees; and limp, weak, and fearfully dirty, I staggered to my feet. Half an hour afterwards, a dejected-looking Englishman might have been seen mustering his thick ring of dark-skinned coolies. How it was got through goodness only knows. I have an indistinct remembrance of placing a finger on each long native name, and reading it over three or four times to get the right sound, while everything swam before me; and when the end of the column came suddenly, I went straight to my hut, locked myself in, and, just as I was, got supperless to bed.

It is curious to see how distinctly the races of the natives are marked off, although they have been living side by side for many years. Now, most of our coolies were Canarese, and a miserable, dirty, gaunt race of scarecrows; but the men of Wallenghay, who are Tamils and come up here on contract, showed a much finer set, tall, muscular, and of a pleasant coffee colour. Their women in the plains go about clad in purple and fine raiment, with bangles tinkling on their ankles and big nose-rings—an ornament, by the way, which the Canarese women do not wear. The very fact of the Wallenghay men only taking contract work shows they like to be their own masters and to do as they please. They are also great sawyers, and we had several couples at work cutting up logs into planks for permanent buildings, for which they were highly paid. Another race are the Malayalims, of which I had come across none until, by special invitation, I went with L—— to the "Bitter End," to see three women of that type, and was much impressed. We found them watering the young plants in the nursery, and they were noticeable directly by the way in which they kept close together and shunned the other coolies. One was an old woman, bent with age and grey-haired; another was a matron of middle age; and the last was a really good-looking girl of sixteen or seventeen. Their skins were much lighter than those of any other natives I ever saw, more approaching the tint of a native of Southern Europe than of the tropics, and their features were more finely cut than the Canarese or Tamils. Their dress, or rather lack of it, was the same; but I noticed they made the most of their scanty sarees when we approached them—a thing the other women never do, apparently deeming clothes are simply to keep one in fashion, and needless for any other purpose. L—— says he had considerable difficulty with these three Malayalims, as he knew nothing of their language, and neither did his maistries. Where their men were he cannot tell, as they came on to his place with fifty ordinary coolies, and he knew nothing else of them. Poor creatures! they never went more than fifteen yards away from each other, and seemed very solitary.

L—— told me one thing which amused me much. His Christian name happened to be Samuel, and when a new lot of coolies came up to his place, he set them to work and gave the head man some orders, at which he salaamed, and replied, "All right, Samy; it shall be as you say." This familiarity took my friend considerably aback; but he said nothing, until presently, giving a fresh order, a small coolie girl, fresh from her native village, observed, in reply to his mandate, "Very well, Samy." This was too much, and there would have been a disturbance, but fortunately it occurred to him suddenly that it was "Swami," the Canarese for "Lord of Wisdom," by which they were calling him; and such turned out to be the truth.

Beyond our estate there was a wonderful view down the Manalora river, here of quite a respectable breadth, with dense green banks of trees on either side, and tall ferns and creepers overhanging the water; but the jungle grew so thickly it was scarcely possible to penetrate any distance without bill-men. L—— said there was one red cedar tree on top of a hill near here, the only one he had ever seen. The trees we called "white cedars" were plentiful enough, and amongst our largest timber. I roughly measured one as it lay on the ground, and found it was a hundred and ten feet from where it had been cut through to the first branch. The total height of the tree must have been nearly double. It was, perhaps, fortunate nobody took any interest in keeping the course of the Manalora open and free from obstruction, or my friend might have chanced to get reprimanded, since he had made a clearing in one place directly on the edge of the stream, and all his big trunks had fallen headlong into the water, where, of course, they would not burn. So for the next five years or so the channel will be a wild tangle of branches.

Amongst this *débris*, on the day of my visit, I noticed a pair of beautiful little black-and-white birds, which were probably the rare *Parus nuchalis* of Jerdon, besides some small blue kingfishers, a small heron, and a sandpiper. But, in truth, no part of these jungles is very productive in bird life: a morning in the plains shows one twice as many new species as a month up here.

A large tiger had just been killed on Pardagherry,

in a patch of jungle which I could see quite plainly from the windows of my hut. It seemed he was an old and well-known animal, with a decided taste for fresh beef, and had already made considerable havoc amongst the herd of cattle belonging to the native estate next to ours. One day the cows were driven up in the morning, according to custom, to graze on the grass hill under charge of a Tamil cow-boy. All went well until three o'clock in the afternoon, when the animals were spread out and their guardian was resting under a tree, dozing in the warm shade. At that time he was soon roughly aroused, for a sleek, well-fed red heifer, intent on the most succulent young grass, strayed away from the others, and wandered along the margin of a shola, or patch of low jungle. It was strolling towards death! There was a fierce growl—something yellow and black rushed forth—and the petrified cowherd saw the animal roll over with the tiger on top of it, its back broken by a single stroke from those mighty paws. But the "royal animal" does not like his meat too new, so he lapped a little blood, and then left the body for supper. Meanwhile the native had driven away the other cattle, and told the tale to a sporting maistry of the Dewan's estate, who forthwith took his rifle, and, getting to the dead cow, climbed a tree at dusk and waited. He sat there for several hours, but at last his patience was rewarded; for the tiger stalked out of the jungle into the moonlight, and, after sniffing the air, was about to commence his repast, when a single well-directed shot from the tree-top caught him between the shoulders, and ended his hunting for ever. Of course L—— and I were disgusted at having lost such a chance, and sent our servant over to know if the skin was to be bought; but we found the Dewan of Cochin had desired his agent to keep it for him, so we had to wait another opportunity.

That same rocky hill must be a gamey place, as I saw a very fine bison up there a few mornings afterwards, and watched him through my glass as he stalked slowly down among the date palms, stopping every now and then to graze, or whisk his long tail about to frighten away the flies. His hide was shining black, and his horns of splendid proportions; but he was quite safe from me at that distance, so he still wanders in his native wilds. On that morning I was too far, on a former one I was too near to one of these noble animals; for, walking on the latter occasion silently down a deserted trace, with nothing but a light gun loaded with small shot, I suddenly put up a large solitary bison, who immediately charged at random. For a moment it was impossible to say in which direction he was moving, as the jungle was dense and nothing could be heard but the breaking of the branches and snapping of bamboos; consequently I was naturally much relieved when I caught a glimpse of the animal galloping down the valley below, and saw the tall bamboos shaking as he broke through them further and further away. Had he charged me there can be little doubt that this account would never have been penned.

An institution very usual in most districts is the Sunday outing—already alluded to—on which day the planters don their best clothes, and ride to some central spot where the bungalow of a sociable neighbour serves them for the occasion as a club-house, and they sit about chatting and smoking, till the short Indian twilight warns them to get home again. On our hills there were, unfortunately, so few English, and most of the estates were so new and required so much attention, that we had not yet started a proper club, but contented ourselves with utilizing W——'s bungalow. Thus, when Sunday morning came, we converged from all parts to Palm-tree Bungalow, and made ourselves completely at home. W—— was always in the same position, with his heels on the back of a neighbouring chair, and a cheroot invariably in full blast between his lips. He nodded to each new arrival, and waved his hand towards the table, on which stood the cigar-box and brandy and water. This was the utmost he could manage; but if absolutely forced to say anything, he replied in mono-

THE SUNDAY RENDEZVOUS.

syllables, and at once enveloped himself in a cloud of smoke. So we had to entertain ourselves, and were generally successful.

While the sahibs derived what amusement they could in this way each Sunday, their coolies were also enjoying themselves after a fashion, and laying in a store of provisions for the next week. They had received pay on Saturday afternoon, so when Sunday morning came they put some castor oil on their hair, decked out their persons with all the bangles and finery they possessed, and then, with empty gunny bags and cocoa-nut shells, they streamed by my hut—men, women, and children—on their way to the head of the ghaut, where a great weekly bazaar was held, and merchants and grain dealers from the lowlands came up with strings of white, rice-laden bullocks and packs of gay-coloured cloths and native jewellery. They also brought up with them what we should have been better pleased if they had left behind, namely, plentiful supplies of arrack—a coarse sort of rum distilled from the palm tree—and cheap and bad but very fiery brandy; and on these dreadful liquors the coolies spent their hard-won annas, and drank in a day what should support them for a week. The result was that on Monday our morning muster was always very thinly attended, and we never hoped to get much work done. At these fairs the coolies bought their rice and chillies for the next week, and the maistries even purchased sheep and chickens occasionally; but the only form of animal food which I ever saw a coolie purchase was a badly cured fish, which looked much like a pike that had been split open and roughly dried between boards. Once I walked home behind a party of workmen who possessed one of these "appetisers" amongst their other provisions, and it was an experience never to be forgotten. It would not have surprised me if all the tigers, wolves, and foxes in the neighbouring jungles had been attracted by the scent, and come sniffing after us.

It seemed these bazaars, with their fatal supplies of arrack and cheap brandy, stirred even the mild-tempered coolies up to deeds of violence; and free fights sometimes took place. Of this we had an unpleasant proof once, for while at breakfast, I was astonished to see three native peons and a sergeant come into my verandah and make their salaams. The head-man was dressed in black, with scarlet braid and a scarlet turban. He had a long curved talwar at his side, while his satellites were equally well dressed and armed. They presented me with a document written in English and Tamil, to the effect that there had been considerable disturbances in the last bazaar at the head of the ghaut, in which "sundry and several" Pardagherry coolies had attacked the stall of a grain dealer suspected of giving bad measures, and had stolen the grain and beaten the native merchant; wherefore the Englishman in charge of the said estate was requested to hand over the "undermentioned natives" to the Raja's peons who brought the warrant. Then followed the names of many of our men and of all the maistries. Now, we could spare a few men, but the maistries were too valuable, and I told the officer so; whereupon he said, "What the sahib wished must be." So the coolies were mustered, and then the peons secured their astonished prey. I was sorry for them, but it was not civil to disregard the warrant, as the authorities had taken the trouble to send it up, and our coolies shortly afterwards returned to the hills none the worse for a short detention.

Perhaps the reader will say "*toujours* Pardagherry" if I write anything more about that big mountain; but the truth was it formed so prominent a feature in our landscape, that we could not be indifferent to its various changes. In the monsoon it was emerald green and ribbed with white stripes of falling streams; and when the hot weather came and dried up the shallow soil, the grass seeded, withered, and turned brown, and we knew sooner or later it would be burned. Perhaps the jungle-men might fire it, or two bamboos, dry and brittle, rubbed together by the north-west breezes might kindle the flame, while our recent experiences in firing another grass hill told how quickly the conflagration would spread. So an eager watch was kept; and sure enough, returning from work one evening, a heavy column of smoke was ascending into the sky from the very summit of the grey old hill. As darkness came on the fire rolled into sight, and we sat long in the verandah in our armchairs, watching the beautiful scene. The flame sprang over the hill, dyeing the moonless black sky a blood red, and then advanced slowly down the cliff-side in a wide semicircle. But it was actually going against the wind, and, consequently, there was not the furious rush which I have mentioned in a similar instance. Instead of this, the long array of crimson light fought its way down yard by yard, now going out in one place, and anon shooting up high and bright from a thicket of date-palms and cuscus grass, and then rallying its forces and carrying in a sudden rush the patches it had left unburnt. At one time a thousand separate fires were gleaming in the blackness of the night, and it looked like nothing so much as a big camp. Again the hill was encircled with a complete halo of blaze, all reflected on the smoke overhead; and then the flames would creep into the dry bed of a grass-grown nullah, and, finding there plenty of fuel, would outstrip the rest of the advancing line, and pour rapidly down towards the valley, like a stream of molten lava. All night long the hill flared, and its crimson reflection still lit up our rooms when we fell asleep. But the conflagration was over by the next morning, and there was our stout old friend, scorched, blackened, and naked from head to foot, the ugliest object that could be, his shamefaced head hidden in a shroud of thick smoke. We were positively downhearted about it, and L—— expressed our common feelings when he said mournfully, "Poor old mountain! I wish it would rain, so that he might get himself another green coat. It is shocking to see him so!"

When the hills burn the planters know the worst of the fever season is at hand. Already we had heard from the Wynnaad that three-fourths of the men there were down with fever, and our own jungles were very unhealthy. D—— and L—— had fever constantly, and the former assured us cheerfully that in May we should be able to "cut the malaria with a knife," and might expect an attack of fever every other twenty-four hours. This set me thinking of a holiday, in order to recruit my energies for the encounter; and, as D—— had been away again at Palghaut—this time to celebrate his birthday—leaving me to look after four or five hundred coolies, I was beginning to think my "outing" should come next.

CHAPTER XVIII.

JUNGLE FESTIVITIES.

THE coolie is not entirely without religion, though it is one chiefly made up of superstitions and deeply contaminated with the strange and fantastic fetish worship of the aboriginal tribes—peoples who have roamed these jungles since the remotest ages, and have been overcome by succeeding waves of northern invaders. But these wild superstitions are grafted on the stock of Hinduism, which is the prevailing religion of the south of India. Thus, our coolies wore the red spots and parti-coloured trident of Vishnu on their forehead, and would yet eat the flesh of monkeys, when they could get it, or drink strong spirits without a misgiving. Perhaps on our hills they were on their worst behaviour, and the famine had made them careless of strict rules—it is very hard to be virtuous on an empty stomach.

All over the estate there were samee trees at conspicuous spots, and generally at cross-roads. Under these, strange little shrines were built just big enough for a man to kneel in, and made of green boughs plastered over with mud. The figures inside varied considerably. In one close to my hut there was a slab of wood with a roughly carved image of a cross-legged deity on it, and a three-pronged fork with the two outer prongs painted white, and the inner one red, stuck in the ground by the side. This lay right in our track as we went to work every day, and each coolie, as he or she passed, salaamed to the little idol—a proceeding which hindered the march, but they would not work well until it had been gone through. In another little temple, not so well endowed as the former, there were two small mud cones on the floor, on the top of one of which white paint was poured, and on the other red. At this shrine a bit of ground had been cleared of weeds and leaves, and there every Tuesday afternoon (apparently the coolie Sunday) they congregated and killed a chicken or a sheep, if they had one, and made a *burra puja*, or offering, afterwards salaaming and rubbing their foreheads on the ground in front of the mud pyramids, which, however, it should be clearly remembered, they no more worshipped than a Christian worships the altar when he kneels down in front of it. It was simply that the shrine was the abode of a divinity, and they represented the Invisible according to their means.

For myself, I always reverenced these little places, and would no more have thought of disarranging one than I would blow out the tiny votive lamp of an Italian wayside chapel. The men killed sheep and ate them there, but the women also made small offerings; and on a pointed stick by the entrance of the temple were a number of glass bangles freshly taken from the wrists of the votaries; these remained there untouched by any hand for many months. Whether or not coolies had much faith in charms was difficult to say; they did not wear them about their persons; but there was a handsome brown-and-yellow flower, the Indian marigold, which seemed to find especial favour, and one of the prettiest habits of the native women was the way in which they twined bunches of these gay buds amongst their shining black tresses. The effect was very pleasing. These flowers did not grow wild in the forests, but there were plenty of them about the older bungalows, whence they were fetched on grand occasions, to deck the women-folk and strew the floor of the temples.

As for birth, marriage, or death ceremonies, I can say very little from observation. The population of the "lines" had been increased by various small brown babies, but without any visible rejoicings. As for marriages, they were probably put off until better times; and though there had been very many subjects for burying, these were interred with few funeral honours. In fact, even the nearest kindred of a departed coolie seemed to think the sooner he was forgotten the better, for they raised no memorials over his narrow cell. There seemed to be some sort of ill-defined desire to put the dead on a peninsula with running water on as many sides as might be—a trace, perhaps, of that wide-spread and strange idea that a stream is a safeguard against evil spirits, whereof there are fragments in the legends and superstitions of every land, from the "bush" of Australia to the forests of North America.

A veritable "burra tumasha," however, came under my notice once, and was an interesting spectacle. The time for which some two hundred of our coolies stood engaged having expired, their headman begged permission to go away, with all their belongings, and plant rice in their own country. This was granted, and they informed us of their intention of holding a grand feast before they left; so Saturday was a holiday, and, having received all arrears of pay on Friday afternoon, they owned plenty of rupees. Myself and L—— were away all day, but, getting back at dusk, we found a large square of ground at the top of the ridge overlooking the settlement carefully prepared and raked as smooth as a flower bed. This was the banqueting hall, and was thickly hedged round with green branches, while some three hundred little holes were made in lines inside—the plates of the expected guests. Adjoining this was another enclosure for a kitchen, with ten stone fireplaces, and here all day long twenty men had been at work cooking rice and various curry stuffs in red clay chatties, and as they were done, piling them up in huge heaps on palm-leaf mats, the odour from which was really so satisfactory as we walked by hungry and tired, that we wished we had been invited. L—— dined in my hut, and we missed the first act, which consisted of dressing a coolie up in satanic costume to represent the evil spirits of the jungle, and, after subjecting him to all sorts of indignities, expelling him from the lines, by beating and kicking him until he took refuge in the forest beyond. But though we only heard the noise and the shouting, our servant explained this opening to us, and we hurried through our meal to be in time for the next scene.

Just as our cheroots were lighted, the uproar at the "lines" increased, and a procession came up the hill towards us, escorted by several hundred coolies, a couple of hundred of whom were bearing lighted torches. At the head of the column were five men, wearing all but no clothing, armed with long bamboos, with which they fenced with each other and beat the ground, all the while shouting and dancing in the wildest manner until the perspiration poured off them. Next came the handsomest coolie boy on the estate, Bulgoor Jowra, with all the male finery the "lines" could muster piled on his little body, and the broad trident of the mighty Vishnu painted clear and fresh on his forehead. He looked very sedate and calm, keeping a perfect control of his countenance, all his individuality being sternly merged in the character assumed. By the hand he led the prettiest little brown-skinned girl we possessed, by name Jowrie, and about fourteen years old. She was equally sedate, and came wrapped in a brilliant scarlet saree, with silver and glass bangles all up her arms and on her ankles, her black hair done up in a tight knot behind and adorned with bright samee flowers; on her head a broad shining brass lotah, piled up with jungle fruit and bright leaves, and in her nose and ears bright gold stud-like ornaments. She looked very fascinating under the flaring light of the torches—a real brown rural goddess. Meantime, tomtoms were beaten, crackers fired, and rockets let off, the coolies shouting at the top of their voices, and everybody dancing wildly, except the grave little pair in the centre, while the procession went up the hill and took its way to each samee place in turn. At every fifteen yards little platters of green banana leaves were placed in a line on the ground, and a small quantity of boiled rice piled up on each. When the advance-guard of bamboo men reached these, they left off shouting and capering for a moment, and, stooping down, ate the grain from the leaves, carefully keeping their hands behind their backs meanwhile. At last, but not till near midnight, the procession reached the banqueting floor, where the torches were stuck in the walls of green boughs, and the three hundred coolies sat down to a grand feast; and for a long time we, the lonely masters, listened to their simple merriment, and watched the happy shadows under the brightly illuminated forest trees, glad to see our people for once so "jolly."

I slept very well until about 3 a.m., when the revellers came back on their way to the "lines," and the idea occurred to them to serenade me, which they proceeded to do, Vishnu and his little associate standing in my verandah and singing an impromptu song about my little-worthy self, which I thought so very courteous of two such exalted individuals, that I rose to make them salaams and gave them some bright new silver rupees, thereby pleasing the small deities considerably.

There was not much novelty now in the estate work. The pitting was almost done for the season, most of the fresh clearings had been burnt, and presently we should begin to think of planting and opening new roads, the usual wet weather labour. My own experiences swung backwards and forwards between heavy daily work and frequent attacks of fever, which left me hardly strength to walk. On one of these occasions, being half delirious in the hot stage, I called my boy in, and, giving him a pair of lamp scissors, ordered him to cut my hair off. He was not, however, a gifted hairdresser; and though the process was refreshing at the time, I was not fit to be photographed for some while afterwards. In spite of the fever, it was necessary to look after the whole estate, as D—— went away again to Calicut, to see the doctor about his liver, which always had something wrong with it. After a month of very severe work, things, however, became considerably easier, owing to the departure of two hundred of our coolies for their own country, and the arrival of the superintendent, with his family, from a long absence in the lowlands. They quartered themselves on Bungalow Hill, in a rough wooden shed which had been hastily run up for them; and thus there were now two ladies in our jungle, Mrs. F—— and Mrs. R——, with two small children of the latter.

The heat of the noonday was only equalled by the chilliness of the early morning even in this hot season. Thus, turning out on the 3rd of April at 5.30, the whole forest was enveloped in a dense white veil of mist, impenetrable to the eye at ten or twelve yards' distance. As it happened, this was the Telugu New Year's Day, and the coolies, always glad of any pretence for a holiday, had "struck" in a body. No one would do a bit of work, so I went up Bungalow Hill to pay my respects to Mrs. R——. Following the winding upward track which had recently been made, the mist grew thinner as the elevation increased, until, reaching the clearing in the centre of which the bungalow stands, the sun was shining brightly overhead and the air blew fresh and pleasant. But looking back a most singular and beautiful sight was seen. The whole of our district, lying like a huge ditch between two great ridges, was enveloped in grey mist, nothing being visible of the forest, but all its dark folds hidden in a smooth milk-white sea of vapour. Far away, however, to the northward, like islands in a deep bay, stood out the bungalows of Polyampara, Poothpara, Comlocoda, and Varlavachen, each on its hill. In fact, it looked exactly like a Norwegian fiord at sunrise—the mist most perfectly resembling water, and the great mountains on either side hedging it as high cliffs shut in those inlets. This lasted a long time, even after the sun was well up in the sky; and when at last the fog melted and the trees gradually appeared, the forest stood dripping with moisture, and the moss and ferns were as bright, fresh, and green as after the first monsoon shower.

Among the vegetation fed by this moisture is a

broad-leafed bush, which comes into life in a most curious way wherever light is let into the jungle; indeed, the powers of suspended vitality possessed by its germs would be an interesting study for a better botanist than myself. Even the fall of a tree and the consequent gap created in the sun-proof ceiling of the forest causes this bush to spring up on the spot, but it is to be seen in greatest profusion along the sides of the older clearings, where it grows in undisturbed peace, its light green foliage forming a wide ribbon between the brown soil and the darker tree-tops.

Another plant following the planter's footsteps, and hateful to him from the persistency with which it grows amongst the coffee, is the Spanish-needle, a plant imported, like many other things, by the Portuguese. Unfortunately it has outlasted the raj of that nation, and has established itself firmly in its adopted country. Being provided by nature with seeds armed with innumerable small hooked spines, every passing animal or human being assists in propagating it by carrying to "fresh fields and pastures new" the unwelcome germs, which, once established, are anything but easy to eradicate. But the great dread of the coolies in the jungle is another plant of quite a different kind—a tall, pale-stemmed, sickly looking bush, with long-pointed, whitish-green leaves. Woe to the luckless mortal who lets those same harmless-looking leaves touch his bare flesh! He will not forget it for many a day, for this bush is the dreaded Mealum-ma, or stinging shrub—the nettle of Timor, or "Devil's leaf"—which here, as in the forests of Nepal, produces deadly effects on any person brushing against it. Our coolies said they got fever if stung only very lightly, and they consequently avoided the bush with the utmost circumspection.

Up amongst the branches, and well-nigh out of sight,

there hung many orchids—*Dendrobia* and parasitical plants—but they are not commonly beautiful. If the orchids somewhat fail to strike the observer, there are lovelier vegetable products on the ground which deserve his attention, and if he be a specialist in that way, he will find plenty of employment amongst the fungi and moulds. The most common of these was a small branching fungus which might be mistaken for moss by a careless observer. It was very conspicuous, as its own colour was a pearly white, and it throve nowhere, according to my observations, except on the black and charred logs of wood lying about the clearings. These relics of the fallen forest it decked with sheets of the finest and most delicate white lace, prettier and more faultless than anything man could make. Other fungi were purple or vermilion, and clustered thick on the stems of dying trees; and a small white variety, with a hair-like stem and a very mobile bell-shaped head, sprang from trunks already returning to mother earth. Wherever such a stem lay on the ground covered with leaves and moss, the little fairy stools grew up along it, and accurately marked out its grave to the passer-by. Then there were larger and more striking sorts, one of which was a spongy-stemmed structure with a bright vermilion head, shaped much like an inverted teacup, from the rim of which hung down a most curious crinoline of open lace-like material, with meshes too small for a bee to get through, but not so close as to prevent the stem in the centre from being seen.

At this season or a little later the weather is apt to be very treacherous in our mountain passes. I remember once, returning in a bullock bandy to the forests after a brief holiday run, having been completely overwhelmed in a sudden storm. We had left Palghaut late in the evening, and scarcely had we got so far from the town as to make it useless to turn back, when the sky became overcast, and it was obvious we were in for a monsoon storm, which in another ten minutes duly began. The sky grew black as pitch, and the rain descended in torrents and found its way through the bamboo matting overhead without any difficulty. It was so dark, as we plodded slowly along, that I could only just make out the outlines of the white bullocks in front, while the dusky form of the native driver was quite swallowed up, although he had deserted his usual uncomfortable perch on the pole and backed into the bandy to try and get some shelter. In this way we wandered along all the early part of the night, jolting fearfully, and getting our wheels first into one rut and then into another, every now and then running into the bank or a fig tree, and going elsewhere, goodness only knows whither. At midnight the storm seemed at its worst, and the thunder and lightning raged incessant, so that I was wet through and profoundly uncomfortable. While wondering how it would end, suddenly a flash of lightning illuminated the whole district; I say a flash, but it seemed as if the whole sky split open from east to west, and a river of blue flame poured forth. For one moment everything leapt into view. The wide lonely rice land all around, with miles of watery swamps; the black outlines of the grove of fig trees in which we were; the two white bullocks with their gleaming wet hides; the cowering driver, and the road cut up with gurgling streamlets —all were as visible as though it were midday for an instant, and then everything vanished in profoundest darkness, and the thunder broke out directly overhead with as wild and awful a sound as the lightning had been a terrible sight.

To add to the unpleasantness of the situation, the driver whined out that he had lost the road—did the sahib know where they were? But the sahib hadn't an idea, so ordered the man to go on straight ahead, in the hope of finding some village where shelter might be obtained. It must have been nearly one o'clock when the dim outlines of a hut were made out at the roadside, and, pulling up in front, I jumped down and went to get our "bearings" from the owners. But all was dark and silent. Groping my way to the door, I was just entering when there was heard a most unearthly hoot; I saw the gleaming of two pale-green eyes, and some big bird—an owl, probably, that had been sheltering from the storm—dashed out into the dark night. Judging from this the place was empty, I walked inside, but before I had gone many feet, tripped over something heavy on the ground, which from the feel and particularly "high" odour, I judged must be a coolie; so I stirred him up again with the toe of my boot, and called out to him to wake; but he never moved. Thinking this strange, a wisp of rice straw from the bandy was lighted, and by that uncertain torch, held above my head, I made out the bare mud walls, the palm-leaf roof, and mud floor of the deserted hut, and at my feet a bundle of dreadful rags, wrapt round the thin form of a coolie. Poor fellow! it will be a long time before he wakes again; for when I turned him over to see why he slept so soundly, I saw he was dead—dead of starvation, and had crept in here, lonely and forgotten, to finish his life. While I looked at him the straw went out, and we were in darkness again, with the certainty of having to stay there for the present. The bandy man was crouched under the cart, with all his clothing round his head—the usual way in which a native keeps himself warm—and for a time I tried walking up and down under the eaves of the hut, and watching the moon struggling with the watery rear-guards of the army of clouds; but, being dreadfully sleepy, I made up my mind that, dead man, or no dead man, I would lie down inside, so entered the hut, pushed the poor old coolie into the most remote corner, and, wrapping myself in a rug, with a revolver conveniently at hand in my belt (for my departed friend against the opposite wall was odoriferous enough to attract all the jackals in the neighbourhood), I stretched myself on the bare floor, and was soon sleeping delightfully, with pleasant dreams of fair English homes flitting through my mind.

Needless to say, we did not linger long in these quarters, but with the first pink streaks of the fresh welcome dawn we "harnessed to" and followed the road to the southward, keeping the lightest parts of the sky on our left. This, by the way, was my birthday, but I was almost forgetting it myself until it suddenly occurred to me as an odd sort of celebration.

Presently we fell in with some landmarks which the bandy-wallah knew, and so bore gaily up for Wallanghay, while the sun dried my wet clothes, and things looked much more cheerful than they had appeared last night. Finally, about 10 a.m., the Vladimir Bungalow was reached; and after a substantial breakfast, for I had eaten scarcely anything since the morning before, I lay down for a rest on the shaky charpoy which formed almost the only article of furniture in the widow's guest-room.

The evening was spent in company with D——, Cecil H——, S——, and L——, who were all bound for Palghaut, to attend the funeral of an old Englishman who had died there the day before. Poor L—— was a mere scarecrow of skin and bones, after a month's fever, and scarcely able to stand, while the others were all more or less shaky and hollow-eyed. They described the malaria up above as fearful. Nevertheless we spent a pleasant evening, seated round the rickety table in the little bungalow, drinking bottled beer and punch out of cracked cups and saucers, while the widow and her little daughter trotted backwards and forwards in the moonlight outside, with their bangles tinkling and their slim forms wrapped in white sarees, attending to our wants, until the time came for the others to start northward. Then, with a lot of "good nights," they tumbled into the line of bandies standing in the road, and went off down the deserted native street, leaving me to my meditations—not very pleasant ones, perhaps, as I foresaw a certainty of sickness in store for me, and lately the fever had considerably undermined my strength. But the night was beautiful, and it was impossible to be gloomy under such a lovely sky. High overhead the moon soared, shining amid countless stars, as big and bright as they only are in the tropics; and, descending to our tiny earth, the little village was asleep from one end to the other. Even the bananas round each compound hung down their broad leaves, and for once had ceased fluttering, for there stirred not a breath of air, and the fields of tall green rice stretching away to the foot of the forest-clad Annamullies were still and deserted by every sign of life except the fireflies. Of these there flickered countless myriads; if the rice had seeded and every grain grown luminous with pale-green fire, the sight would not have been more wonderful. It was like nothing so much as the phosphorescence to be seen on a calm night at sea, and I smoked my long cheroot, watching the oscillating swarms of little lamplighters, and thinking how much a man may bear without losing heart or the enjoyment of life.

CHAPTER XIX.

DEATH AND BRIGHT LIFE.

ONCE more in harness and at the hard grind which usually falls to the lot of the coffee planter in new districts, I was now entering on all the discomforts of my second wet monsoon.

The coffee had just finished flowering on the older estates, and it was a fine sight while it lasted. I have said that the trees are about three or four feet high, and densely covered with broad, glossy, dark-green leaves, very much like those of the orange. From the junction of each of these leaves with the twig bursts forth a great cluster of ten or twelve blossoms, also closely resembling the orange flower in colour and form; yet not, alas! in odour. The former is delightful, but the latter is faint and sickly; the coolies declare the scent gives them fever, and those that had to carry my messages through the flowering estates begged double pay, as though it were a service of danger. The scent is undoubtedly unpleasant, though the sight of a wide extent of clearing covered with a carpet of green leaves and a wealth of snow-white blossoms is very pleasing, and reminds one of the country at home when the hawthorn hedges are in full bloom.

The malaria at that time was wonderfully bad, worse than anything I had known before. Every time the sun came up, and when he went down again, the heavy fever mist was drawn out of its lurking-places amongst the decayed vegetation, and rolled over the ground in bluish-grey sheets. All day long it lay in the deep glens and river hollows, and became so dense as to be perfectly nauseous to breathe. Once, while crossing the jungle, I came to the steep banks of a reedy nullah, and descended to wade across; but no sooner was I down into the fog than my head swam, my breathing grew painful, and my throat rough and dry, so that I was glad to scramble back before my senses left me, as they were rapidly doing. In this same nullah, hanging from the trees overhead, was a wonderful creeper, which is rare in these jungles. Its leaves, as usual, were so high up as to be an undistinguishable green mass, but the stem, as thick as a man's arm, was covered with big grey knobs, all rough and thorny. These creepers are very useful to the monkeys, who employ them as though they were ropes, and climb up them in a most extraordinary manner.

Of course this weather affected the coolies even more than the Englishmen, and my sick list every evening was a heavy one, while, as D—— was very unwell himself on Bungalow Hill, and R—— away collecting coolies in Madura, though we had five hundred already, I rapidly acquired some fresh practical medical skill in the diseases most common on the estate. Then the "lines" were in a vile condition, and we were so hard at work road-making and planting, that we could spare no time to construct fresh ones. The natural result was that small-pox and cholera soon appeared. Very few of the coolies were vaccinated, and we had no means of performing the operation for them, so we jogged along as well as we could.

One morning, while sitting at breakfast, I heard a tinkle of bangles in the porch, and, getting up, found a coolie girl—a very comely girl as coolies go—of about seventeen or eighteen, kneeling on the ground. When she saw me, she threw herself down full length and cried out something in Tamil so unintelligible that, calling my "boy," I asked what she wanted whereon she lifted her head a few inches from the ground, and again spoke in her own language. "Sahib," said the boy, translating with his usual total disregard of genders, "this girl here he say he has had small-pox very bad. He's too sick, too thin to do any more work, and has got no food. He say no one will help him but the sahib, and if he doesn't get food, he is going to sit on the sahib's doorstep and die." And truly the girl was thin and haggard, and the few glass bangles on her arms slipped up and down them as though they were sticks. She, however, was more in need of food than medicine; so, by way of commencement, I gave her a substantial breakfast, subsequently placing her in my private relief camp, in which were included all ages and both sexes; she rapidly picked up strength, and was at work again two weeks afterwards.

The cholera was even more serious, and many coolies died of it, though it did not spread rapidly, but contented itself with a few victims each week. The stables, a few yards from my hut, furnished the hospital, and I am bound to say "the stoker" took the greatest interest in the patients, who—considerately enough—either died or got better in a very few days, and so made room for more. He borrowed all my chatties to cook them conjee in—needless to say, I never asked for the chatties back—and even told my servant to look after them. This was too much for that poor wretch, and so one night, after placing my dinner on the table, he stood in front of me, shuffling about with his feet, his face a bluish tint, until, asking him what was the matter, he said he was frightened of the cholera. He had seen two men die that afternoon, and he wished to start for the lowlands the next morning, where his wife and child were. Not a very pleasant prospect for me to have to cook for myself after each day's hard work, but I saw he was just in the right way to get the disease if he stayed, so I told him he might go for a week, and the next morning he went.

When I came back from work that day at noon and flung myself into an armchair, forgetting for a moment the state of affairs, I called out, "Boy, breakfast quickly!" but there was no answer, and the misery of my position dawned upon me. Carlyle has said the great distinction between man and beasts is that the former only uses implements; and, allowing this, I should add that the chief distinction between savages and the civilized was that the latter employed others to cook for them. Certainly I never felt so barbarous as I did that morning, when I crouched in the grubby little hut that served as a kitchen, blowing hard at a stubborn fire, and half choked with the dense wood smoke, which enveloped and made my originally white clothes terribly black. But, somehow or other, I cooked a chop in great discomfort by running a stick through it and twisting it over the fire, and then bolted to the hut with it and ate it, all booted and unwashed as I was; after which some water was boiled in an empty beef tin and a rough brew of tea made. I was extremely uncomfortable that week, and learned by bitter experience how much of one's enjoyment depends on the domestic department. The breakfasts were not so bad, for there was at least enough light then for my operations; but cooking the dinner in the dusk after a long day's toil, and being sickened with the smoke, and, after all, having to be contented with a little dirty, underdone meat, was not the least of many drawbacks to a "frontier" life.

The coolie graves in the jungle near by were at this time growing terribly numerous; there were more already than we had opened of acres, and the number increased daily, but even they did not represent the complete total of deaths, as I was sometimes only too well aware. For instance, a coolie woman died, and I ordered her to be buried in the jungle by two of her kinsmen, and paid them the usual two rupees to do it. But they had a mind to save themselves trouble, and so took her down to the Manalora stream, when there happened to be a freshet in it, and threw her in. She floated a little way, but was caught on the limb of a tree, and then the river sank into a single thread of water. About two weeks afterwards, I was walking up the nearly dry nullah bed, when my olfactory nerves told me there was something wrong, and going a little further I found out the cause—it was the body of the poor coolie woman still hanging to the branch! Then, again, many of the graves were made shockingly shallow, and the wild dogs and wolves tore them open and partly disinterred the inmates. In fact, I saw things which will not bear describing; and, pretty well hardened as I became, my breakfast was often left untasted, and, with gun on my shoulder, I wandered away to the open grass hills, to freshen myself up by a little sweet air and undefiled nature, after some such dreadful sights and experiences.

But to turn to pleasanter subjects. This was the season for the entomologist. It was a sort of border time between the dry and wet monsoons, and the Lepidoptera of the former and the Coleoptera of the latter were in almost equal abundance. My collections grew rapidly whenever I was fortunate enough to get a couple of hours' holiday, and amounted to some two thousand beetles and a couple of hundred butterflies, captured on odd occasions. On a single occasion I secured six varieties of *Bacteria trophinus*, or walking-stick insects, in half an hour, of most wonderful forms and shapes—some so like dried twigs that it was impossible at first to recognize them, and others so accurately resembling green leaves that they would have been safe from my search, had I not sent them tumbling into an open umbrella beneath the bush in which they lodged by a few vigorous strokes with a stick. These insects seem to find their curious vegetable appearance useful in two ways. Firstly, it protects them from their foes amongst the birds; and, secondly, enables them better to obtain their food by surprise. Indeed, one of the most noticeable points in the insect world of the jungles was the way in which each small creature was protected by nature from its foes in some ingenious manner. The instances of this which I observed were well-nigh innumerable, and would fill a long chapter. Thus, when I have been searching under the bark of dead trees, it has been very observable that all the beetles harbouring there, and most of the other insects, have let themselves fall immediately they have felt the disturbance, and have become lost amongst the long herbage below. The success of this *ruse* when they are attacked by their chief foe, the woodpecker, is obvious. Many species of Heteroptera are so strongly scented, that doubtless no bird of any delicacy would think for a moment of eating them. One large brown specimen scented my hand with an odour of bitter almonds for several days, and another had a wonderfully strong smell of musk about it. Besides these scents, they are ungainly looking things, with spikes and thorns on the thorax, enough to make a bird's throat feel rough even to look at them. Another little beetle, one of the *Phytophagæ*, though its "christian" name is unknown to me, lived on the leaves of a small jungle shrub, in close companionship with a gaily striped yellow-and-black caterpillar. The beetle was steel-blue, and about the size of a pea, but a most curious thing was the trust it placed in its strange associates as watchmen. "A little more than kin and less than kind" does not apply here, for the caterpillars are less than kith and more than kind. Several times I have approached one of these bushes, but no sooner have I shown myself to one of the caterpillars than it has left off feeding, thrown itself back on its rear claspers, and violently swung its body from side to side. At this strange movement, which might alone repel a bird, a gentle vibration has been communicated to the neighbouring twigs and leaves, and the blind-looking beetles have hastily let themselves drop to the ground, where they are quite safe; while, after passing the signal rapidly round the bush, so that every twig at last was in a tremble, the caterpillars would each take a turn round the nearest belaying-pin, and let themselves down after their strange associates by a thousand silken threads.

A much larger beetle, of a grey colour with a few orange spots, known to science as *Batocera rubus*, had the curious habit of squeaking loudly when touched, and doubtless this afforded it protection from some of its enemies. Now, the first time I caught a specimen of this beetle the squeaking puzzled me, since no insect has the power of making any sound from its throat and mouth, as vertebrate animals do. Every noise coming from an insect rises in its exterior parts—from its wings, its legs, or, as in the cicada, from drums or threads which it causes to vibrate; but none of these would explain the sound arising from my beetle. So I took him home and investigated. He squeaked most strangely all the time, moving his head backward and forwards and waving his antennæ. This gave me a clue; and I dipped a small feather in oil, and passed it lightly round the junction of the head and thorax, and in a moment all sounds ceased, though the insect still continued his movements, and it was plain the sound had been caused by friction of his head and neck.

Then there is the mighty *Spirosireptes cinctatus*, as long as a man's hand, and belonging to the same family as the common English millipede, but of giant proportions, and, when touched, giving out from every ring of its body a thick yellow fluid, equally unpleasant to sight and smell, though I never found it to cause any physical pain, as is sometimes supposed. Another of these strange jungle creatures bears much resemblance to an English woodlouse, but when rolled up, as it always is when anything approaches, it equals in size a hen's egg; and if it happens to be on a fallen tree-trunk or on sloping ground, it rolls away, and it is ten to one that it cannot be caught.

Among the Lepidoptera there does not seem to be quite so much mimicry, though there exists a brown butterfly which flits amongst the low herbage, and on being alarmed shuts its upper wings and lets them lie under the lower pair, then becoming so exactly like a dead leaf, that even when captured and lying on white paper, it is a matter of considerable difficulty to say whether it be insect or vegetable. But, as a rule, Nature has endowed this order with gay wings and great powers of flight. In general, they flit singly in sunny glades, and along the borders of the clearings, but occasionally I have come across marvellous companies of these bright insects. On one occasion, in the hot weather, when the streams were at their smallest, and everything lay dry and baked under the fierce sun, while all the trees and plants sagged down their leaves for want of moisture, I lit upon a quiet nullah meandering through the jungle. The bed, by chance, just there was broad and sandy, and the stream a single thread that seemed every moment in danger of vanishing. But to my astonished eyes the whole place appeared a garden of flowers of a thousand colours, and crowded so close by the water that the sand could scarcely be seen. I looked and looked again, and then stepped down to observe the *parterre* closer; but as I did so these animated blossoms sprang into the air in a vast cloud, and the truth was plain that they were a countless host of thirsty butterflies, collected from the forest all round to drink at this thread of liquid. The sight was wonderful as they wheeled round and round amongst the hanging creepers, and enough, in itself, to delight any naturalist—hundreds of varieties and tens of thousands of specimens, all intertwining in mazy gambols; every size and shape and colour was there, and as they flew backwards and forwards in the sunlight, with their wings shining and flashing, it was like a shower of jewels. I had often seen a few drinking before, but never such a mighty concourse. Perhaps the popularity of the stream was owing to the ease with which the flat sandy bed enabled them to come at the water.

Some may say that there is not much coffee planting in all this, but the truth is on an estate the work remains very much the same for the first three seasons. It has been mentioned how we planted out the young coffee shrubs, during the previous monsoon, first into baskets, and then into the square holes in the already felled and burnt clearings where they were to continue; and now again we were hard at work at the same thing, *i.e.* planting up the new enclosures made during the hot weather.

Some of our trees, however, in the oldest clearing were now nearly full-sized, and had even made a few attempts at flowering, but of course there was no crop worth picking; yet as they grew it became necessary to remove all shoots and suckers likely to interfere with the uniform shape of the plant, and this was done by small parties of our most trustworthy coolies, armed with short curved knives—the chief portions to be cut away being all suckers coming up from the ground round the chief stem, and any secondary "ascending axis" which would tend to make the centre of the bush too thick; for the great thing to aim at is to have a neat round tree, nicely filling the space of ground allotted to it, and with the branches so disposed as to let each get a fair supply of air.

This was our own idea; but on F——'s estate and another the bushes were under "shade," *i.e.* a few of the forest trees, here and there, had been left standing and protected the plants from the direct glare of the sun. Of course, on these estates the clearings were never burnt, as the fire would have destroyed the shade trees; but instead, the forest was felled, and the lighter material carried away to the borders by hand labour—a long process, which, however, is said to leave the valuable top soil of vegetable *débris* uninjured; though against this we thought that that same *débris* harboured a world of insects hurtful to the coffee plants which a good "burn" would kill, and also promoted the dreaded leaf disease so common in Ceylon. But I do not pretend, with my short experience, to say which may be the best way, though since coffee in its wild state grows in the deep jungle, it seems natural that a certain amount of shade should be good for it. Let those interested look the subject up in some of the numerous technical works, such as Spon's "Tropical Agriculture," or "The Experiences of a Coffee Planter in the Jungles of Mysore," by R. H. Elliot. The latter, though written many years ago, is an excellent book, containing a vast amount of good advice, and should be in the outfit of every coffee planter, as it was in mine.

CHAPTER XX.

ROAD-MAKING.

ROAD-MAKING now came also into full swing again, and most of my time was taken up in carrying on the new ghaut trail, which during the hot weather had been at a standstill, past the borders of the next estate, through it and all the others, to the head of the ghaut. This, of course, was hard work both for the men and myself, as we now had a long walk in the early morning before we reached work, and a long trudge back in the evening. It was also feverish, as we kept close along the side of the Manalora stream, in order to make the road as level as might be, and the malaria which rose as we worked was often sickening. It proved, however, interesting, as my bill-men broke into untrodden nooks and corners of the virgin woods at every fresh spell of work; and we were in very gamey parts too, though the noise of the axes and choppers frightened every wild thing away as we advanced. One day we broke full into a tiger's lair—a smooth, hard hollow at the foot of a shady tree, littered all about with bones and shreds of flesh and hair, amongst which there were some relics astonishingly like human ones. They may well have been such, for not long ago one of our planters rode up the ghaut late at night, and at the top, hearing a woman moaning, he dismounted, and found it was an old coolie too sick to move. He did all he could; he gave her some water from the nearest stream in his helmet, and the next morning sent some of his men to fetch her in, but she was gone, and from the marks round about it was plain a tiger had carried her off. As for the sambour and bison tracks, they were so numerous that when I went half a mile ahead and set a trace with a few men, the main body, who followed behind with mamooties and spades, often turned off to the right or left, and took their work up one of these bypaths, under the impression that I had just made it. To show how numerous the game was, and what good sport might be had by any one who could spare sufficient time, I may say that going to work one morning over the fresh, smooth earth of yesterday's road, there, all newly stamped in the same narrow passage, were a tiger cub's footmarks as big as saucers, the hoof-marks of a full-grown bison sunk deep into the soil, and also those of a sambour and a jungle sheep. All these various animals must have come down to examine our operations during the few hours of darkness. But this abundance of game was of no use to hard-working planters like ourselves, for a shot is only to be had late in the evening or early in the morning, and our exertions during the day left us little inclination for that sort of thing. L—— and I did, indeed, sit up all one night in the jungle, on a rough framework of boughs, by a stream where deer often came to drink, but L—— smoked so much bird's-eye to keep the fever mists away, that probably the animals scented us half a mile off. Certainly nothing came near us, and we got horribly bitten by mosquitoes, and were so very bad-tempered next day that we gave it up in disgust, and came to the conclusion that little is to be done in the shooting way until an estate is several years old, or unless one likes to devote the few and precious holidays to it.

Birds, too, were numerous along this new road, and here I saw the only green paroquets noticed in the jungle. I was standing by the stem of a small dead tree, gaunt, withered, and brown, without a leaf to boast of, and my white clothes were partly hidden from above by a flowering creeper, when there was a rush of wings, a loud screeching, and a flock of at least a couple of hundred of these emerald-green birds came up, wheeled twice round the dead tree, and then settled altogether in a cloud. The contrast was very striking; for whereas a moment ago the branches were bare and leafless, they now seemed buried in green foliage from the highest to the lowest, and the tree had regained its youthful beauty as rapidly as though touched by the wand of an enchanter. But the delusion did not last long, for I was soon noticed by one of the many pairs of sharp eyes, and, with a chorus of deafening shrieks, the whole covey took to flight.

This road-making was dangerous work, on account of the snakes which we often dislodged from the low herbage and rubbish. Many of these I caught and took home, much to the disgust of the coolies. Some of them were agile little creatures, with grey skins banded with black; others as long as whip-thongs, and of the loveliest grass-green, with sparkling gold eyes. These are said to hide in bushes, and dart out at the face of any one approaching, but, as far as my experience goes, they make the best of every opportunity to escape. One big snake I caught and killed, as I thought, and took him back with me in my coat pocket. I subsequently rolled him up very neatly, and tied a label round his neck, with his scientific name, and putting him into a bottle of spirits, corked it up. But the spirits seemed to have revived him, for in the night he drank up the greater part, pushed the cork out of the bottle, and returned to his native jungles none the worse for his little adventure. How astonished some one will be if he catches him again with that label round his neck and smelling strongly of native brandy!

Although never actually meeting with an accident, I have killed several deadly snakes at close quarters. On one occasion Mrs. R——'s smallest boy, very fond of collecting for me, brought me a small grey snake with a square head, which he was holding by the tip of the tail. Directly I saw it I knew it was the deadly tic-polonga, and, though a small specimen, possessed of poison powerful enough to kill a horse. I took it safely from him, but it was a dangerous moment for the little fellow. On another occasion, when walking down a jungle-path with L——, my companion actually strode right across a black cobra, five feet long, which was lying across the path. This snake gave chase to L——, who "made tracks" as fast as he could go, until I got a chance and killed the enemy with a single shot from my rifle. His skin, though not brilliant, was very striking, blue-black with a velvety spectacle-like mark behind the head.

Sometimes, however, the snake gets the best of the encounter. I once lent some coolies to a surveyor working on the other side of the river, and one of these men trod on a tic-polonga some four feet long, whereupon the reptile turned at once and struck him in the ankle. The Englishman's remedy was prompt and effectual, but terribly painful. He at once cut away the flesh all round the wound, as though he were operating on an apple, and then poured in boiling water from the camp kettle. This rough treatment was successful. The man was sent back to me to be nursed; and although he subsequently came out all over his body with spots, as though he had contracted smallpox, and spent the greater part of his time in a state of coma, he eventually recovered, and went away well to his own country.

When the sun was at its hottest and straight overhead, though we still worked on at our road-making, most of the birds hid themselves in the thickest gloom of the jungle, and the woods were very silent and gloomy, with only the sound of our own ringing axes to be heard. Yet there was twittering and singing enough in the early morning. One big hawk sailed over us for many days, no matter what the heat was, until at last I got to look out regularly for his graceful flight and wide-barred wings high up over our heads. In the evening the birds came out again as we wandered homewards, and the curious rocket-bird, with feathers in his tail twice as long as his body, thin and thread-thin up to the tip, where there was a paddle-like enlargement, played about on the tops of the trees, and enlivened the scene with its gambols.

One evening, instead of returning with the coolies, I sent them home, and, mounting a pony which had been brought over for me, rode away to W——'s, to have a look at the newspapers and see how our friends at home were getting on. I did not mount to return till late, as by chance my host seemed not so sleepy as usual. But at last I was in the saddle, and by the time his estate was left behind the sun had set and the jungles were buried in profound gloom, which the full moon did little to dissipate. However, I pressed on, and the horse willingly made for his stables. We brushed through the dewy coffee of a couple of estates, forded a moonlight nullah, and frightened a fox out of his wits as he was coming down to drink. We cantered downhill and scrambled up the rises, thoroughly enjoying the cool fresh air and the silent darkness, until we came to a lonely hollow, through which a little rill ran tinkling downwards, and the forest trees crowded in and shut out all the light, while the wild sago waved about, as it seemed, of its own accord. This place was supposed to be haunted, as six coolies had died of cholera by the side of the little stream, and a robbery had been committed there some years before. Besides that, it was a great place for bears, who have a liking for horseflesh; and my little "tat" seemed to know this, for he snorted and shook his head, and, without a word from me, started off at a canter up the rocky path. At one place the bridle-track passed under a strange fantastic pile of rocks, looking silent and grim under the occasional rays of the moon; and I was just thinking what an excellent post it would make for dacoits, and letting the pony have all the rein he wanted, when, without a moment's warning, a rope was thrown over my neck, and I was dragged right back to the crupper of the saddle. To say I "saw stars" would be putting it very mildly. The whole sky seemed to burst into a blaze of comets, and my own eyes seemed to flame with blue light. But I kept in the saddle, and reined the horse right back on his haunches, at the same time drawing a long hunting-knife from my belt, the only thing I had with me. Of course, I expected it was dacoits—what else could it have been?—but they did not put in an appearance, and, lifting up my hand after a moment of suspense, I found something round my neck, very rope-like, but not twisted, and hard and smooth, which a little more investigation showed to be the long pliant stem of a rattan creeper. Thus the mystery was solved; I had run my neck into the loop of one of the creepers which hang in graceful curves from tree to tree everywhere in the forest. But I suffered from a sore throat for a week afterwards, and, as may be supposed, finished that dark ride at a more moderate pace.

No clearer or sadder proof could be required of the feebleness of the coolies, and the constitutional ruin wrought on them by the famine, than the way in which they succumbed to fever and sickness. There was no other reason why I should hold out better than they did, for my hut was almost eave by eave with their "lines," and we both shared the same weather, and yet they died around me from simple attacks of fever which only staggered me for a day or so. Lately they had been going off at an astonishing and piteous rate. A great number of Tamils came up during my absence in Bombay—miserable famine-stricken wretches, thin and weak. They had been too suddenly exposed to the deadly air of our jungles, and half of them had died in less than a month. On one side of the Bungalow Hill stream there was a living population above ground, and on the other an almost equally large population underground.

The remainder of the coolies, very naturally, had enough of this sort of thing, and feeling a "foolish hankering for existence," they took all their small belongings with them to the bazaar at the head of the ghaut one Sunday, and when the fair was over, instead of returning to us and dying like straight-forward folk according to their agreements, they went away to their own country and dissolved amongst the lowland villages of Mysore. I had seen them start that Sunday morning, for I was sitting in my verandah, according to custom, reading, with a gay English flag flying from a staff above the hut, and I noticed that several of the old coolies and maistries to whom I had been kind salaamed lower than usual as they passed me, but attached no importance to it. However, the next morning D—— and I were surprised to see how few natives mustered when we rang the big bell. We rang again and again, and "the stoker" got wild with rage, but as the coolies were thirty miles away by that time no wonder they did not hear. This was rather a loss to the company, as each coolie took away the cumbly or coarse goat's-hair shawl we lent him by way of monsoon clothing, and nearly all had gone away owing the estate the two or three rupees' advance which had been made not long before to induce them to come up to the jungles. I should put this loss at about Rs. 1500, twice as much as it would have cost to build the poor wretches good "lines" and keep them on the estate. After this, operations came to rather a standstill, and we were forced to wait until R—— sent us up two or three hundred men—Canarese this time by way of a change—from the lowlands.

Meanwhile, I was beginning to wonder how long I could hold out myself. Hitherto I had accepted the repeated attacks of fever as a thing which must be, and had anxiously watched to find them decreasing in strength, but they got worse and worse. I had been delirious twice, and had now had fever often and badly.

This I could have stood perhaps, were it not for the leeches, but those wretched things were "the most unkindest cut of all," and very nearly reduced me to the condition of skin and bones. I bore them, as a naturalist, no particular or personal antipathy, but their conduct in return was outrageous, and their bloodthirstiness insatiable. Nothing checked them; nothing satisfied! I tried against their assaults top-boots, gaiters, two pairs of socks, and tying the bottoms of the legs of my trousers with string; I even painted my boots with tar, oil, and lime; but they laughed everything to scorn, and the jungles swarmed with their thirsty armies. They attacked me directly I went out, and it was hopeless to escape them. They were so numerous that, if one stopped in the shadow of the trees, they might be seen converging from all points, and regularly racing to get the first suck at the stranger. It is a melancholy fact, but I have felt my own blood squelching in my boots as I have walked home after a long morning in the jungle; and any one who has had the misfortune to feel a single half-dozen of leeches applied for medicinal purposes will understand how the loss of blood affected me. When my hut was reached, I could do nothing but fall into the nearest chair, while a servant pulled off my boots and crimsoned socks; nd then the horrible bloated creatures rolled about the floor like ripe cherries, little thin streams of blood meandering down my feet for half an hour afterwards. On one occasion I took eight leeches off one leg, and eleven off the other, but many others had fed and rolled away. Of course, it is impossible to eat much breakfast under such circumstances, and mine was often left scarcely tasted, though I felt always wonderfully thirsty. There would follow a brief respite for writing letters and reading, but then the sodden boots had to be pulled on again, and I went forth to hobble through the forest, about as comfortable as though I were walking on red-hot plates.

This sort of thing had gone on for a long time, until at last the fever came on my bloodless frame very badly one day. No amount of quinine would stop it; I was alone and unattended in my little hut, tossing about in all the miseries of the hot stage, and feeling, to tell the truth, considerably "played out" and broken down, when by a fortunate chance F—— came over on his white pony, and dismounted at my verandah. He showed himself, as usual, cheery and considerate, but said he considered me very ill, and advised me to come away with him to Varlavachen Bungalow. I explained that I could not leave everything to D——, who was then on the estate, without warning; so F—— stayed by me a little longer, and then rode away, and I relapsed into my former condition. But in half an hour F—— was back. He had galloped up Bungalow Hill, interviewed D——, told him I was really very ill and persuaded him to take care of everything for a few days, and now came down with violent kindness on me—would not listen to my protests for a moment, but wrapped me up in an astonishing number of coats, put me on the pony, and walked at the side as we made for his eyrie. A curious thing about the fever is that, though it saps the strength and greatly disarranges one's internal economy, for a little time after each attack one feels very well, and has an excellent appetite. Thus a night on F——'s mountain-top, and a good breakfast with all the little comforts which only flourish where a lady presides, set me up, and I could hardly believe I had been so ill the night before. Even F—— noticed the improvement, and, wishing to make the most of my short holiday, invited me to come and try for an ibex with him on the nearest grass hill; and we started, though I was conscious it was a rash enterprise on my part.

We crossed two valleys to the southward, with some coolies behind carrying our rifles, and presently found ourselves on a grassy ridge at the edge of the ghaut overlooking the lowlands. Here, as I might have expected, the exertion told sharply, and I felt the well-known fever creeping back over me. There was nothing to be done but let it take its course; so F—— went ahead with the coolies and guns, and I lay down on a sloping slab of rock, on which the sun was shining fiercely, making it much too hot even for the lizards. But as long as the cold stage lasted I shivered and shook in a frightful manner, with no power to keep myself still; and then suddenly a change arrived, and the hot stage set me perspiring and half mad with the heat, though I had been freezing a few minutes before. Thus things continued until F—— came back, having seen three ibex, but lost the chance owing to the cartridges missing fire in both barrels. The walk back before the fever had left me was a woeful experience; the headache left by the hot fit was intense, and every joint in my limbs worked rustily with rheumatism. The last hill all but finished me. It was a very rough experience, and I have never suffered more than I did in mounting that rocky slope, with my head reeling, my blood boiling and shooting to and fro in my veins.

But at length we gained the Varlavachen plateau, and a coolie F—— had sent ahead for brandy and water hove in sight. I had drunk nothing all day, and my thirst was intense. Once I had filled my helmet at a stream; but the water was bright green —concentrated essence of decayed vegetation—and I had poured it back untasted, so my feelings may be guessed when the brandy-pawnee arrived. I asked F—— if he wanted any, and he looked at me and shook his head; so I took the silver tankard, and tilted it up and up until I could see the kites in the sky overhead through the glass bottom, and I never before tasted so bitterly earned or so delightful a draught.

This bungalow, which I have described before, is a delightful place, but it had one drawback, which was the rats. Even down in my own hut they were very numerous, and a trap, which I set every night, often sprang with a clap before I had left it a minute, so that I was constantly hopping in and out of my cot to remove the victims and reset it. But up at F——'s the rats simply swarmed, and at night they came forth from their hiding-places and ate up everything left within their reach. On the evening after the ibex expedition, no sooner had I put out the lights and rolled myself up comfortably, than they were pattering all over the bed; and though I kicked vigorously every now and then, it only caused a temporary scare. I fired off all the boots and slippers in reach, a lot of hats and helmets, all F——'s shaving materials, and several brushes and combs, then the pillow, and finally the bolster, which brought down some crockery, and drove them away for a good ten minutes; when, making use of the opportunity, I went to sleep. But they soon returned to the charge, getting so bold that one woke me up by actually sitting on my forehead. There was no mistake about this, for I seized him there, and threw him to the other end of the room. However, they are harmless creatures, though remarkably inquisitive; so that, after the first novelty of the thing had worn off, their gambols over my couch and reckless leaps about the furniture did not long keep me awake.

The next and subsequent days were spent reading in the verandah, though I had two more sharp attacks, which even the fresh mountain air could not mitigate; and F—— earnestly advised a long holiday at Ootacamund, on the healthy Neilgherry Hills, or even a return to England, as I had come to that state in which my strength no more rebounded after each attack. I passed now each interval in a strange sort of sleepy condition, careless of everything around, and doing everything in a listless, lackadaisical style, which my kind host said was a very bad sign.

My exercise was confined to circumnavigating the terrace round the hilltop and revelling in the wide prospect. From my chair I saw one morning a string of six wild elephants cross the brow of a hill four or five miles away, and disappear over the sky-line. They looked like great brown mice, and followed one another in Indian file to their distant retreats. Had I been well, we would have given chase to them, and made a nearer acquaintance with these jungle monsters. Another time, while meditating on the wonderful expanse of virgin forests to the eastward, a brown cloud, like the smoke of burning bamboos, appeared in the valley below, and rolled rapidly up the hillside, accompanied by a strange humming sound. When it came nearer, it developed into a mighty swarm of wild bees, so large that, in all my apian experience, I had never seen the like. As they were taking a "bee-line"—nothing indeed could be straighter than their flight towards my position,—I stooped down on one knee, and soon they were spinning overhead like a brown hailstorm, and actually dimming the light of the sun. There must have been many thousands all following in the flight of the queen-bee, and I watched them until they were lost in the forests beyond.

On the fourth morning of my visit, having had no fever during the night, I felt duty-bound to get back to my own jungles, and take some of the work off D——'s shoulders; so, breakfast over, and due thanks having been paid to my generous entertainers, I slung my rifle, took a last look round and a long breath of fresh air, and plunged down into the fatal jungle. That same rifle had grown wondrously heavy lately. Not so long before, it hung light as a feather at my back, but now it felt a ponderous mass of wood and iron, and I shifted its position twenty times in a mile.

The jungles were fearfully hot and close after Varlavachen, though it was just the weather for the collector. Insects of all sorts were abundant, and enjoying themselves while the warm weather lasted, for we were on the brink of the wet monsoon, and they would soon have to hybernate or die. One dead tree was a magnificent sight, being surrounded by hundreds of the lovely brass-green *Chrysochroa fulgida*, an almond-shaped beetle nearly two inches in length, and each green wing-case adorned with a rosy stripe running down it. As these insects flew round and round the withered stem, they made a beautiful display in the bright sunlight, and one not easily to be forgotten.

Then I came across a bright emerald-coated lizard of large size, with gold eyes and a wonderful prismatic throat, sky-blue, orange-yellow, and vivid red, all fading into each other; but the gaudiness of this dandy lacertan made him shy, and he would not stop to be closely investigated. The smaller grey lizards were, as ever, very common, and glided over and under the fallen timber in every direction. One attracted my attention particularly by his violent contortions, and, capturing him easily with my hand, I found a very large, soft-bodied beetle was firmly fixed in his mouth. He could not swallow it, as it was stuck in his teeth, and could not eject it for the same reason; so, not liking to leave him in such an uncomfortable predicament, I took the liberty of pushing the beetle down his throat with a grass stem, for which he seemed very much obliged when placed in freedom once more.

In many places the sandy drifts were pitted with the little hollows made by the ant-lions, the curious little larvæ of a clear-winged fly. At the bottom of each excavation crouched the small lobster-shaped creature, buried up to his eyes in sand, with nothing showing but a long and sharp pair of forceps. Woe to the foraging ant that ventured on the brink of that treacherous pit, for he is sure to slip in and be devoured by the vigilant monster below, who sits expectant all day, with a good appetite always at command against the time when a victim arrives.

Then there were many birds about—a fine black thrush haunting the underwood, whence, when disturbed, he rose with a long-drawn and melancholy whistle. Although his general colour was the deepest velvety black, he had on each shoulder an epaulet of bright sky-blue feathers, wonderfully conspicuous by contrast. This was the *Myiophonus Horsfieldii* of science, a well-known bird of Southern India. A brisk little nut-hatch, of a slaty blue colour (*Dendrophila frontalis*), was also very busy about the decaying trees, and exhibited all the wonderful clinging and climbing capabilities of his family. Really it seemed to be a matter of the most profound indifference to him which way his head was when he swallowed a fat grub or a juicy beetle, and he appeared to gaily defy even the law of gravitation.

But the most remarkable and beautiful birds seen during this walk were those of a family of six jet-black woodpeckers, with flaming crimson crests, which were hard at work hammering at a dead tree as I passed. These birds were probably the *Picus Hodgsoni*, though there are two or three Southern Indian varieties of woodpeckers very much alike in general plumage, and it was only the second time I had observed them in these jungles.

During the next few days after my return, two hundred Canarese coolies arrived on the estate, and R—— came back with them. They were a poor lot, even worse than the Tamils who had recently run away; but when the superintendent showed them the deserted "lines," and told them to take up their quarters there, they said they were much too dirty, and would not move into them until they were thoroughly cleaned out—an expression of opinion which made R—— doubtless feel small, but pleased and amused me. By the way, while the "lines" were being cleaned, all these men and women camped round my hut, and, having no servant just then, and nothing but a latch on the door, they could have made off with anything they wished during my absence; but nothing was touched.

When that "boy" of mine did come back, after having got over his fear of the cholera, I was very glad, as he relieved me of the distasteful job of cooking my own meals. He had asked permission to get his wife and baby up from the lowlands, which I had readily given, as he assured me his wife was "very small," and would not eat much of my food; so one morning my breakfast was interrupted by the arrival of a very diminutive woman, half hidden under a load of cooking-pots and sleeping-mats, with a brown baby perched on top. "Who is this?" I inquired. "Oh, sahib," said the "boy," "he's my wife." So we exchanged salaams, and the new additions to my household took up their quarters in the rear. It was a matter of some curiosity to me how they lodged in the tiny kitchen, until, going to doctor my servant one day, when he was ill with fever, I found him and his better half coiled up like a couple of squirrels on the two rough boards which served as dresser and table, and the baby suspended from the roof in a shawl. On that day the "boy" was too ill to cook me any dinner, so it was done, and done very well, by his wife. But she was much too shy to place it on my table, and instead seized the opportunity, when I was having a wash, to put dishes, crockery, etc., just inside the door, and, placing the cloth on top, bolted back to the kitchen; so the arranging was left to myself.

The brown baby was very inquisitive, and occasionally crawled into my verandah to take a good stare at the burra sahib, whom he seemed to think a most curious object; but his mother generally interrupted the contemplation by snatching him up by his waistcloth and bearing him howling away. His parents were equally amusing. For instance, for about a week everything sent in to me was roasted or fried, nothing was ever boiled; and when I came to ask an explanation, it appeared that my servant had imported some chickens from the lowlands, and one hen had undertaken to make a nest and hatch some eggs in my only saucepan; so the "boy," not liking te disturb her, had resolved to do all my cooking in a fryingpan or before the fire. On another day his wife volunteered to prepare me some soup for breakfast, as her husband was ill again; but by mischance, instead of taking a cake of preserved soup, she got hold of a square of brown Windsor soap, and knowing nothing of this material, she carefully boiled it up with carrots and plenty of salt and pepper, and sent it in to me. I shall not easily forget my first and last taste of that horrible saponaceous broth.

The "boy" seemed to share the usual indifference of the natives for the fate of their countrymen and former friends, and, excepting as it put himself in danger, seemed totally careless of suffering and sorrow —very likely the effect of seeing too much of both. Thus, amongst the creatures I had collected round me to relieve the solitude of the jungle, was a fox-terrier and three half-grown puppies, all of them a present from W——, of Poothpara. It was an amusing sight to see the old dog lead out the young ones to hunt in the jungle, and when I shot them anything they used to go frantic with delight. But they were also much given to foraging on their own account. On one occasion they were out all day, and it was only when I was seated at dinner that there came the patter of canine feet in the verandah, and the truants filed in, and, sneaking under the table, went to sleep at once, appearing to suffer from fearfully bad dreams. "Boy," I said to the servant behind my chair, "how is it my dogs look so full and sleep so badly?" "The sahib's dogs," he said, "have been hunting in the jungle and found dead coolie. They not want any more dinner for very long time;" and this he said with perfect placidity, as though it were a very ordinary occurrence.

Another of my pets was a cat, but she was only nominally mine, although I gave eight annas for her in the lowlands. From the very first she utterly refused to recognize me as her owner, but made herself a nest in the thatch of the roof, whence she sallied forth at night, killed my chickens, upset my lamps, and ate my provisions in a truly lawless way. I only saw her once after I let her out of the basket on her arrival, and then it was to fire at her with a rifle as she was darting up a tree, under the impression she was a new species of wild jungle cat.

Speaking of cats and trees reminds me of a slight adventure I had some time before with a large member of the feline tribe, which might easily have resulted disastrously. The weather was particularly hot, and, having done a long morning's work in some clearings far to the southward, I was slowly taking my way homewards to breakfast; but, being in no particular hurry, I thought I would rest a little under a beautiful spreading tree which grew close beside a dry nullah, nearly choked with long reeds and wild sago. I shut my umbrella up, placing it against the trunk, and then, for want of something better to do, took out my pocket-knife and proceeded in the British way to carve my initials on the smooth bark. I am rather skilful at carving initials, the result of practice, perhaps, and it was five minutes or more before those of mine pleased me sufficiently to be thought finished. But when there was nothing else to be done to them, I shut the knife with a click, and slipping it into my pocket, let my eyes wander up the beautiful smooth trunk of the tree. Judge of my feelings when I saw crouching on a branch scarcely six feet above my head, so low, indeed, I could have poked it with the ferule of my umbrella, a full-grown and gleaming-eyed panther. His body was partly hidden by the branch, but his tail hung over one side, and his head looked over the other, and in the deep shade his eyes shone like opals. When our glances met, his lips curled up slowly into a fierce snarl, showing all his white teeth, and I saw his claws grip into the green bark ready for a spring, and instinctively my hand went down to the hunting-knife in my belt. For a moment things hung in suspense, and the next second might have pitted his vast strength, great weight, and superior position against my knife and fever-wasted muscles. But he kept his place, though his eyes watched every movement; so I judged discretion was in this case the

AN ANXIOUS MOMENT.

best part of valour, and, slowly taking up my umbrella and keeping my eyes full on his, I backed off until the tree was hidden by others, and then took a swift "bee-line" for my hut to fetch a rifle. But by the time I was armed and back at the tree, the panther was gone, and I never saw him again. Had he chanced to be hungry, or a fraction more ready for a fight, he would doubtless have saved you, courteous reader, all the trouble of wading through this chapter, by putting a final stop to the author's wanderings in the jungle.

CHAPTER XXI.

THROUGH WATER AND FIRE.

At last the hot weather ended, and the ragged grey clouds, which had been hurrying over the sky like the skirmishers of a vast army, banked themselves up and flooded the thirsty land. The first few heavy drops fell one day while L—— and I were smoking in my verandah, but they were only the forerunners of the great downpour, though they made the withered leaves on the ground hop and rustle, and frightened the lizards horribly before they stopped, leaving the air full of a wonderfully fragrant smell, as of wet wine-coolers.

But the monsoon burst that night in serious earnest. It was impossible to get to sleep—the air was very dense and hot, and the mosquitoes were busy and furious in every direction. Up to eleven o'clock there was a profound hush outside, and I was almost asleep, when there came a blinding flash of lightning, and immediately afterwards a loud peal of thunder, and the wind crept up from the valley and began to rock the tree-tops. Then down came the rain in continuous sheets, followed by white lightning which enabled me to catch glimpses of the path and hillside streaming with water, the tree-trunks shining as though they were carved out of silver, and everything far and near dripping and hanging down limp under the tropical midnight downpour. I sat wondering what the monkeys were doing outside, and all the dry-weather creatures, but soon found that charity begins at home, and that it was quite unnecessary to pride myself on being safe under shelter. The thatch of my roof had been put on early in the year, and during the dry weather it had shrunk considerably, so that, instead of forming a compact mass, as old thatch should, it was more like fresh straw loosely laid down. Consequently, when the rain began to descend in earnest, it found its way through into my sleeping compartment with very little difficulty.

I was sitting up in my charpoy listening to the howling of the wind, by this time blowing a regular hurricane, and watching the bright long forks of lightning playing about the tree-tops, when I was suddenly aware of a little trickle of water running down my back, and then another and another rivulet developing. It was necessary to act promptly; so, springing up, I rolled all the bed-things into a mass, and covered them with a waterproof. Then, opening an umbrella, I sat on top in my flannel sleeping-suit, and calmly watched my property being flooded. It was a profoundly uncomfortable night, and my position was both cold and ridiculous. The rain came in everywhere, and soon everything was afloat, while as fast as I lit lamp after lamp, the rain-water put them out and left me in darkness. When the roof of your house plays you false, it is hopeless to contend against the elements. I made two or three attempts, and found a little shelter for some of my best books under the dining table, but the greater part of my belongings were soon hopelessly saturated. My bed was also converted into a sort of tent, more or less dry, by crossing cords from the four posts and throwing coats and shawls over them. Into this harbour of refuge I crept, and watched the water coming down the walls and descending (in cascades from the roof, for there was no sleep for me. The tempest howled overhead, and the trees rocked and groaned, until every moment I expected one to come crashing through the roof of my deluged hut. Indeed, a great trunk did fall a little higher up the ridge, and I could feel the concussion, so near was it. Then another matter kept me awake. My hut, like every house in India, was a great harbourage for all sorts of strange creatures in the insect way, besides bats, snakes, rats, lizards, and so on. All these creatures were flooded out of my walls and roofs, and wandered aimlessly about the furniture and floor. Such a chance was not to be lost, and, careless of being wetted through and through, every now and then I emerged from under the shelter of my tent to secure and box a strange centipede, or give chase to a big spider, or to paddle about with bare feet after a lizard which looked something out of the ordinary. In this way I made some considerable additions to my collection that night, and with the exception of being wet through all the time, with no chance of sleeping, I was not so desperate as may be supposed. Nevertheless, I felt glad when dawn broke and daylight made it possible to move about freely, and, finally, a good breakfast with plenty of hot coffee set me up again.

With the breaking of another monsoon the work relapsed into its old channels, and nothing was done now but constant "planting out" of the young seedlings in the places they were to occupy—a dreadfully monotonous labour, which goes on day after day without stop or variety. Thus we had passed through a whole year of a new estate, and some idea of the round of operations may be gathered. Afterwards it would become more varied, and when there arises a prospect of a crop it is necessary to build "pulping houses," where the ripe cherry-like berries are subjected to constant streams of water and freed from the soft fleshy outer part, the hard stone inside (which is the coffee of commerce) being roughly dried on carefully levelled plots of ground, and sent down to Calicut or elsewhere, on the backs of bullocks, to be divested of a thin silvery skin which still enwraps the bean. Thus it is prepared for exportation and consumption in the European markets; and little the comfortable homefolk, as they sip their after-dinner *cafè noir*, think or know by what hard work the rough material has been grown and prepared for their use!

On July 21 an accident happened which forced a holiday upon me, whether I would or no. Perhaps it was even fortunate it occurred, as otherwise I should not have left the jungles until perchance carried down the ghauts feet foremost.

I was busy writing, and the evening being cold and wet and fever still hanging about me, on that eventful day I had made a fire in the stove in my little hut, the chimney of which passed up through the thatch of the roof. The dinner was standing ready on the table and the lamp was burning brightly, but, as the next day was mail day, I wrote on and on, absorbed in my occupation. The temperature of the room suddenly increased very rapidly, and a sort of red glow came on the paper, which I remembered afterwards, but at the time thought little of. However, the heat became so noticeable, that I at last started up to attend to the stove, which I supposed was the culprit; but, to my dismay and astonishment, directly my eyes were raised, I saw the whole roof of my hut already in flames, and burning fiercely under a wind which was howling through the trees outside.

What followed was very brief and decisive. My "boy" was just coming round from the kitchen with a dish of curry, but when he saw this astonishing sight he stood spell-bound for a moment, and then down went the curry, and he flew to the big bell hanging on a tree close by, and rang a peal which brought the coolies swarming up the hill in a dusky yelling crowd from their "lines." Half a glance showed me it was impossible to save the hut, for it was now well alight, and the strong wind increased the flames every moment, while the nearest water was at the bottom of the hill, and I knew well that before we could collect chatties and organize a fire brigade, it would be all over. So I proceeded to save what was possible. The estate books were got out first, along with a lot of my own, which will bear the marks of the jungle mud, into which they were thrown, as long as they last; and then I unlocked some drawers and salvaged several parcels of money. By this time the place was like an oven and burning "fore and aft," and the wild-looking crowd of coolies outside were yelling and dancing about quite at their wits' end. One old woman rushed bravely in, and making for my sleeping compartment, seized a blanket and pillow, which she gripped tight in her dusky arms and carried about with her for the rest of the evening, being much too excited to put them down anywhere. Fired by this example, some coolies made a rush into the porch. Unfortunately, my door opened outwards, and in the scuffle it banged to and was kept hard shut in my face by the great crowd outside, of whom the men nearest the door were pressed close against it by the others further away. In vain I kicked and shouted; it was shut firm, and the dense yellow smoke was blinding me and getting down my throat. At length I called out to the head native maistry, who I knew was outside, "Jowra maistry, knock some of those fools down and clear my door." Then there came the refreshing "whack, whack!" of his stick, and the crowd parted and the door opened, but not a moment too soon. Already the flaming mass of the roof overhead was rocking on the slender uprights which supported it. Any moment it might fall. The last I saw of the interior of my jungle hut was the ready-set table, the lamp still burning placidly in the thick yellow smoke, the white tablecloth on fire in twenty places, and big flakes of matting falling, smoking, to right and left. Scarcely had the door opened and freed me, when I heard the sharp crack of my revolver, which hung up loaded at the side of my bed, and the bullet whistled overhead. The pistol had become red-hot, and now added to the general confusion by falling to the ground, and every now and then leaping up and firing a shot promiscuously into the crowd. This reminded me of my unfortunate guns, which there had been no time to save, and they, in turn, reminded me of a new, unopened five-gallon tin of kerosene oil which stood in my bedroom. I would have fetched it out, though it were red-hot, had there been any chance of its staying the fire; but, as it was, I was so disgusted with the loss of my property, I thought it might as well take its chance and end the *tomasha* by a grand final firework. And so it did! The coolies had scarcely obeyed my warning and got behind trees, when there was a terrific thud, which was heard right up on top of Bungalow Hill; a great column of smoke, flames, and sparks leapt up to the tree-tops, singeing the leaves; and then, dying down, the roof fell in, followed by what remained of the walls. For a moment everything was brightly illuminated, and then the fire went out with a sudden swirl, and I was standing in my slippers, bareheaded, in the rain, falling fast now, by the smoking cinders of the poor little shed which had sheltered me for ten or eleven months.

That night I slept rolled up in a blanket on the floor of L——'s bungalow on the hill, and the next morning, after a melancholy search amongst the ruins for treasure trove—in which I found rupees and annas fused into lumps, and only the metal-work of my guns remaining—I confided my servants, my dogs, all my belongings that could be got together (and the cat if she could be found) to the care of my friend, borrowed a pair of boots and a hat, and, mounting the estate pony, turned my back on the Pardagherry jungles, meaning to go to Calicut to refit and see a doctor, and perhaps take a holiday, if he prescribed one, at that great resort of the broken-down Southern Indians, the Neilgherry Hills.

CHAPTER XXII.

VANQUISHED BY FEVER.

NEVER was a more melancholy ride than that of mine the day after the disastrous fire which thus forced leave of absence upon me. And yet it has left a very slight impression on my memory; all that occurs to me when I think of it was that I was racked with pain, and so weak it was difficult to sit in the saddle. I can remember the blinding torrents of rain which poured down unceasingly as the lonely jungle paths leading to the head of the ghaut were paced, and the torrents of water cutting the road up with innumerable rills. But although wet through before being in the saddle many minutes, it made no difference to me; all my thoughts were full of regret at leaving the estate unfinished, and turning my back on friends and companions. Whether we went slow or fast, I have no idea; but presently the horse stopped of its own accord, and, looking up, I saw we were in front of the Comlocoda Bungalow, which lies a little off the main road at the head of the ghaut. A night's lodging was begged of the owner, a brother of my lively friend, C. H——, and readily granted, and together we dined and spent the evening, beguiling the time with rival stories of past adventures. H—— gave me a history of all his guns and hunting gear, and the great numbers of animals he had killed in various wanderings.

I had spent a good many uncomfortable nights lately, but perhaps that at Comlocoda was the worst of all. The only "shake-down" which my host had to offer me was an old sofa which stood in one corner of the room; and belonging to the straight-backed sort which our forefathers seem to have liked so much, even in its very remote youth it must have been uncomfortable. Now nearly all the stuffing was gone, and there were three deep hollows and three sharp ridges in it. To lie on it full length was most indescribably miserable, and it was almost as bad to repose with your chin between your knees. During the long dreary hours of that stormy night, while the wind howled outside and the rain pelted on the "shingle" roof, I tried every position I knew of to get just so much rest as would let me go to sleep; but it was quite impossible, and the last night of my sojourn in the jungles will never fade from my memory. At last, racked with rheumatism and dysentery, and feeble with long-continued fever, I went out into the verandah, and, sinking into an armchair, felt my sand was nearly run out. It was a fearful night, the wind howling like legions of ghosts among the dead and fire-blackened trees along the margin of the clearings and the white mist sweeping in sheets over the waving coffee, drifting this way and that, and twisting like a monstrous serpent amongst the fallen logs. Once a tall spectral form was seen hurrying up the pathway, with the dead leaves eddying about it, and in the darkness of the night came straight towards me, mounted the steps in so ghostly a way that I had half risen from my chair, when a gust of wind came rattling off the roof and dissolved it into mist. It was in this very chair and on this spot that a brother of H——'s died, little more than a year ago. He was a great shikaree and a friend of F——'s, who had told me how he came out from England and opened this estate single-handed. But the fever found him out, and at last he was so ill that he was obliged to go down to Calicut, where the doctors told him he must stay for a long time; but he was naturally impatient, started for the jungles before he was completely recovered, and walked up the ghaut from Wallenghay one hot day to his hut. There did not seem to be anything the matter with him when he arrived; nevertheless, half an hour afterwards, when the "boy" brought him the coffee which he had ordered, he was found sitting in this chair, with his head sunk forward and quite dead! All that night the wind howled and the lightning played about amongst the forest trees, until a little before dawn the moon struggled forth and the rain began to fall more lightly; and when at last the welcome day did break, the sun found our part of the world very misty and dripping with last night's rain, but otherwise quiet and pleasant.

A light breakfast disposed of, and thanks made for the night's shelter, I found myself in the saddle again, and bound down the ghaut. The only thing of interest, until the bottom was reached, was a miserable coolie boy, lying across the path in the hot sunshine and almost hidden by swarms of flies. At first he seemed dead, for it looked almost impossible that such a hideously dirty and skeleton-like frame could hold any life. He had been out all night in the pelting rain, and the mud and sand was heaped up on one side of him. It would have been best that he were dead, but as I reined in my horse for a moment, he slowly opened his eyes and moved one hand! What could I do? I had no food with me, nothing but money, which would have been mockery to him. I might have taken him on the crupper, but the rivers below were all flooded, and I knew it was as much as the horse could do to get across unburdened with anything but myself; so the wretched creature was sadly left behind.

The smaller streams, though much swollen, were swam without serious difficulty, but when the broad nullah between the foot of the hills and Wallenghay was reached, it was a different matter, and a halt was made on the brink to consider where the passage lay. For, though the stream was a rapid brown flood, scouring down between its banks, and whirling along trunks of trees, dead cattle, and small islands of rubbish, turning back could not be thought of, and the river had to be crossed at all hazards. So I drove my nag in, though he did not like it much, and kept him as well as I might to where the ford seemed to be; but we went wrong, and getting on the rocks, where the dhobies wash linen in the fine weather, we floundered ahead with the water just up to the stirrups, for a few yards, and then the "tat" missed his footing, staggered forward, and down we plunged into deep water with a prodigious splash. Of course, I was drenched through and up to my waist, while the horse was swimming, and nothing but his head showed. The turbid river looked wonderfully broad from the centre, and the stream nearly lifted me out of the saddle twenty times, while as we neared the opposite bank the horse began to pant and blow as though the current was becoming too much for him. But he held out well, and, after narrowly missing getting foul of a floating mass of broken boughs and jungle *débris*, that went swirling by, we climbed on to the far bank, in a very pulpy condition, but with the worst part of the journey over.

At Wallenghay a woman and small girl came into the compound of Vladimir's bungalow, where I was resting, and, after a deal of salaaming, the woman, who was clearly starving, asked, in a trembling voice, if the sahib, "whose bounty was the refuge of the poor," would buy the little girl of her. She was rather a nice damsel, about twelve years old, and very brown, with big black eyes, and her hair done up in a knot behind; while to increase her attractiveness the woman had spent their last cowries in cocoa-nut oil, with which she had rubbed her all over, until she shone like a little statue cut out of polished marble. She was clearly much more astonished at the six-foot sahib, all in white clothes, than frightened, and held tight to her mother's saree, while she stared with all her might. I asked how much money would purchase so fascinating a young lady, and, after a moment of hesitation, the woman said I might have her for four rupees—not quite seven and sixpence in English coinage! She was certainly not over-priced; but I had reluctantly to decline the bargain, and gave the woman a note to one of my friends on the hills, begging him to find work for the unfortunate couple and take special care of the little girl, and then sent them away with enough money to last until they reached the hilltops. From Palghaut the train was taken to Beypore, and an hour's ride through the flat rice lands and bamboo clumps subsequently brought me to Calicut.

I had then no intention whatever of finally leaving the jungles; but when the English doctor came to my quarters in this quaint Indian seaside town, he did not take long to undeceive me, and, in fact, expressed his opinion that, weakened as I was by constant fever, a delay of a few days more in the jungle might have been fatal. He prescribed a long visit to Ootacamund, and would not hear of my returning to the Annamullies for several months to come. So there was nothing to do but submit.

A few days were spent in Calicut, partly at the club, and partly at the comfortable house of F—— and his family—the great centre of the local society; and then once more the train was whirling me away from Beypore towards Central India, and the scenery, which had become as familiar to me as though it were all my own back garden, flew rapidly by the windows of the carriage. It was strange to pass Palghaut at midday, and see the lofty mountains to the southward blue and grey in the distance, on the summits of which I had been living so lately, and then to take a last look at them and be rushing forward over the lower India plains, which seem to lie flat as the bed of an ancient sea between the coasts on the east and west.

The night was spent in the little waiting-room of the station at Poothanor, whence a branch railway goes nearly due northward through Coimbatore, a pretty fresh-looking English settlement by the side of a wide river, to Metapolliam, where it ends; and the traveller getting out and turning his glance to the northwards, sees the lowermost tiers of the Neilgherries, rising one above another in green forest-clad undulations, and trending back towards some misty grey hills, which are the topmost peaks of the southern barrier of the plateau.

The very word Metapolliam is associated in my mind with roasting, remorseless heat. What the place must be like in the "hot season" Heaven only knows, for even in the south-west monsoon it is fearful and unbearable. Even the dogs seemed to have rubbed and scratched off most of their shaggy coats after finding them too oppressive, and lie about helpless in the shadows of the station, with their tongues hanging out of their mouths. Imagine a ruinous old building in a stony compound, surrounded by a broken-down wall, and just one ragged old tree hanging in a dejected manner over the fragments of a dried-up well. Such is the Station Hotel; but unless you can also picture the fierce glare of the sun overhead, making half the ruins black as ink and half dazzling white, you will only form a partial idea of it.

I had certainly fancied that everything on the road to the fashionable "Ooty," the great holiday place of all the Madras officials, would be well kept and clean; yet Metapolliam is utterly ruinous, and the changing place at the foot of the hills fearfully dirty, littered up with old and broken-down conveyances of all sorts, while coolies, dogs, and children grovel on all sides in the hot sand. But if man and his works were vile here, Nature was undoubtedly lovely; and after breakfast I was soon ascending in my comfortable munchiel, borne on the shoulders of a half-dozen Tamils, by a really beautiful road, winding amongst an astonishing tangle of tropical vegetation. It was one continuous thicket of cocoa-palms, plantains, bamboos, and *Butea frondosa*, all matted together by a wonderful labyrinth of thick or slender creepers, some with bright flowers, and hanging in graceful curves from stem to stem.

These jungles, although fairy-like, are very dangerous at night, on account of the fever mists, and the numerous wild animals which wander about the hill-sides; indeed, before the road was cut and much traffic disturbed the solitudes, they were the best place for tigers in the south of India, and there are still a considerable number of the striped jungle monarchs in the neighbourhood. So they should be passed in the daytime whenever practicable. As we went ever upward, now backwards, now forwards, according to the winding of the road, the scenery was beyond description. At times the path led us along the brow of a ridge, from which we could look far down into a deep valley with a foaming torrent at the bottom, breaking into sheets of silver among the fresh green foliage, and then up the rugged, rocky side of the opposite mountain, where, perhaps, the land was being cleared for a coffee plantation. There were telegraph wires along the roadside in places, and strings of birds sat on them, so that at a distance they seemed to be suspended in the sky by some invisible power. Gradually the air grew cooler as we rose above the plains—most refreshing after the scorching heat in which I had breakfasted. We saw various coffee plantations, until the lowland vegetation gave place to more European-looking trees—the first I had seen for a very long time; and at last we were six thousand feet above the sea-level, and entered the outskirts of the upland town of Coonor, having done the nine or ten miles from the plains in three hours, which was good considering the precipitous nature of the ascent.

Early the next morning, when I arose and threw open my bedroom window, the fresh air was so enchantingly soft and cool, that it was difficult to think this was India, and not England in May. Truly, amongst all those things which most of us enjoy every day and are rarely thankful for at home, stands fresh air. To me, newly from the Annamullies, where the stuff we breathed was a nauseous compound of decayed vegetation and carbonic acid gas, it was indescribably refreshing. Then, too, everything looked neat and

English,—the pretty villas rising one above another up the side of the church-crowned hill, the road with willow-like *Eucalyptus globulus* on either side, and horses—not humped cattle—munching the short grass of the banks. Even the flowers were English, and as I drank in their sweet scent the picture was made complete by a bright little English girl coming down the road with her father, her arms full of flowers and convolvuli, the spoils of an early morning walk, and her yellow hair floating on the wind, while she laughed and talked and looked so truly delightful I felt proud to be her countryman.

Then came a hasty breakfast, and a delightful ride over an undulating road for twelve miles into Ootacamund. It was so pleasant, in fact, that my "tat" was allowed to walk the whole way, and the fresh air entered my fever-shrunk veins and exhilarated me in a wonderful manner. Certainly it is a beautiful region. The road winds along the side of steep hills, now grass-covered and swelling with as smooth and even undulations as any English downs, and like them carpeted with close green grass, and then, perhaps, changing for a time to high rocky hills and richly coloured precipices, nourishing a scanty growth of low bushes and tufts of the common bracken, with numerous subalpine flowers and bright lichens clinging amongst the rough, disjointed stones. For the greater part of the way the road overhangs a wide valley, where one rubs one's eyes and wonders to see waving fields of yellow barley in real hedge-enclosed English fields. Perhaps the crops were not very heavy, but they delighted me; and so unlike the usual Indian scenery was it, that with astonishment I saw brown-skinned children frightening away the birds from the ripe corn, or native beggars sitting at the path-side. But undoubtedly the most striking sight was the hedges of geraniums and roses, miles long, and as high as the head of a man. Every one who has read of the Neilgherries has heard of those beautiful hedgerows, but they must be seen to be appreciated. How and why these two English-looking plants came to flourish here to such an extent, it is difficult to say. Both were natives of Persia before they were taken to Europe, and perhaps here they have found again a soil and climate much like their old home in the Circassian uplands. At all events, they thrive wonderfully. The roses are not the five-petalled English wild rose, but a pink many-petalled variety, and the geraniums show two or three shades of bright red, with such stems as would not do discredit to a stout bush. Thus, when the two, both in full bloom, combine together and fringe the road as far as the eye can note, or frame in the fields of ripe barley, the sight is altogether novel and delightful.

This charming scenery continues right up to the outskirts of Ootacamund, and then two or three varieties of coniferous trees are met with, for the elevation is now some eight thousand feet above the sea, and at certain seasons, in the early morning, the grass is even covered thickly with hoar-frost on these open downs.

The town itself is a curious place, the villas and bungalows being scattered about at haphazard, each in their own compounds, and generally separated from their nearest neighbours by a tract of grass or rocky ground. There are good roads in plenty in every direction, but streets nowhere. Government House stands in haughty solitude on top of a green hillock of rising ground, and close by, on another small hill, is the English church, with the handsome Library and Assembly Rooms. Then the main road turns to the right, and leads along the face of the ridge, past the "Ooty" Club, and finally brings one full in front of Sylk's Hotel. Here I soon settled down with a comfortable sitting-room, bedroom, and bath-room opening into each other in the "bachelors' quarters," and board and lodging with this accommodation was Rs. 200 per month.

CHAPTER XXIII.

HOMEWARD BOUND.

OOTACAMUND is really a very pleasant spot, amidst beautiful scenery, and with a delightful climate for the greater part of the year. The mornings are charmingly fresh and pleasant in September, and the early riser throws open his window and, as he inhales the sweet air, his eyes wander over the great undulating Neilgherry plateau, extending from the very town itself far away over a long succession of grassy curves, broken by scattered sholas, or patches of brushwood, with tumbled fragments of old rocks, to the distant mountains which form the buttresses of the uplands, and are themselves, under the changing lights of sun and cloud, wonderfully picturesque. Perhaps the best view of all is from the Library, looking north-east, where the hills rise up step by step, in even tiers of tree-clad slopes, to the highermost summits. But one can hardly look in any direction without being pleased, and the town of white houses dotted over the green expanse and broken up by clumps of trees always shows fresh and cheerful.

Neither in the way of society is "Ooty" deficient, and when the Governor-Bahadur and the Madras officials are "on the hills," there are plenty of parties and *tumashas* every week. There is a capital polo-ground, where many good games are played by officers and civilians before "store of ladies," whose presence leads to fiercely contested struggles and total disregard of wounds. There is also a concert-room, where auctions are held of the guns and properties of gentlemen "going home," and bazaars, where the English ladies keep stalls for charitable purposes. There is also some good mixed shooting in the neighbourhood, chiefly of snipe, duck, woodcock, and plenty of hares; while if the sportsman goes beyond the limits of the town and up into the neighbouring hills, there is no knowing what he may not meet.

Sometimes the shooting is too "mixed." Only a short time ago a party of gentlemen were out snipe shooting about half a mile from the back of Sylk's Hotel, and while the beaters were going through a shola, a fine ten-foot tiger came quietly out a few yards from one of the Englishmen. Being an old shikaree, he knew what to do, and—the story is his own—quietly substituting ball cartridges for his "No. 8," killed the beast with a single shot as it was staring at him. When out shooting on these hills, one should always be prepared for emergencies such as this.

Amongst the sporting capabilities of the place are those which the lively hill jackals give for hunting; and a pack of dogs is kept—I had almost written for their amusement; but although the hounds are nominally maintained for the enjoyment of the English residents, they kill so seldom, owing to the swiftness and cunning of their tawny-skinned quarry, that really it is very doubtful if the jackals mind being hunted very much.

The first meet of the season took place soon after my arrival, and I witnessed a very good morning's sport, though, *sub rosâ*, it was a thing strictly forbidden by my worthy doctor. It came about in this way. The solitude of the "bachelors' quarters" had been broken by the arrival of two or three gentlemen, and amongst them a chik-doree, such as myself, on the way to a distant estate, who brought with him a host of luggage and servants, and two grey "tats," on one of which that morning he offered me a mount. Feeble as I felt, I was yet totally unable to refuse; and as the dawn was breaking over the distant hills, and half the country lay in shadow and half in the faint grey light, we turned out, swallowed some hot coffee, put biscuits into our pockets, and joined the hounds and red-coated huntsmen as they came through the compound from the kennels on the hill-side above. It was so cold that I could hardly feel the reins at first; nevertheless, we were met by several plucky ladies and many gentlemen, and ten minutes' ride brought us out into the open beyond the town, where we were soon hard at work.

As usual, the difficulty was not to find a jackal, but to keep the dogs together; for they sprang up on every side, and there seemed to be one behind every heap of stones. It was a treat to see the ladies riding amongst the foremost, with their hands down and heads up, and obviously enjoying it thoroughly; neither did the occasional stone walls or banks of peat turn them from the straight course, and it was plain they had not forgotten the lessons learnt in far-away English fields. I saw one or two saddles emptied in crossing a nullah, but without any serious consequences, and in a short time the field got scattered far and wide, the jackals springing up every now and then under the dogs' noses, until it was impossible to keep them packed any longer. In a little time I found myself quite alone, with one dog and a wise old jackal ahead of us. As I looked at him and noticed the easy slinging trot at which he was going, though *we* were doing almost our best, I had to confess to myself that it was very doubtful if I should carry home his brush with me that morning. He was clearly not in a hurry, and took us up and down and round about for half an hour or more, at one time leading the way through a shola, where I had great difficulty in keeping the hound in view, then down a steep hillside across a nullah, over a wall, through a rose hedge, and up the other side, where I was obliged to jump off and lead the "tat" up, as the incline and heavy dew on the grass made it more than he could do to keep his footing. But we would put the pace on over the next bit of level, and catch up our two friends, the jackal still a few yards ahead and going at a comfortable canter, while the hound was flying signals of distress and obviously doing all he knew. At last the jackal seemed to think it was getting tedious, or that he had given enough sport for the morning; anyhow, he shook himself together, and, lying down to his work, put on a pace which in five short minutes fairly ran his pursuers out of breath, and left them looking very foolish on the slope of a hill, while his tawny form disappeared over the sky-line. I need hardly add that I got the punishment I well deserved, and paid the forfeit by being very much knocked up for several days after.

But it is as tedious to be ill as to speak of it, and especially distasteful to me in a new district where there was much to be seen and done. Not being permitted to walk more than half a mile at a time, it was impossible to explore the country round about; I, itching for the fight, had to look on at the polo as though I were an old Greenwich pensioner; tennis was forbidden, though the court was under my very windows; and the great Marcoorti peak, 8400 feet high, frowned down on me all day long, and tempted me vainly to climb it.

Sometimes I wandered to the Botanical Gardens, very pretty and neat, but somehow affected with that uncomfortable formality which always hangs about British public gardens; a sense of too much order, and of being requested not to walk on the grass or smoke in the conservatories, oppresses the visitor. Still they were very well kept and richly stocked with plants of various zones of temperature. Here one might see the *Eucalyptus pendula*, a tree which exudes a thick gum with a strong smell of peppermint; besides many others,—lovely camellias growing in the open air, and a daisy-like Australian *Erigeron*. The birds also had an English look, wagtails running about near the ponds, finches in the thickets, and a blackbird (*Merula simillima*), almost the exact prototype of the British species, feeding on the lawns.

The handsome new Library deserves and obtains a large share of patronage from the English residents. There one sees all the latest telegrams from England and Europe posted up on the doors, as might be said hot from the journey half round the world, and at tiffin-time we know in this way all that those at home knew while they read their morning papers. Of books in the shelves upstairs there were some six thousand, and works amongst them in every branch of literature, science, and art, though the novels show, perhaps, most signs of wear and tear, and from the way in which they are "dog's-eared" and written upon it was easy to guess that the ladies are their chief patrons. Doubtless they find it very hard to pass the hot midday hours, when they are perforce detained indoors, and so novel-reading is perhaps less blameworthy in India than anywhere else.

This was my special haunt when the weather changed to wet, as it did some time after my arrival on the hills, and I spent many grateful days amongst the books.

Of course, messages were sent from the jungle inquiring about my health, and charging me with plenty of commissions, as I was in a civilized place. Some of my former associates wanted ammunition for guns and rifles; some, sides of bacon and hams—luxuries only to be obtained on the Neilgherries. In fact, it taxed my whole abilities to successfully carry out all the various orders.

L—— wrote to me to say the coolies on our estate were much impressed with the burning of my hut, and the suddenness with which I had vanished from the scene of my former labours. The general feeling seemed to be that I had mounted to the abodes of the blessed in the smoke of the flaming bungalow, and the coolies applied for leave to build a shrine and kill a chicken at it every week to appease my wandering spirit! Some of them went so far as to declare they had seen me go up through the tree-tops when the flames were at their fiercest, and the coolies on other estates, that had only heard half the story, firmly believed that the "burra-wallah" disappeared in some supernatural way.

On one occasion, too long a walk in a tremendous downpour of tropical rain round the Ootacamund lake had brought on a return of the fever, which in my very feeble health told on me considerably, and the next day, when a little recovered, I determined to go to the doctor and take his advice. There was no carriage to be had, and as walking was out of the question, a powerful brown horse was borrowed from one of the gentlemen staying in the hotel. Climbing into the saddle with great difficulty, we started off at a very orderly walk for Church Hill. Unfortunately, just at the hotel gates was an old coolie woman talking to a gossip, and as I passed she turned round suddenly, letting the chatty in her hand fall to the ground with a loud clash. This was too much for my horse, fresh from the stables and unlimited grain; he started off as hard as he could go—luckily in the right direction—and I could no more have reduced his desperate pace than stayed a whirlwind; in fact, my whole energies were spent in remaining "on board." In this wild way we charged past some native huts, half killing some pigs and chickens, and sending the small children howling to right and left—past the Club, where the members who happened to be in the verandah must have judged my news was very bad from the pace at which I rode over Church Hill—and eventually to the point where Dr. F——'s carriage drive joins the main road. By a great effort I turned the horse up this path, and in a moment more he had come, of his own accord, to a standstill in front of the house. Dr. F——, who had been walking in the garden, said somewhat sarcastically he was glad to see I was so much better; but I replied with a good deal of awkwardness that my errand was to say I was much worse, though the tale fell rather flat in face of my wild riding. In fact, it is not every one who gallops to fetch their own doctor when seriously ill.

The crows were nearly as bad up on the hills as they had been in the lowlands. They are little influenced by change of climate, and have none of the virtues usually supposed to be possessed by dwellers on mountains. When I first took up my quarters at "Sylk's," I thought it would be pleasant to have some pets of some sort or other; and there being nothing else handy, I made some friendly advances to the crows, feeding them occasionally with bread and scraps. But the result was anything except satisfactory, for in two days at most the news of my philanthropy seemed to have spread to the whole corvine population of the town; and no sooner did I venture outside the verandah than all the crows on the roof-ridge began cawing, and the chorus was taken up far and wide, till the trees in the compound rapidly filled with crows, all croaking at the top of their voices and following me about; so that at last I was heartily ashamed of them. Ceasing to feed them was of no use; I had earned a character for benevolence which was not to be shaken off easily, and my popularity was overwhelming amongst my black friends. At last they became so troublesome and unruly that something had to be done; so, after trying to lower myself in their good opinions by giving them bread soaked in brandy, which only made the noise worse, I sent down to Madras for a small blow-tube, firing a small charge of powder and a swan-shot. My popularity entirely disappeared the day it arrived; and after I had upset two or three birds, and taken some feathers out of the tail of another, they saw that I had changed my mind about petting crows.

One makes strange friends at these Indian hotels, the majority pleasant, but some few very much the reverse. However, the pleasant ones *are* much the most numerous, and when Englishmen meet in India they "fraternize" more readily than in perhaps any other country, not even excepting "home," which is a result very likely of nearly every one in the country being on much the same social footing, since, of course, poor or low-class English are very rarely seen "up country," and seldom even in the big towns. The quickness with which friendships are made is astonishing. For instance, the silence of the "bachelors' quarters" was broken one day by the arrival of a Mr. H. R——, a barrister of Calcutta, coming up to the Neilgherries for a month's shooting, with tents, ponies, and a number of servants, with which the verandah was soon littered. The request for the loan of a pocket-knife was sufficient to introduce us; half an hour later, we were hard at work relating shooting adventures, and before we parted for the night Mr. R—— had taken me by the button-hole, and said,

"Look here! you can do something for me. I am going away at daybreak to-morrow with the greater part of my baggage and the tents, and may not be back for two or three weeks. But there are two portmanteaus, full of books and clothes and so on, which I do not want to take with me. Here are my keys. If you will permit those portmanteaus to be placed in your room, and will open them and send me any little things I may write for from time to time, you will place me under an obligation to you." Of course, I expressed my pleasure at being of any use to him, and subsequently received several very interesting accounts of his doings and tent-life. I merely mention this to show how rapidly friendships grow up when strangers have mutual ideas and thoughts.

But even hotel life at "Ooty" is not without its drawbacks. The charges are very high, and the food not particularly good, though the chief grumblers on that score were the old officers, who make a point of grumbling at anything and everything, and will probably grumble at the fit of their wings in heaven when they some day get them. Thus it took little more than a month to tire me of the town and the hills. I had visited the curious little village of the Todas, or aboriginal inhabitants; had seen the Mussulman burying-ground with its silent city of little white-domed graves; and "done" everything in the near neighbourhood which was to be done, and at last received, with great satisfaction, the doctor's permission to go down to Coonor, on the way to Madras, whence to take steamer home, for I had finally decided the many months of rest declared absolutely essential to the recovery of my health might as well be spent in the dear old country as here in India.

By half-past seven one bright morning I had taken my place in the mail tonga, with my belongings at my feet; and with a parting shake of the hands of those many kind ones who had come to see me off, the driver blew a blast on his horn, and away we went down the road towards Coonor.

I had chosen the tonga dak because it is a much faster mode of travelling than by private carriage, and the mail-cart being very like an Irish jaunting-car, one gets more fresh air and a better view of the scenery. The pace was certainly not disappointing. Our first pair of horses were young and fresh, and, by way of commencement, ran the pole deep into a high earth bank before we had gone a hundred yards. Freeing ourselves, we dashed down the hill at a gallop, the driver occasionally blowing lively blasts on his horn, which brought every one out to stare at us, until we had threaded the winding roads of the outskirts of the town, by some wonderful chance without knocking down any of the old men and women, who would keep in the centre of the road in spite of all the warning we gave them. Here we were free of the town, and began to descend rapidly. Soon a toll-bar came in sight, and a loud blast on the horn brought out the man, who flew to the gate and opened it just as we charged down; it certainly seemed to me that there were not six inches between our wheel and the gatepost when we passed. However, the driver was expert and experienced; he kept both horses carefully in hand, and by his side was a powerful brake, to be used on the steeper declines, and an arrangement of screws and levers by which the pole could be raised or lowered at will, according to whether we were going up or down hill. So, feeling an able pilot was at the helm, I was free to enjoy the really beautiful scenery and the fresh morning air. In places the view was like the wildest parts of the Scotch moorlands, with green swampy valleys and small burns trickling down the hillsides; in others, precipitous rocks towered above the road, like the Norwegian fjelds; and elsewhere were wide-spreading hollows, with fields of barley and little wayside huts amongst the geraniums and roses.

At one of these little changing-houses we pulled up and got fresh horses, and then continued the rapid descent again. Many times it seemed that we must inevitably come into collision with some of the numerous country carts which were toiling up to Ootacamund with lowland produce in charge of sleepy drivers, who would only wake up just as we were upon them, and then shout to us to stop, or pull the tails of their cattle, who were at least as sleepy as their masters. Of course, we did not stop, but shot by as best we could. On one of these occasions a bandy was passed, out of which a long pole was projecting. We cleared the cart, but the stick caught in the sheet of strong canvas placed across the side of the dak, scarcely more than a foot from my head, and rent it from side to side. But we never slackened speed for a moment, except to change horses again and for the last time, and then did the remaining stage into Coonor, sweeping round the sharp curves of the road, and close to the very brink of deep nullahs, sometimes passing a few sons of the Celestial Empire boring holes in the rocks for blasting purposes with an iron "jumper," and by some very beautiful nooks of tropical vegetation, with bright birds and butterflies on the wing amongst the trees and shrubs. Finally, we pulled up opposite the post-office of the ghaut town.

The two best hotels are both on top of a high ridge, which necessitates a long climb to reach them; but the exertion is repaid by the freshness of the air and the beauty of the scenery. The native town and bazaars are seen down below in the hollow, and a long succession of undulating ridges beyond. The "Camel's Hump" mountain, in the distance, rises some ten thousand feet above the sea, and occasional glimpses open of the flat Madras plains far away to the southward.

In fact, I think this neighbourhood is much superior to Ootacamund, charming as the latter is, especially in botanical riches, as, being just at the head of the ghaut, and more than a thousand feet lower than that town, the vegetation includes more tropical forms of great beauty, besides European plants and trees. There are some really noble oak trees, which would be a credit to any English wood, growing side by side with the Australian *Eucalyptus globulus*, which, during the few years since they were first planted, have attained great height and proportions. The roses bloom as plentifully as ever, and the heliotrope forms great hedges and envelops small buildings in clouds of its pale-blue, sweet-scented flowers and leaves. There are also lovely orange gardens on the hillsides, reminding one of the south of France and the islands of the Mediterranean; while, besides all these natural charms, there is plenty of agreeable society, and the arrangements of Grey's Hotel, where I stayed, were everything that could be desired in the way of comfort and convenience.

Two or three days' rest at this pleasant town somewhat accustomed me to a heat greater than that of "Ooty;" and, though a rather heavy recurrence of fever threw me back, I was able to pay my bill early on the morning of the 15th, and, hurrying down the hill, to secure a seat in the mail-cart when it arrived from inland.

The descent was made by the new road, not the bridle-track by which I had come up, though the scenery was much the same; the most striking thing being the wide views we occasionally obtained of the far-spreading plains below, seeming as even as a billiard table, with a few little mound-like eminences scattered here and there, looking so out of place amid the surrounding levels that it was difficult to think they were not human works.

We passed many English soldiers with nets and boxes, reaping a rich harvest amongst the splendid butterflies and bees of the wayside jungles, which grew hotter and hotter at every turn of the road.

At last the heat again grew well-nigh intolerable, for midday found us only halfway down the ghauts, and the blazing sun overhead, and the clouds of choking white dust raised by the native carts which we passed, made my eyes and throat smart till I could hardly draw my breath. The guide-books say the road is an excellent one, and so it is as far as concerns the engineering skill which made it; but the surface in the dry weather is very shifting, and the natives in charge of the upward-bound bandies are constantly stopping and placing stones under the wheels of their carts while they rest. These they never think of removing when they go on, and consequently we were continually going over these obstructions with an amount of jolting which, with the thermometer at 100°, was more painful than amusing. The driver, a tall, white-clad Mussulman, was continually saying to me, "Now, sahib, hold tight;" and then we would give a fearful plunge, which would send the mail-bags all down into one corner, and would have undoubtedly "unshipped" us had we not been prepared.

However, the longest road must come to an end, and by 2 p.m. we reached the lowlands, where everything looked terribly dry and withered under the fierce sun. Half an hour's gallop over the blinding white road brought us to Metapolliam, hot, tired, and dusty, but just in time to catch the mail train to Madras, which was standing with steam up, impatiently waiting for the letter-bags.

There is nothing to record of interest for the

remainder of the journey, but nearly my whole night was spent at the open carriage window, watching the moonlit country as we flew along, and the bright white reflections and deep shadows of the little villages and temples dotted over the land. Never shall I forget, amid all my memories of India, two things—the endless beauty of the open country under the moonbeams, and the splendid daybreaks.

At 6 a.m. we rattled into the station of Madras—just twenty-four hours after leaving Coonor, on the summit of the Neilgherries—and I immediately took a fly and hurried to the office of the British India Steam Navigation Company, as one of their ships was advertised to sail on the 16th at midday. But I might have spared myself so much haste, for it was only to learn that the steamer had been detained in the Hooghly, and was expected "to-morrow." By a curious coincidence, when I came to inquire what ship was expected, it turned out to be the *Almora*, my old sea friend; so, securing a berth in her, I took my way to an hotel facing the beach, and spent a decidedly hot and close night in the open verandah, tormented by mosquitoes.

There is little more to be said. I watched the horizon of the sea all the morning hours of the following day, and at last my patience was rewarded by a thin line of smoke to the northward. It grew and grew rapidly; at first the funnels and masts, and then the hull, of the big ship coming into sight, and in an hour more the *Almora* lay at anchor off the pier. That night we were off the Coromandel coast; the next day, in the pearl and coral waters of Ceylon; and a month afterwards our anchor rattled down off Gravesend Pier.

Hic longæ finis chartæque viæque.